P9-AGM-794

mrs. delany's menus, medicines and manners

mrs. delany's

menus,
medicines
and
manners

KATHERINE CAHILL

NEW
ISLAND

Mrs. Delany's Menus, Medicines and Manners
First published 2005
by New Island
2 Brookside
Dundrum Road
Dublin 14
www.newisland.ie

ISBN 1 904301 77 0

British Library Cataloguing in Publication Data. A CIP catalogue
record for this book is available from the British Library.

Typeset by New Island
Cover design by New Island
Printed in the UK by CPD, Ebbw Vale, Wales

10 9 8 7 6 5 4 3 2 1

Special thanks to David Skinner who kindly gave us permission to adapt his 18th-century
'Bellamont' wallpaper design for the jacket.

Illustrations by Sinead McCarthy nbarch@eircom.net

in memory of my mother and father

silhouette of mary delany

aged 87

CONTENTS

acknowledgments

❦

My thanks go to Mrs. Delany for writing her letters in the eighteenth century. To Lady Llanover, who collected and edited them in the nineteenth century. To all the writers since then who have kept Mrs. Delany alive, especially to Ruth Hayden, author of *Mrs. Delany: Her Life and Her Flowers,* and to Angelique Day, author of *Letters from Georgian Ireland: The Correspondence of Mary Delany, 1731–1768.*

In making my contribution to Mrs. Delany's life and legacy, I would like to thank my sisters, especially Mary and Aileen Cahill, who have given me enormous assistance, also Carmel and Joan Cahill for lending every possible support. Thanks go to Tony Farmar, author of *Patients, Potions and Physicians: A Social History of Medicine in Ireland,* who read my chapter "Rotten Apple Water: Mrs. Delany's Medicines" and guided my path. Patricia McCarthy, author of "Vails and Travails: How Lord Kildare Kept His Household in Order" read "Fatty John: Mrs. Delany's Domestics", and I am very grateful to her.

My thanks go to Joseph Hoban, PR and Marketing Director of New Island, for bringing this idea to the attention of the team there and to Emma Dunne, my editor, for her enjoyment and encouragement of the project.

Last, I want to thank my husband, Frank Corr, for patiently putting up with Mrs. Delany and me for the past eighteen months and for making some very apt suggestions.

MRS. DELANY: (*née* MARY GRANVILLE) became MRS. PENDARVES on her first marriage and MRS. DELANY on her second. Addressed as A.D. or AUNT DELANY by her nieces and nephews.

ALEXANDER PENDARVES: Mrs. Delany's first husband. During the period of her first marriage and widowhood there are many references in the correspondence to MRS. PENDARVES or PEN or PENNY.

DR. PATRICK DELANY: married Mrs. Pendarves in 1743. Made Dean of Down shortly after his marriage. Affectionately known in the correspondence as THE DEAN or D.D. or "MY OWN D.D."

ANNE GRANVILLE: Mrs. Delany's sister. Became MRS. DEWES on her marriage to John Dewes in 1740. Mrs. Delany's principal correspondent and beloved confidante until her death in 1761.

BERNARD GRANVILLE (sometimes called BUNNY): Mrs. Delany's older, intractable brother.

MARY GRANVILLE (*née* Westcombe): Mrs. Delany's mother, referred to as MAMA.

COURT DEWES: Anne's first child. Nephew and godson to Mrs. Delany.

BERNARD DEWES (called BUNNY or BANNY): Anne's second son and Mrs. Delany's nephew.

JOHN DEWES (also called JACKY): Anne's third son and Mrs. Delany's nephew.

MARY DEWES (nicknamed Pauline): Anne's only daughter. Beloved niece and goddaughter of Mrs. Delany. Married John Port in 1770 and referred to as MRS. PORT from then on in the correspondence. Had a large family, the most important of whom was G.M.A. or Georgina Mary Anne Port.

G.M.A. or GEORGINA MARY ANNE PORT: grandniece of Mrs. Delany. For several years called G.M.A. and a variety of names until the name GEORGINA was finally decided upon.

SALLY CHAPONE: daughter of Mrs. Delany's girlhood friend Sally Kirkham. Joint goddaughter to Mrs. Delany and Anne. Spent a large part of her life with the Delanys.

DUCHESS OF PORTLAND: Margaret Harley Cavendish, wife of the second Duke of Portland, William Cavendish. Mrs. Delany's great friend.

ANNE DONNELLAN (called PHIL or PHILOMEL): Mrs. Delany's friend. Sister of Katherine Clayton, wife of Robert Clayton, Bishop of Killala and Achonry, hosts to the then Mrs. Pendarves on her first visit to Dublin in 1731.

MISS SPARROW (Frances Mabel Sparrow): niece and ward of Mr. John Port, husband of Mrs. Delany's niece Mary Dewes.

principal places

❧

Throughout her life Mrs. Delany made long visits to friends and relations and consequently her letters are addressed from various locations. She moved house several times in and around London and had addresses ranging from Northend in Fulham, which was the home of her Aunt and Uncle Stanley, to her own homes in Lower Brook Street, Clarges Street, Thatched House Court and finally St. James's Place. The principal addresses Mrs. Delany wrote to or from throughout her correspondence are as follows:

BULSTRODE, near Gerrards Cross, Buckinghamshire: home of the Duchess of Portland where Mrs. Delany spent six months of every year after the death of Dr. Delany, generally from spring to autumn, until the duchess died in 1785. The Duke and Duchess of Portland had apartments in Whitehall where Mrs. Delany also spent some time.

CALWICH: the country home of Bernard Granville, in Derbyshire on the Staffordshire border, situated close to the town of Ashbourne. Bernard Granville also kept a house in town.

DELVILLE: the Delanys' famous home near Glasnevin in Dublin.

ILAM in Dovedale near Ashbourne, Derbyshire Peak District: the ancestral home of the Port family and home to Mrs. Delany's niece Mary (Dewes) Port after her marriage and home to G.M.A. and the extended Port family.

MOUNT PANTHER: the deanery house close to Downpatrick, Co. Down – headquarters for the dean's northern visits.

WELLESBOURNE: home of the Dewes family in Warwickshire, near Kenilworth and Coventry. Most of Anne's letters centre round the family and Wellesbourne.

Variations in spelling have been preserved in all extracts from Mrs. Delany's letters as reproduced by Lady Llanover and in all other quotations from contemporary sources. Mrs. Delany sometimes spelled a word differently in the same letter – for example, Sevil and Civil oranges for Seville oranges. She also frequently used abbreviations – Dss for Duchess and so on. Dates have been standardised to the Gregorian calendar with the New Year beginning on 1 January, though Mrs. Delany used both the Julian calendar, with the New Year beginning on 25 March, and the Gregorian. The address of "Mrs.", meaning mistress, was a term of respect and did not necessarily imply married status. The term "friends" meant the wider family group of blood relations and interested parties.

introduction:

S. Basite Feb. n? Aug? 1784.　　　*A View of Delville from beyond the Ever-Green Grove.*

how

d'ye

do,

mrs. delany?

Your letter of the 25 January I received last Sunday evening; I had company with me – some ladies of our town of Glasnevin – and when it was brought in, and one from my brother, I laid them on the table before me, expressing joy at the receipt of them, and the stupid Goths never said, "Pray open your letters," or anything civil about them. I staid a full minute for that compliment, and my patience would hold out no longer; so I said, "Pray, excuse me, I must read my letters, as I expect some news of consequence." So, opened them and read them from end to end. (Delville, Dublin, 9 February 1751)

Mrs. Mary Delany was sorely tried when visitors delayed her reading of the letter from her beloved sister Anne, just arrived from England. Separated by the Irish Sea, the sisters could only communicate with one another by letter. The only other possibility of hearing news directly was from a visitor recently returned from one or the other sister with fresh reports, but those opportunities were few and far between. Letters were a lifeline. They were company on a dark day, a friendly substitute for the writer. In an era when a fever could take a life within twenty-four hours, they essentially confirmed the health and well-being of the other. They also provided virtual conversations and for those reasons were read and re-read. The sisters had voracious appetites for news of each other, and of each other's households, and no detail was considered unworthy of notice. In a somewhat apologetic tone, though, Mrs. Delany wrote to her long-time friend and correspondent, Lady Andover: "Writing to a friend is so like conversation that one forgets that what will pass off tolerably well in talk, is dull and tedious on paper" (Thatched House Court, 21 January 1771). Letters were read aloud to family and visitors but not so the more private parts. Those sections were perused later in seclusion and responded to with care.

Pen, ink, paper, franks (pre-paid postage) and a little shake of sand to blot the ink dry were the media through which the astonishing chronicle of Mrs. Delany's life was built up incrementally. She wrote:

> I have been so silly as to forget franks. I must beg the favour of you to get a *dozen or two* for me from Sir Charles Mordaunt; you will find paper in the middle drawer of the walnut table in my closet: a dozen will do if I am to see you soon. I don't know but you will find a few of the Duke of Portland's in the drawer with the paper. (Calwich, 19 August 1749)

Franks were never dated at the period of this letter. Ladies provided themselves with packets of half sheets, folded and signed by members of either house of parliament. These sheets lasted for months and were dispatched to whatever address was required.

A large number of Mrs. Delany's letters were written to her sister Anne. They remained in the family long after Mrs. Delany's death in 1788. They were edited and published in six volumes by a great-grand-niece, Lady Augusta Llanover, almost a century later, in 1861. These volumes are the primary sources for this exploration of Mrs. Delany's life. She was born Mary Granville in Coulston, Wiltshire, over three hundred years ago on 14 May 1700. She was the second child of four, Bernard, Mary, Bevil and Anne, and the eldest daughter of Colonel Bernard Granville. Her mother was the beautiful Mary Westcombe, daughter of Sir Martin Westcombe, former consul at Cadiz in Spain.

Bernard Granville was a third son. Part of his subsistence accrued from his older brother George, Lord Lansdowne, a politician, poet and playwright, who was then head of the Granville family. In the prevailing system of primogeniture, where the family inheritance went to the eldest son, the unequal ranking placed Mary's father down the scale and effectively sealed her fate. She was extremely marriageable on all points of youth, vitality, family connections and accomplishments. She lacked nothing but fortune.

The Granville family had an ancient lineage going back to the first Dukes of Normandy. By Mary's time they were part of the political establishment. Her aunt Anne Stanley, her father's sister, was the wife of Sir John Stanley, secretary to the Lord Chamberlain. Aunt Stanley, so called because the use of a Christian name was too presumptuous, had no children of her own. She often took Mary for extended visits to her London apartments in Whitehall. These visits had the dual purpose of providing youthful company for the Stanleys and of training Mary in the social graces requisite for a court career. Mary was being groomed to be a lady-in-waiting, a position of great prestige. Staying with the Stanleys, she mixed with the daughters of peers and politicians and the most influential families in the land. She had a gift for friendship and held the friendships she made in childhood fast for life. The Stanleys' sophisticated world of political manoeuvrings, manners and lifestyle gave her a decided taste for city life and she was loath to leave it when the time came.

The great friend of her life, Lady Margaret Harley, later the Duchess of Portland, prevailed on Mrs. Delany to write her autobiography and it is thanks to this partially completed work that we know so much about her early life. Lady Llanover included this autobiography with the collected letters. In it Mrs. Delany described Aunt Stanley as a hard taskmistress.

> My Aunt was a woman of extraordinary sense, remarkably well-bred and agreeable. Her penetration made her betimes observe an impetuosity in my temper, which made her judge it necessary to mortify it by mortifying my spirit, lest it should grow too lively and unruly for my reason. I own I often found it rebellious, and could ill bear the frequent checks I met with, which I too easily interpreted into indignities, and have not been able wholly to reconcile to any other character from that day to this. Nevertheless, the train of mortifications that I have met with since convince me that it was happy for me to be early inured to disappointments and vexations.

The death of Queen Anne, the last Stuart monarch, in 1714 marked a huge change in family fortunes. The Granville family had supported her reign and been rewarded with posts and emoluments. The political wind shifted, and a new Whig government swept in with George I of Hanover, supplanting the Granvilles and many other families loyal to Anne. Mary recounted those events many years later. "We were of the discontented party, and not without reason; not only my father, but all my relations that were in public employments, suffered greatly by this change." Her uncle Lansdowne, who had been Secretary of State for War, was arrested for inciting rebellion and sent to the Tower of London. Mary's father's attempt to escape the city was foiled.

> My father, who then resided in Poland Street, upon this change in the affairs of his family,

determined upon retiring into the country. He ordered two carriages to be at his door at six o'clock, and gave a charge to all his people not to mention his design. The man from whom the horses were hired proved to be a spy. I was sleeping in the same bed with my sister, when I was suddenly awakened by a disturbance in my room. I looked round. I saw two soldiers standing by the bedside with guns in their hands. I shrieked with terror. When we were dressed we were carried to my father and mother, whom we found surrounded by officers and messengers. My father was extremely shocked by this scene, but supported himself with utmost composure and magnanimity, his chief care being to calm and comfort my mother, who was greatly terrified, and fell into hysteric fits, one after the other.

On learning of their plight, Aunt Stanley came flying to the rescue. In defiance of the soldiers posted at the door, she marched into the house and demanded to take the two young girls to her own home. Bernard Granville was taken captive. We are not told where or for how long Bernard Granville was incarcerated, but by November of that year he was allowed to leave London with his family. They made a miserable five-day journey to their new home at Buckland, near Campden, Gloucestershire.

Anna [usually known as Anne], who was then a little girl, too young to consider how such a retirement might prove to her disadvantage, was delighted with a new scene. I may own, that I left it with regret. I had been brought up with the expectation of being Maid of Honour,

Queen Anne having put down my name for the office with her own hand.

To make their exile even more bitter, a few days after they arrived at the farmhouse they were assailed by as severe a frost as ever was known in that country. All comings and goings were stopped. Bernard Granville exerted himself to entertain the family by reading aloud to them and playing cards in the evenings, but his wife's despair at the turn in their affairs cast a pall over them all. Out of the gloom came the first of Mary's suitors, Robert Twyford. He was twenty-two, tall, handsome, lively, good-humoured and a political refugee of their own colour. "The first Sunday after he came he met us all at church, and my father asked him to eat beef and pudding with us." This invitation was extended to a longer stay during which Mary noticed a change in his demeanour. "He was often silent and thoughtful. When I came down in a morning to practise my harpsichord, he was always in the room, and he would place himself beside me while I played." This behaviour was noticed, and her mother forbade her to leave her room until she sent for her and ordered her never to take a walk without a servant or chaperone. Foiled in making a personal declaration, Robert applied to her father, who told him he would be happy to have him as a son-in-law, but that he should know his daughter had no fortune and Robert must first lay those facts before his own parents. Mary wrote: "After some months' trial to get his parents to consent he wrote that they were inexorable." The intrepid lover pressed her to marry him privately, but she was offended at the suggestion and sent him packing. She declared herself "very easy when this affair was over". However, she did not escape her next suitor with such equanimity.

Lord Lansdowne, recently freed from the Tower, wrote to invite Mary to stay with him at Longleat in Wiltshire, the magnificent country seat of his wife, Lady Mary Villiers, widow of Thomas Thynne. Mary's parents considered the invitation highly advantageous, and her father delivered her in person into his brother's care. The house was a lavish showpiece, filled with company. There were card parties, theatricals, music, dancing and witty discourse every night. Mary thought her "present state and future prospects as happy as this world could make them". This munificence did not extend to her father, though, who was sent back to Gloucestershire on a reduced income.

> The day before he left, my father opened his mind to me, and I afterwards wished I had returned with him that I might, by tender duty and affection, show him that I preferred his house and company to all flattering views that were laid before me — but it was his pleasure that I should stay.

Lady Lansdowne was a vain, flighty creature who quickly became jealous of the tender girl who captivated her husband. Lansdowne had found in his niece a kindred spirit. They delighted in books together, and Mary read to him "every day, till the ladies grew angry at my being so much with my uncle". One day while the company was at dinner, word came that an old friend of the family, Alexander Pendarves of Roscrow in Cornwall, was at the door. For the mischievous ladies the visit proved timely.

> I expected to have seen somebody with the appearance of a gentleman, when the poor old dripping, almost drowned Pendarves was brought into the room. His wig, his coat, his dirty boots, his large unwieldy person, and his crimson countenance were all subjects of great mirth and observation to me.

Pendarves' discomfiture on arrival was partly on account of an argument he had had with Francis Bassett, the husband of his niece. He had offered to settle his entire estate on him should Bassett take his name, a common practice for an heir at the time, but Bassett refused. Lansdowne saw a golden opportunity and paved the way for the old swain.

> He was then nearly sixty, and I seventeen years of age. I thought him ugly and disagreeable. He was fat, much afflicted with gout and I dreaded his making a proposal of marriage. In order to prevent it I did not in the least disguise my great dislike to him. I was often chid by my aunts for this behaviour.

Undeterred, Pendarves applied for Mary's hand. The bird came home to roost. Aristocratic wedding settlements of the time were essentially a barter, and Lansdowne triumphed. He secured, as he thought, a fortune for his niece and a Cornish faction to his own political interest. Pendarves, for his part of the bargain, secured a seventeen-year-old bride.

> One night, at one of our concerts, all the company went into the room where the music was performed ... my uncle called me back. My spirits forbode what he was about to say, and when he bade me shut the door, I turned as pale as death. He took me by the hand, and after a very pathetic speech of his love and care of me, of my father's unhappy circumstances, my own want of fortune, and the little prospect I had of being happy if I disobliged those friends who were desirous of serving me, he told me of Pendarves' passion for me, and his offer of settling his whole estate upon me ... I was not entreated but commanded.

There was no way out. Mary knew that denying her uncle's wishes would damage her parents' already precarious position. Filial duty was a fixed principle of her life. If this match would relieve her mother and father of the burden of her care and secure their future, she owed them that obligation. "I was married with great pomp. Never was woe drest out in gayer colours, and when I was led to the altar, I wished from my soul I had been led, as Iphigenia was, to be sacrificed … I was sacrificed."

The newlyweds stayed at Longleat for some months before heading for Cornwall and Roscrow Castle. Mary's one consolation was that her brother Bernard, whom she called Bunny, was permitted to accompany them on the wedding journey. Pendarves did not improve on acquaintance.

> He was excessively fat, of a brown complexion, negligent in his dress, and took a vast quantity of snuff, which gave him a dirty look. His eyes were small, black, lively, and sensible; he had an honest countenance, but altogether a person rather disgusting than engaging. He was very sober for two years after we were married, but then he fell in with a set of old acquaintances, a society famed for excess in wine, and to his ruin and my misery was hardly ever sober.

The sight of her new home was far from encouraging.

> When we arrived at Roscrow Castle I was indeed shocked. I was led into an old hall that had scarcely any light belonging to it; on the left hand was a parlour, the floor of which was rotten in places, and part of the ceiling broken down. Here my courage forsook me and I fell into a violent passion of crying.

Her tears were in vain. There was nothing for her to do but submit to her fate, which she did with a fortitude that characterised her entire life. She never pretended to love her husband – her honest nature would not permit that hypocrisy – but in Christian duty she resolved to be a good wife to him, and she was.

Two years later, Pendarves, beset by financial problems, went to London in an attempt to repair the damage. He sent for Mary to join him. Delighted at first at the prospect of a return to London, she was disgusted to find he had taken a house in Rose Street, Hog Lane, a very unpleasant part of Soho. He had installed his crabbed old sister in the house as duenna and, with mounting paranoia, had charged the servants to report on all of Mary's comings and goings. Drinking and dissipation grew in tandem with the money worries, and she was given many hints that he had some very near relations to maintain. "This was the last misfortune I could have expected; I thought myself at least secure of an easy fortune."

While Pendarves lived, there was no option but to perform the duties of nurse-wife.

> He was never at home but when the gout confined him, and then I never left him. When he had the gout he could never bear (even in the midst of winter) the least fire in his room, and I have read three hours together to him, trembling with cold all the time. He has often been confined six weeks together; as soon as he was able to go abroad, he returned to his society, never came home sober, and had frequently been led by two servants to bed between six and seven o'clock in the morning.

Mary had leave to mix with her old set while her husband was out carousing. This freedom was a double-edged sword that "exposed me to the impertinence of many idle young men". Mrs. Pendarves was perceived as a new beauty come on the scene, the fresh young wife of an old cuckold, ripe for the plucking. This was excellent sport for the jaded fops of the town, and she ran their gauntlet. In one episode worthy of the most lurid Gothic romance, the Hanoverian ambassador, Mr. Fabrici, aided by the king's favourite, Lady Walsingham, lured Mary into one of the enclosed royal gardens at Windsor. Compromised and outraged, she saw the wretch off with a threat to expose him to the king. The offence was greatly compounded by her horror that Pendarves might get to hear of it and misinterpret her part in it.

Changes were afoot and deliverance at hand. Mary's beloved father died. Her mother and Anne moved from the country and settled in the city of Gloucester. Anne, seven years Mary's junior, now became her closest confidante and supplied that role for the rest of her life. "From that time I had perfect confidence in her, told her some of my distresses, and found great consolation and relief by this opening of my heart."

Coming from supper with Lady Sunderland one evening, Mary found Pendarves home before her. This was most unusual. He was agitated and wanted to talk, to assure her she had been a good wife and he was grateful. He told her he wanted to reward her and was set to re-write his will that very night. Thinking he was maudlin and depressed, Mary persuaded him to go to bed and put it off until the following day. The next morning, she found, to her complete horror, the old reprobate dead in bed beside her, his face completely black. He had been dead for about two hours. Lansdowne's scheme had not come off. Mary was left a young widow, all right, but not a rich one. Alexander Pendarves' estate went to his niece Mrs. Bassett, and Mary was left a relatively modest income of a few hundred pounds a year. She had been married for seven years and was as old as the century. New suitors flocked, but her opinion of marriage was as might be expected: "I marry! Yes, there's a blessed scene before my eyes of the comforts of that state. A sick husband, squalling brats, a cross mother-in-law, and a thousand unavoidable impertinences."

There was now some compensation. Widowhood gave her a measure of independence. Six years later, she made her first visit to Ireland. In the intervening years she moved between the Stanleys' homes at Whitehall and Northend and Mama's in Gloucester, but she had freedom to come and go as she pleased. In London she reclaimed the giddy town life. "Next Wednesday the Duke of Norfolk gives a masquerade; everybody is to be extravagantly fine, and to pull off their masques before they leave the house." She attended the opera and concerts: "I was yesterday at the rehearsal of Mr. Handel's new opera called *King Richard the First* – 'tis delightful." Royal birthdays and royal occasions were opportunities to cut a dash and study the fashions. "The Queen never was so well liked; her clothes were extravagantly fine, Lady Fanny Nassau, one of the ladies that bore up the train looked exceedingly well; her clothes were fine and very becoming, pink colour satin the gown (which was stiff-bodied), embroidered with silver, the petticoat covered with a trimming answerable [matching]." The world of books, theatre, fashion, scandals, suitors, engagements, births, weddings, settlements, deaths, wills and all the tittle-tattle of society absorbed her. Of her many admirers, only one made any real impression: "I thought him more agreeable than anybody I had ever known, and consequently more dangerous."

This was Lord Baltimore, Charles Calvert, one of the inner circle. He paid an erratic court and yet sparked a flame in her bruised and battered affections. Mary described him as a young man in great fashion at that time, very handsome, genteel, polite and unaffected. For five years he threw her into confusion while he flirted and dissembled. She flirted back but lack of fortune proved yet again the stumbling block. Shortly after making a disingenuous declaration, he turned tail and married Mary Janssen, daughter of the wealthy Sir Theodore Janssen of Wimbledon. This was a severe blow, and Mary's cruel representation of her rival clearly shows a woman scorned. She described her as looking "like a frightened owl, with her locks strutted out and most furiously greased, or rather gummed and powdered" (22 January 1740). When Baltimore met his death in 1751 she wasted little sympathy on him:

> I saw in the newspapers that Lord Baltimore
> was ill: is he dead? He had some good qualities;
> I fear his poor children at Epsom have been
> sadly neglected: I suppose he suspects they are
> not his own, but that cannot justify his neglect.
> (12 January 1751)

Ireland now beckoned. Mary's great friend Anne Donnellan (variously called Don and Phill), daughter of the Irish Chief Justice, had invited her to come and stay with her relations. Her sister, Katherine Clayton, was married to Robert Clayton, Bishop of Killala and Achonry. The bishop and Mrs. Clayton lived in some magnificence in Dublin. Mary wrote, "the real reason of my going was entirely locked within my breast". She needed an escape. Ireland, she hoped, would restore her; she could repair her broken heart in privacy and avoid the scorn of a society that had sniggered at Baltimore's cynical courtship. On the eve of the journey she drew a sad picture of herself: "thirty years is enough to wear off the bloom, and I must submit to be tarnished by time".

The expedition to Ireland across land and sea was a hazardous undertaking and Mary first canvassed the family:

> upon my mama's approving of my Irish scheme
> I plucked up my courage and spoke again to my
> brother. He answered "I was to please myself,

he had nothing to do with it," and after that was
as mute as a fish to all I could say.

Bernard's lack of approval became a constant theme of Mary's
life, but she proceeded without it and wrote to her sister on a
lighter note. "I pick up by degrees the things I shall want for
my Irish expedition. I have bought a gown and petticoat; 'tis a
very fine blue satin, sprigged all over with white" (13 July
1731). Men were off the menu and Irishmen no less so; Mr.
E. she lampooned without mercy, "with his Irish fash as
round as a potatoe, and with a sufficient stock of Corinthian
mettle to denote the 'nashion' he belongs to".

Dublin and the change of scene proved to be the balm she
needed. Mary wrote of her everyday activities. "Phill [Anne
Donnellan] and I walk three times round Stephen's Green,
which is two English miles. I never had my health better than
since being here." The Claytons lived right in the heart of
what is considered today the fashionable centre of Dublin
City in a newly built townhouse. She described their new
house, 80 St. Stephen's Green:

> The chief front of it is like Devonshire House.
> The apartments are handsome, and furnished
> with gold-coloured damask – virtue, and busts,
> and pictures that the Bishop brought with him
> from Italy. A universal cheerfulness reigns in the
> house. They keep a very handsome table, six
> dishes of meat are constantly at dinner, and six
> plates at supper. (22 September 1731)

The social round was hectic: there were balls, concerts,
picnics and parties. Dublin was eager to welcome Mrs.
Pendarves, the young widow who was cousin to the former Lord
Lieutenant, John Carteret. Family connections were only half
her attraction: she had wit and beauty and accomplishments

enough to dazzle any company. Her old vivacity returned, and she wrote of Irish informality: "there is a heartiness among them that is more like Cornwall than any I have known, and great sociableness". Dublin Castle was the court and command centre of English authority to which all the Anglo-Irish paid their respects. Mary reported on a gala day there:

> Yesterday, being the anniversary of the king's coronation, we, like loyal subjects, went to the Castle. There was a ball, very decently ordered, and French dances in abundance. I danced three country dances with Mr. Usher in a vast crowd; after that we were summoned to supper, where everything was prepared with great magnificence. (9 October 1731)

She was welcomed into Dublin's literary set by the famous dean of St. Patrick's, Jonathan Swift. *Gulliver's Travels* had been published five years earlier, and Swift's reputation as a writer and satirist was immense. Holding ground with this eccentric genius would be daunting, and she was cautious in her early impression: "Swift is a very odd companion; he talks a great deal and does not require many answers" (Dublin, 24 January 1733). But she persevered, and a mutual admiration was hatched between them. Swift, for his part, flirted and flattered when he wrote:

> Nothing vexes me so much with relation to you, as that with all my disposition to find faults, I was never once able to fix upon anything that I could find amiss, although I watched you narrowly; I kept my eyes and ears always upon you, in hopes that you would make some *boutade,* a French word which signifies a sudden jerk from a horse's hinder feet. (Dublin, 7 October 1734)

It was through Swift that she met her future husband, Dr. Patrick Delany. She liked the good clergyman very well and reported, "I was extremely pleased with him. His sermon was on the duties of wives to husbands, a subject of no great use to me at present." That was all to change.

Mary's visit to Ireland was intended to be for six months, but she was so well pleased with it that she stayed for eighteen.

> I hope my dear sister will endeavour to make herself and my mama easy at my staying so much longer in Ireland than I at first designed, for I never had my health better in my life; this country agrees perfectly well with me. (27 May 1732)

On her return to London she rented a house in Lower Brook Street where she set up home, in between paying the obligatory visits to relations and friends. Her great friend from this time onwards was Lady Margaret Harley Cavendish, wife of the second Duke of Portland. The family ties went back to her uncle Lansdowne, who was imprisoned in the Tower with Lord Oxford, Edward Harley, father of the duchess. Mary virtually became one of the family and spent several months of each year at Bulstrode, the country seat of the Cavendishes, near Gerrards Cross, Buckinghamshire. She wrote to Anne of a typical day there:

> We have variety of amusements, as reading, working, and drawing in the morning; in the afternoon the scene changes, there are billiards, looking over prints, coffee, tea, and by way of interlude, pretty Lady Betty [one of the Duchess's daughters] comes upon the stage, and I can play as well at bo-peep as if I had a nursery of my own.

Into this "palace of delights" came the first news of Anne's impending marriage. It caught Mary off guard, and she confided in their good friend Lady Throckmorton: "You that have a tender heart can easily guess what agitations of spirits I have been under, for marriage is *serious* and *hazardous* and you know what my fondness is for my sister" (Bulstrode, 5 December 1740). Anne Granville's choice was John Dewes, a steady, worthy man, neither handsome nor rich, but of good family and moderate means. The lovely Anne, now thirty-five, had in her younger days rejected numerous suitors. Her life was that of a dutiful daughter living with her mama in a gloomy townhouse in East Gate Street, Gloucester. She had, however, been persuaded that marriage and a home of her own would suit her better. By extraordinary omission, Mary was not party to these negotiations – possibly because of her fixed aversion to marriage. It was their bachelor brother, Bernard Granville, who brokered the deal. The prospect of losing her principal confidante disturbed Mary greatly; she knew only too well that Anne's first duty after marriage would be to her husband. Girls of their class were commonly married in their teens, while sufficiently young and healthy to deliver the necessary heirs, and the prospect of Anne childbearing in her thirties was alarming. Anne was not strong, and Mary had accompanied her to Bath on more than one occasion to take the waters. All these considerations tempered her response when she wrote to Anne on 22 April 1740 in a sober vein:

> I think Mr. Dewes behaves himself like a man of sense, and with a regard for you which must recommend him to all your friends. As soon as we have met, and he has settled with my brother, then we may proceed to particulars, buying wedding clothes, and determining where the ceremony is to be.

Despite Mary's reservations and worries, the couple were married. Their first-born son, Court Dewes, arrived safely the following year to the great satisfaction of all.

In her own life, Mary was becoming increasingly restive. Anne's marriage had not diminished the intimacy between the sisters – rather, the growing Dewes family provided a new focus for them both. She wrote with great animation:

> I have had no trouble about any of your affairs, but much pleasure; I shall send the box this week. The band box, basket and pincushion you must be so good as to accept from me. I will keep myself perfectly informed of the new dress for the bantling [a baby in swaddling bands]. I suppose you will have the cradle lined with dimity or white satin quilted.

Compared with this busy family life, Mary's social round was beginning to pall. She was actively seeking a new direction, and had confided her disappointment that influential friends had not exerted themselves sufficiently to secure her a position at court, when a bolt came out of the blue.

> You madam, are not a stranger to my present unhappy situation, I have lost a friend that was as my own soul, and nothing is more natural than to desire to supply that loss ... I know it is late in life to think of engaging anew in that state, in the beginning of my 59th year. I am old, and I appear older than I am; but thank God I am still in health, tho' not bettered by years, and however the vigour of life may be over, and with that the *vigour of vanity*, and the flutter of passion, I find myself not less fitted for all that is solid happiness in the wedded

state – the tenderness of affection, and the faith of friendship.

I have a good clear income for my life; a trifle to settle, which I am only ashamed to offer; a good house (as houses go in our part of the world), moderately furnished, a good many books, a pleasant garden (better I believe than when you saw it), etc. Would to God I might have leave to lay them all at your feet.

You will, I hope, pardon me the presumption of this wish, when I assure you it is no way blemished by the vanity of thinking them worthy of your acceptance, but as you have seen the vanities of the world to satiety, I allowed myself to indulge a hope that a retirement at this time of life, with a man whose turn of mind is not foreign from your own (and for that *only* reason not wholly unworthy of you) – a man who knows your worth, and honours you as much as he is capable of honouring any thing that is mortal, might not be altogether abhorrent from the views of your humble and unearthly wisdom.

Your most humble and most obedient servant,
Pat. Delany.

P.S. I hope to be in London on Monday night, and to have the happiness of finding you either in Clarges Street or Northend on Tuesday morning. I beseech God to guide and guard you. (23 April 1743)

Mary had liked Dr. Delany when she first met him in Dublin ten years before. She had reported to Anne: "Mr.

Delany will make a more desirable friend [than Swift], for he has all the qualities requisite for friendship – zeal, tenderness, and application; I know you would like him, because he is worthy" (20 February 1732). At that time he was about to be married to Margaret Tenison, a wealthy widow. At the age of forty-five, it was his first venture into matrimony, and Mary had related this news not once but twice. The marriage was a happy one. When he found himself a widower, after a decent interval he looked about him and his eye fell on Mary, now forty-three and widowed for nineteen years. Mary, true to form, applied not to her head or heart but to filial duty and her family.

Dr. Patrick Delany was a learned clergyman of humble and uncertain origin. A brilliant scholar, he had been educated in Trinity College Dublin, where he took orders in the Church of Ireland and became a senior fellow. He was chancellor of St. Patrick's Cathedral, Dublin, and a great friend of Swift's. A noted preacher and author of theological and literary works, he was a convivial and generous host – his "Thursday Society" gatherings at his townhouse in Stafford Street were famous. Ten days after his spirited proposal, he wrote again. From the tone of this letter it is clear Mary was not prepared to give her answer until Mama and Bernard had first given theirs, but it did show her inclination: had it been otherwise the matter would never have come before them.

> 3 May
> Permit me, madam, to beg to know my fate as far as it depends upon your friends in Gloucester: if it be favourable, be so good as to signify it to me, by *allowing* me the honour to call them *my friends*.

> 6 May
> Though I can scarcely hold a pen in my hand, I cannot help attempting to inform you that I

apprehend, from a moment's conversation with your brother this morning in the street (for he was gone out before I could reach his house), that his visit at Northend has made some change in his sentiments in relation to me. I beseech you, madam, leave me not to the caprice of any of your friends; and much less to the mercy of every humour of every friend. When you *owe duty*, pay it; and let me rise or fall by the determination of *duty*; but let not the decision depend upon the fickle, the uncertain, and the selfish. God has blessed you with noble sentiments, a good understanding and a generous heart; are not these, under God, your best governors? I might venture to pronounce that even a parent has no right to control you, at this time of life, and under your circumstances, in opposition to these; and a *brother* has no shadow of right.

The haughty Bernard Granville had gone out of his house to avoid Dr. Delany's call but instead ran into him on the street. The meeting was awkward but a change of attitude was detected. Uncle John Stanley at Northend had been persuaded, and the house of cards fell. Family hostility was put aside but never entirely overcome. Mama and Anne were reconciled to the match, but Bernard never completely forgave Mary for marrying so far beneath her station.

Mary's striking out cannot be underestimated. She had written that Dr. Delany "is as agreeable a companion as ever I met with, and one who condescends to converse with women, and treat them like reasonable creatures". A partnership of equals was a mightily attractive prospect. Their union decreed a removal to Dublin where a warm welcome awaited them, but the old life in London would be left behind. Mary would be leaving the little rented house in Clarges Street, the proximity of her beloved sister, the company of her fine friends and all familiar ways, but she was ready for a change. Widowed for nineteen years, she was bored with her vapid social existence. D.D., as she fondly called him, told her she had "seen the vanities of the world to satiety" and it was true. Dr. Delany had given up his house in Stafford Street much to the annoyance of Jonathan Swift and now resided at Delville. As wife of Dr. Delany and mistress of her own miniature estate, Delville, she would no longer be the obliging satellite circling Northend or Bulstrode. In an earlier letter to Swift, she recollected no entertainment with as much pleasure as that at Dr. Delany's: "it has made me lament very sincerely the many hours in my life that I have lost in insignificant conversation". It would be good to pit her wits against them again. Parting from family and the uneasy relationship now fostered with Bernard were drawbacks in the exchange. Anne dreaded the separation:

> Alas, my dear Penny, it makes me tremble when you say 'tis *three weeks* before an answer can return from Ireland! What an age to an impatient heart anxious for the health and circumstances of a belov'd friend! But that's a thought I must not, dare not, trust myself to encourage.

The Gentleman's Magazine reported that the couple married on 9 June 1743, and Ireland beckoned again.

The departure was not immediate – the new Mrs. Delany had work to do. Advancement in the Church would be to D.D.'s credit and improve his standing with the Granville family. Political patronage was the order of the day, and her connections should be useful for something. She determined to wring what she could for her new husband. After much lobbying, the following year she was able to write:

> Yesterday, just as dinner came upon the table, Lord Carteret came to the door. He desired we

> would send the servants away, and when they
> were gone he told D.D. he was come from the
> Duke of Devonshire to offer him the Deanary
> of Down. (Clarges Street, 8 May 1744)

Carteret had come through; Mrs. Delany had found her mark
and secured promotion for her beloved D.D. Her work in
England was done, there could be no more delays and Ireland
was now in their sights. They packed up and set off.

Mrs. Delany was very well disposed to like her new home.
On her first visit to Dublin, she had written: "This morning
we are to go out of town to a house of Dr. Delany's called
Delville: we carry a cold scrap with us, and propose spending
the day very agreeably; it is about three mile off" (9 October
1731). She had even more reason to be delighted with it now.
Refurbishing the house, making improvements in the garden
and managing the household totally absorbed her, and she
went to the task with all the energy of a new bride.

> I expected a great deal of business, but not so
> much as I find; I have workmen of all sorts in
> the house – upholsterers, joiners, glaziers, and
> carpenters – and am obliged to watch them all,
> or their work would be but ill-finished; and I
> have not been one day without company since I
> came. (26 July 1744)

She was never idle, prompting the dean to write:

> She hath works for all hours and occasions, and
> finds full employment for her hands even
> between the *coolings of her cups of tea*. (Character of
> Maria [Mrs. Delany] by Dr. Delany, sent as a
> Christmas present to Mrs. Dewes. Lady
> Llanover's footnote says that "The portrait
> alluded to of Mrs. Delany under the name of

'Maria', was evidently intended for the periodical publication called the *Humanist*, of which the Dean of Down published fifteen numbers; commencing in 1757... [These portraits were intended to inspire others to emulation.] On Mrs. Delany's discovering that the model given for imitation was intended for herself, she objected to its being published.")

She superintended elaborate new decorative schemes and hand-worked chair covers, carpets, curtains, fringes, knotting and, on a larger scale, candle sconces and festoons in shells. The house itself, near Glasnevin in Dublin, was demolished in the 1950s with some of her exquisite shell-work still extant.

Dublin's social scene was as hectic as ever and the Delany's were naturally sociable, but their interest now revolved around home. Delville opened its doors to visits long and short – the artist Letitia Bushe was one of the long-stay visitors and Delville became her second home, as it did for Mrs. Delany's godchild, Sally Chapone.

All visitors were pressed into service when great works were afoot.

On Monday, two Mrs. Hamilton's, Bushe, Miss Hamilton, Mr. Sackville Hamilton, came to breakfast. As soon as that was done, *I set them all to work*; gave each a dusting-cloth, brush, sponge and bowl of water, and set them to cleaning my picture-frames. Bushe undertook cleaning the pictures, and egging them out, whilst the *carpenters and I fixed up shelves for* my books and china: everybody that popped their head in, was *seized to work*; no idler was admitted; a very merry working morning it was, and my dressing room is very spruce and handsome. (22 September 1750)

Callers were not always so welcome.

> A strange gibble gabble woman has plagued me
> all the morning; I never was more nearly
> provoked to be rude in all my life. I crammed
> her with chocolate and plum-cake, and then
> sent her packing, but she has robbed me of
> what is not in her power to restore, a good hour
> of *my time*. (13 February 1746)

The new dean and his wife had to introduce themselves to
their deanery, and a removal north in expeditionary style took
off for Downpatrick.

> The Dean and I travel in our chaise, which is
> easy and pleasant; Betty and Margaret, the cook
> and a housemaid in the coach and four, and Peg
> Hanages (who I am breeding up to be a house-
> maid) in a car we have had made for marketing,
> and carrying luggage when we travel. Our new
> coach will be ready when we come home, but
> now we hire one for the northern expedition.
> (20 May 1745)

There was no deanery house, so they stayed at Mount
Panther, some miles from the town. The Delanys were
shocked at the sorry state of the parish. Mrs. Delany wrote,
"The last Dean was here but two days in six years ... the
curate has been so negligent as never to visit any of the poor
of the parish." This complaint rang somewhat hollow later on,
when they were accused of similar neglect themselves.
Accounts of the neighbourhood were faithfully communi-
cated to Anne:

> As Down is three miles from hence, and we
> cannot go to prayers in the afternoon if we dine
> at home, the Dean designs to dine every Sunday

at Down. There is a public-house kept by a clever man who was butler formerly to one of the Deans; he has a very good room in his house, and he is to provide a good dinner, and the Dean will fill his table every Sunday with all the towns-people and their wives by turns, which will oblige the people, and give us an opportunity of going to church in the afternoon without any fatigue. (11 June 1745)

Anne, living at Wellesbourne in Warwickshire, had three thriving boys, Court, Bernard and John, when her only daughter was born in February 1746 to the great joy of all the family. The child, Mary Dewes, was named after her aunt Delany and became her "own little girl". They shared responsibility for the rearing of this child, familiarly called Pauline (this was after the granddaughter of the great seventeenth-century letter writer Madame de Sevignée, who was the keeper of her letters). No detail of her development was too small for notice; Mrs. Delany was consulted on all matters.

The Delany marriage was a very happy one. The couple were devoted to each other for twenty-five years, until the Dean's death in 1768, but their lives were not without disappointments and sorrows.

There is murmuring at his [the Dean] not living more at his deanery, and being absent so long from it when we go to England. This you may believe is vexatious to me, as it is entirely on my account he goes, and he is so generous as not to retract in the least from his promise to me and to my friends of my going to England every third year, though I am very sensible it is not quite convenient to him. (3 January 1752)

This was a cause of some dissatisfaction among his flock, and there was a dispute over the payment of tithes, but it was a nagging lawsuit that upset their composure for several valuable years. It arose over the will of the dean's first wife, Margaret Tenison. In the aftermath of her death he had foolishly burnt some of her papers. The Tenison family seized on the blunder and accused the dean of spoilation. The slur on his reputation and the threatened loss of income was devastating. Claim and counter claim carried on for six wearying years until it was finally decided in his favour.

> A cause never was so *well attended* nor a more *universal joy seen* than when Lord Mansfield, after an hour and half's speaking with angelic oratory, pronounced the decree in our favour; the "spoilation" *entirely thrown aside* on the very arguments my good brother Dewes always insisted on! The decree that now takes place makes D.D. liable to pay 3000 pounds, and there are some other accounts to be settled, but of *trifling consequence.* (7 March 1758)

Mrs. Delany had lost none of her bite when, the following year, she found herself in company with the Lord Chancellor of Ireland, John Bowes, one of the dean's greatest adversaries in the lawsuit. She described him as being in a miserable state of health, "with legs bigger considerably at the ankle than at the calf" (12 May 1759).

Throughout this period, her distress and a growing sense of isolation from family and England was palpable: "some of my friends cannot, others will not take their turn of making me a visit. To you my most dear and most indulgent sister, I should not say this." The complaint was, of course, directed towards Bernard Granville.

> I agree with you perfectly in regard to my brother. I know he has excellent qualities ... As I lay my whole heart open to you I must tell you of a vain foolish chimera of mine; I could not help thinking that he would come to me as soon as he knew of the sudden and unexpected turn of our affairs. (2 September 1752)

Bernard Granville never came to lend support. Anne was excused because of family responsibilities. The family circle was contracting. Mama had died in 1747, and her death had drawn the two sisters even closer together. Bevil Granville, the black-sheep younger brother who featured in the early letters, had been sent out of England to North Carolina for bad debts. He had succumbed to swamp fever and died there. Bernard Granville continued cold and perverse to the end.

The successful outcome of the court case gave way to a deeper crisis: Anne's health was failing. A sense of dread crept into the letters. Mrs. Delany was almost frantic, but she couched her anxiety in all sorts of trivial news and gossip. She was torn between D.D., who was old and unwell, and Anne, from whom she tried to hide her trepidation. Taking the waters at Bristol had been recommended, and Mrs. Delany gave her every encouragement:

> I think I have found remarkable benefit from having chalk in every thing I drank; a lump put into the jug of water, and the tea-water managed in the same way. It is a great sweetener of the blood and in no respect can be bad for you. Since Bristol water is thought proper for you ... I will endeavour to see you there ... provided D.D. is well enough for me to leave him! I thank God he has been very well. I was very glad my brother made you a second visit;

> he tells me you were let blood whilst he was
> with you, and that your *blood* was *very good*. Do
> you think it was of any service to you? I *fear not*,
> as you had a giddy fit or two after it! (13
> December 1760)

It is not surprising that Anne had a giddy fit after being bled. Her condition worsened, and the sister of Mrs. Delany's heart died at Bristol on 6 July of the following year. She was fifty-four.

Those years took their toll. Mrs. Delany drew deep from her well of courage, but she was soon tried again. She confided in her friend Lady Andover:

> I have been sadly anxious for some time past for
> my dear D.D., he has been *very ill*, and reduced
> very low, which, to a man of his years, must give
> cruel apprehensions; however, I thank God his
> good constitution has at present got the better,
> and he is as well as he has been for some
> months past.

The dean's health had suffered during the Tenison affair, and the weight of years now caught up with him. In a tender parting, he died at Bath on 6 May 1768, aged eighty-four. Mary Dewes was with them through this terrible time, and she wrote to her brother:

> The Sunday before he died he was complaining
> of want of sleep ... at six o'clock the night
> before he died, he said to Mrs. Smith [Mrs.
> Delany's waiting woman], "I thought it would
> all have been over long before this time." At 8
> he bid his servant come and close his eyes, he
> prayed for him and blessed him.

D.D. had chosen to die in England so that Mrs. Delany would be among friends and on home soil. Their beloved Delville was sold and Mrs. Delany never saw Ireland again.

She was sixty-eight. She had considered herself very old at three score, but now she felt truly old. "I am tired of the world, and its ways, though a *few* individuals *pull very hard*, and they make me loth to quit my hold!" (3 May 1771). A fierce moral courage, well tempered in the fire, a resolute belief in life after death and the comfort of friends armoured her against the blows. Mary Dewes supplied the place of Anne, and the Duchess of Portland flew to her to offer what succour she could. They persuaded her to settle in London, and settling the house galvanised her energies anew.

Marriage was soon in the air again, this time for Mary Dewes:

> I don't know what to say on a *subject* that occupies my thoughts as much as yours, but ...
> I have nothing to recommend to my dearest Mary during the present state of affairs, but what her own excellent principles and good sense suggest. (15 July 1770)

Mary Dewes' upset was caused by her uncle Bernard Granville, who disapproved of her match. The man in question was John Port of Ilam in Derbyshire. The Port family was of ancient lineage, and the young man's estate and character were good. Mrs. Delany was provoked to write:

> I never can cease wondering at the unaccountable behaviour of [Bernard Granville] ... I must write to him, but with painful reluctance, as I never expect that cordiality which I feel I have a claim to, and cannot guess why it is withdrawn.

The Duchess of Portland stepped in. Bernard Granville was overruled, and the marriage took place at Bulstrode on 6 December 1770. The following year, a daughter, Georgina Mary Ann Port, was born. For years she was called G.M.A., before the name Georgina was finally settled on. Mrs. Delany's grand-niece became her new child and lit up the remaining years of her life.

A year later Mrs. Delany wrote to Mary Dewes (Mrs Port):

> I have invented a new way of imitating flowers. I'll send you next time I write one for a sample. I have done no work but *finishing* the work'd stools, and am now knotting fringe for them, and I have done 3 chimney boards for the drawing-room here, the dining room, and the Dss own bed-chamber. They are meer bagatelles; but the weather has been so fine we lived much abroad, and my *agility* is not now equal to my *imagination*. (Bulstrode, 4 October 1772)

Mrs Delany's industry was such that in her seventy-second year she invented a new art form, making paper cut-out copies of real flowers. She had a genius for detail and, with scissors and coloured paper in hand, made exact botanical representations to scale. This work became so famous during the years that she was employed in it that flower specimens were sent to her from the Royal Gardens at Kew to copy. Her flower mosaics now form part of the British Museum's permanent Enlightenment exhibition.

Her *Flora Delanica*, as she called it, was started as an experiment to pass an idle hour at Bulstrode. It grew into a collection of almost one thousand flower mosaics and brought her to the attention of many interested admirers, including amateur botanists King George III and Queen

Charlotte. The flower pictures, though extraordinary in themselves, were but a fraction of her life's handiwork. She was a gifted artist – in her younger days she had produced the finest spun cloth and exquisite needlework. Her inspiration was always from the natural world: flowers, plants, insects and shells. With the keenest sensibility, she worked the stitches and colours to suit the vagaries of nature. She made intricate black-and-white paper silhouettes, representing everyday family scenes with her signature tool, a pair of scissors. Under the adoring eye of the dean, she had developed her painterly talents, copying works from the masters for the chapel at Delville. In the rococo spirit of the day, she created mystical shell grottos, ingenious follies for the gardens of her friends at Northend, Killala and Delville. She was a musician of feeling and an elegant dancer. She was well-read in all the books of the day, except works considered morally dubious. She was interested in everything: the arts, science, travel, theatre, music, the opera. Her conversation was informed and lively, and her company was sought after well into her old age.

A friend from Ireland, Mrs. Preston, gave the following description of Mrs. Delany in 1787, the year before she died. They had not seen each other since the Delanys' departure for England. She wrote:

> I will not delay giving you the pleasure I know you must receive, my good friend, from hearing such an account of Mrs. Delany, as I can truly give you from having spent two hours with her this morning. I was with her at 9 this morning, and heard (with no small agitation) her *well-known foot* hastening down to meet me. For a few minutes our meeting was silent, as many circumstances rushed into our minds very

affecting to us both. I *dreaded* seeing the alteration in her, that was naturally to be expected from *twenty years' absence!* But I was *soon set at ease,* by seeing the same *apprehension, attention, benevolence,* and comfortable enjoyment of every pleasant circumstance in her situation, that you remember in her. Her enquiries, her remarks, her whole conversation, full of *life* and *ingenuity*; and that kind heart and manner of expressing its feelings, as warm as ever! She is as *upright* and *walks as alertly*, as when you saw her. (13 September 1787)

In step with the century as ever, Mrs. Delany was undiminished.

Into this extraordinary world of refinement and art and grace came the seven-year-old G.M.A. Aunt Delany had undertaken to bring her forward as she had been brought forward all those years before by Aunt Stanley. She reported on her progress:

I have continued G.M.A.'s masters, and I think they will lay such a foundation as will enable her to go on at home with advantage. I believe 3 times more finishes Mr. Bolton, and I shall then discharge him, as she is grown fonder of looking into her books of geography and her maps. I *can* attend to her writing, and her papa I trust will improve her in arithmetic and teach her multiplication table which she is deficient in, but her excellent capacity, when improved by attention, will do all we wish for her; you must not expect too much on the harpsichord. (St. James's Place, 3 May 1781)

Mrs. Delany, whose mettle had been tried many times, well understood that no life was without its sorrows. Bernard Granville had died in 1775 refusing a visit from her, his only remaining sister. From an account of Mrs. Agnew (Mrs Delany's waiting woman):

> her spending the summer at Bulstrode, so offended her brother, Mr. Granville, when he asked her to meet some particular friends that upon her refusal he altered his will, and after awarding Mrs. Delany £300 a year for her life if she survived him, he left her nothing.

Her world contracted to Bulstrode and Whitehall and to the Ports at Ilam, where she made many visits, and to her own home in St. James's Place, London. In July of 1785, her dearest friend, the Duchess of Portland, second only to her beloved sister, died. Her death, which followed a few days' illness, was unexpected and came as yet another shattering blow. Horace Walpole wrote to enquire:

> By a postscript in a letter I have just received from Mr. Keate, he tells me the Duchess of Portland *is dead!* I *fear* it is but *too true!* You will forgive me therefore for troubling you with inquiring about poor Mrs. Delany! It would be to no purpose to send to her house. (Strawberry Hill, 19 July 1785)

King George and Queen Charlotte came to the rescue. They were regular visitors to Bulstrode and had got to know Mrs. Delany there:

> The King and Queen came a little after six. The King drove the Queen in a low chaise with a pair of little white horses. Lady Weymouth

attending them in another chaise and 6 grooms on horseback, but no other attendants. The Duchess of Portland met them on the steps before the hall-door. I was in the dressing-room belonging to the blue damask apartment. They were so gracious, as to desire me to bring my book of flowers, and I have neither time nor assurance to tell you all the things they said. They staid till 8 o'clock. (5 August 1776)

They were as greatly enamoured with her and her flower pictures as she was with them and their large family. After the duchess's death, Bulstrode no longer seemed a home from home to Mrs. Delany, though the duchess's son, the incumbent Duke of Portland, offered it to her with a full heart. To make good her loss, the royal couple offered Mrs. Delany a small house at Windsor to use for her summer quarters and a pension to fund the added expense.

Astley (my servant) I sent to Windsor last Thursday to see what conveniences there might be wanting in the house that their Majesties have been so gracious as to give me; when there she received the King's command that I was only "*to bring myself and my niece, clothes, and attendants, as stores of every kind would be laid in for me*". (August/September 1785)

There was but a short time remaining to enjoy it. G.M.A. was now her constant companion and was with her to the end.

Mrs. Delany was taken ill on Sunday, 6 April 1788. The following day G.M.A. wrote: "My aunt has passed a very bad day, her fever and oppression on her breath increasing every moment. Indeed to so violent a degree, that without waiting for Dr. Turton, at nine o'clock Mr. Yonge *bled her*" (7 April

1788). The following week the doctors were optimistic and all boded well. Mrs. Delany died on 15 April 1788, and it was so unexpected that the shock to her friends was as great as if she had been in the full vigour of youth. To G.M.A., then only a girl of 17, it was completely overwhelming. In a heartbroken letter to Mrs. Francis Hamilton, she wrote: "Oh Madam, she is no more! On Tuesday the 15th she expired at 11 o'clock at night. Were it not for the assurance I have of her felicity, I think it would not be possible for me to exist."

The extraordinary life of Mrs. Delany ended when was eighty-eight. Her legacy to the world was her collection of letters. They were her lifeline, her connection when she was apart from family and friends. The letters to Anne in particular are long, rambling conversations. Family news, generations of births, deaths and marriages, make up a sizeable proportion of them. News of friends was of abiding interest, as were reports on grand formal occasions and grand people. Marriage settlements and matchmaking were related with some energy, as well as deaths and wills. The art and industry of their hands was a huge part of their letters. Music, plays and books were critically analysed. Detailed topographical descriptions of places visited were recounted. Portrayals of comic characters were drawn for sheer entertainment. Sorrows and worries were shared. Clothes were described in detail. In a time of the crudest medical practice, anything relating to health, illness, childbirth, cures, medications, potions or lotions was seized upon. There was delicious gossip for the pure enjoyment of it. Home entertainments, children's balls, concert parties and games were described in detail. The weather, how hot or cold it was and how the garden looked, was reported. The antics of the household cats were told. As the children were born to Anne and then to Mary Dewes (Mrs. Port), the letters contained instruction as to proper child rearing and suitable decorum for young people. The perennial problem of staff and troublesome servants was a lively source of discussion. Home decorating was described with enthusiasm. Supplying the tables for the endless round of breakfasts, dinners and suppers was a theme they relished.

Mrs. Delany might be amazed to discover her letters still in circulation two and a half centuries after they were written, but in life she shared them. Miss Mary Hamilton, a niece of Sir William Hamilton, while staying at Bulstrode, wrote in her journal:

> She [Mrs. Delany] then talk'd of my settling in life; told me the sort of person I ought for my own happiness to marry ... I read her paragraphs out of my letters; I had one from Miss Hannah More ... At half past 12 Mrs. Delany came to me, brought letters she had received from Mrs. Boscawen and she left me two; I promised to follow her into the drawing-room. (16 December 1783)

Letters were common currency. Private passages could be, and often were, removed or destroyed, but as carriers of news or as witty showpieces they were copied and passed around the salons and toilettes of fashionable society.

Years earlier, Mrs. Delany had written to Anne from Dublin:

> I already delight in your garden; pray have plenty of roses, honeysuckles, jessamine and sweet briar, not forgetting the lily of the valley, which I would rather be than any flower that grows – 'tis retired, lives in shade, wraps up itself in its mantle, and gently reclines its head as if ashamed to be looked at, not conscious how much it deserves it. How pretty it is! Who would not be that flower? (30 March 1732)

Mrs. Delany's decided preference to bloom in the shade was not to be. Her exposure is thanks to her great-grand-niece, Lady Augusta Llanover, who, in the 1860s, collated and edited the letters into six volumes of *The Autobiography and Correspondence of Mary Granville, Mrs. Delany* and thereby safeguarded her place in history. Lady Llanover was not the first into the field; Mrs. Frances Hamilton published her correspondence with Mrs. Delany as early as 1821.

Mrs. Delany has fascinated ever since, with condensed collections and biographies appearing almost every generation. Earlier titles tended to focus on the grand side of her life: *Mrs. Delany at Court and among the Wits* by R. Brimley Johnson, for instance, focused on the aristocrat, the *habituée* at court, the friend of Handel and Walpole, the pupil of Hogarth, correspondent of Swift and favourite of royalty. More recent publications have tended to be thematic, such as Ruth Hayden's *Mrs. Delany: Her Life and Her Flowers* and Angelique Day's *Letters from Georgian Ireland.*

Though well documented, Mrs. Delany's life of birth and privilege is remote to most of us. We can identify very much, though, with the trials of her family life and all the domestic flurry that went with it. These were the personal parts of Mrs. Delany's correspondence, not necessarily for reading aloud in the drawing-room, but the parts she revelled in nonetheless. It is our common ground with Mrs. Delany and the focus for this book. The differences between us are only in time and scale. A fifteenth-century ancestor of Mrs. Delany's, Sir Roger Granville, was known as "The Great Housekeeper" because of his improving works and husbandry. She followed in his footsteps when she wrote:

> I had an intention of writing to you last post but
> – impossible – shoals of impertinences made it
> impracticable. A year's absence [from Delville]

makes it so necessary to have a thorough inspection into everything, and I am settling my family in a different way from what it was formerly, which obliges me to be Mrs. Notable, and to do much more than I ever did in my life, and I hope it will agree with me; and own that the bustle of it, (which once I should have thought better executed by a servant than myself,) has been of service to me. (18 May 1750)

Did Mrs. Delany protest too much? The actual drudgery of housework was for the domestics, but she took on the role of housekeeper with some aplomb. This book is not unduly concerned with Mrs. Delany's status but instead explores her food and drink, her servants, her medicines, manners, wardrobe and décor and her excellent alter ego: Mrs. Notable.

This way to the eating parlour ...

leveret
and
cheesecakes:
mrs. delany's
menus

Yesterday was spent in tranquillity at home; and this day may prove so too, for nobody is yet come, and 'tis past 12 o'clock, and a cloudy rainy day; *n'importe*, only bread and butter is spread, and water boiling without mercy. On Monday next we are invited to Mr. Bristowe's and you shall know to a pepper-corn what we have to dinner. (7 July 1750 Delville)

So Mrs. Delany wrote, giving Anne notice of a feast in the home of Mr. Bristowe, a noted epicure. Her concluding line, "This is an impertinent piece of news, is it not?" suggests that the subject of food and eating was too crude or too trivial to communicate. Nevertheless, through her years of correspondence, she described breakfasts, dinners, suppers and in-between snacks in detail and with great relish.

Bread and butter, tea, coffee and chocolate were the breakfast staples, a meal usually taken between nine and ten o'clock in the morning. Mrs. Delany might have a day's work done by then, but breakfast could be a very sociable interlude, as she reported from the home of Richard Wellesley, later Lord Mornington, grandfather to the Duke of Wellington, whom she visited during her first long stay in Ireland:

We meet at breakfast about ten; chocolate, tea, coffee, toast and butter and caudle, etc., are devoured without mercy. The hall is so large that very often breakfast, battledore and shuttlecock, and the harpsichord, go on at the same time without molesting one another. (Dangan, Co. Meath, 5 April 1733)

Caudle was not on every breakfast menu and was probably served on this occasion in honour of the guests. It was a blend of wine or ale, gruel, eggs, sugar and spices, a sort of fortified porridge that would set a body up for the day. In the following century, Mrs. Beeton consigned caudle to an invalid food, but in Mrs. Delany's time it was regarded as both restorative and celebratory, especially after childbirth. Mrs. Delany's great friend and correspondent Mrs. Frances Boscawen, one of the famous Blue Stocking set, whose daughter had just given birth, wrote:

> I set out pretty early and caught Mrs. Leveson [her daughter Elizabeth] in bed; she treated me with caudle which, tho I am old fashioned enough to like mightily, yet the best part of the treat was to come from Audley Street, in the shape of a letter from Mrs. Delany. (Glan Villa, 14 July 1774)

Caudle was still fashionable in royal circles when Mrs. Delany wrote to her niece Mary (Dewes) Port after the birth of Princess Mary in April 1776: "I have written thus far by owl light. The grand assembly at the Queen's caudle drinking fills my little circle every evening."

Tea, coffee and chocolate, beverages now taken completely for granted, were unimaginable luxuries to any but the extremely wealthy, especially in the earlier part of the eighteenth century. High taxes in England ensured that tea remained expensive until the end of the century, when taxation was eased. It was even more expensive in Ireland, so taking tea was a very exclusive status symbol. In April 1724, Lady Dorothy Cobbe, wife of Charles Cobbe, Archbishop of Dublin, recorded in her household accounts for Newbridge House, Donabate, Co. Dublin, tea at sixteen shillings and sixpence per pound and coffee at one pound per pound. In the same month she recorded "two men digging my garden" at two shillings. In relative terms, though difficult to quantify, the value of Lady Dorothy's one pound for one pound weight of coffee would equate to something like one hundred and six pounds sterling today, which makes it a racing certainty the men digging the garden never had a tea or coffee break.

Orders for tea went from the Granville ladies, Mama and Anne in Gloucester, to Mary in London. Fulfilling them was no easy matter, as the then Mrs. Pendarves reported:

> Mrs. Badge [her waiting woman] nor I could not rightly understand you about the Bohea tea, for she does not remember she was ordered to bespeak any, and you say in your letter that I must send the Bohea tea that was bespoke, and a pound more. She imagines the tea mama meant was "tea dust." But she can't get any for love nor money, but has bought two pound of Bohea, at thirteen shilling a pound, which the man says is extraordinary good; but every thing of that kind grows very dear, chocolate especially. I have sent you a pound at three and sixpence, the best in town at that price, but I am afraid it is not such as my mother will like, but I desire her approbation of it as soon as she has tasted it. (5 October 1727)

Merchants' trade cards show Soho to have been a centre for the sale of tea, coffee and chocolate in London. Nicholas Sanders, a chocolate maker in Greek Street, advertised all sorts of fine teas, coffee and cocoa shells, while the neighbouring Whites' chocolate makers, at 8 Greek Street, claimed to be the only makers of Sir Hans Sloane's Milk Chocolate, greatly recommended by many eminent physicians for its lightness on the stomach and good effects in consumptive cases. Hans

Sloane, the son of a Protestant planter born in Co. Down, became the most famous physician of his day. He also had extraordinary success as an entrepreneur. It was on his voyage to Jamaica as personal physician to Christopher Monck, the Second Duke of Albermarle, that he observed the use of chocolate mixed with milk as a remedy for sickly Jamaican children.

Mrs. Granville, who was brought up in Cadiz in Spain, was something of a connoisseur. Chocolate and coffee were the favoured hot drinks in Spain during her time there, and her approval of any chocolate despatched to her was anxiously awaited. Drinking chocolate was made by shaving chocolate parings from solid chocolate tablets or cocoa shells into special little copper or pewter pots. The chocolate was then milled or ground with a chocolate grinder, a gadget that looked like a swizzle stick. The pot was put to heat, the chocolate melted, milk and sugar were added and the drink was made very thick and luscious. It was agitated again to create a crema or froth on top and served in delicate porcelain chocolate cups, like little beakers, specially designed for the purpose.

The troublesome Bohea tea came from Wu-I, a province in China, and the name Bohea was a corruption of the original pronunciation. Bohea was a good quality black tea usually drunk with milk but Queen Anne, whose death had such dire consequences for the wider Granville family, reputedly took her Bohea tea cold with a little gin. As the century wore on, tea replaced gin as a staple beverage in England, but Queen Anne clearly hedged her bets by taking both together. Whether the Granville ladies laced their tea with gin is doubtful, but the whole tea ceremony well became them. The tea craze started the fashion for Chinese porcelain and the Granvilles became great collectors and connoisseurs of china.

Bohea tea was also taken in Ireland. By the middle of the

eighteenth century the household accounts of the Vigors family of Burgage, Co. Carlow, list it. However, they bought in much smaller quantities, probably because of the price. Entries from June, July and September of 1758 show:

> June 21st. My mother bought half a pound of Bohea at three shillings and three pence. July 17th. My mother one quarter and I another of Green Tea at five shillings. On September 4th. I bought a quart of Bloom Tea at three shillings and sixpence.

These accounts also list a "Loafe of Sugar from Mr. Ealy". This tea was so expensive it was locked away in tea caddies. The lining of the caddies was a tin–lead alloy called "tea pewter" to keep the tea-leaves fresh and dry, and the mistress of the house kept the key. Tea-leaves were also dried and re-used.

Mrs. Delany continued to report on her breakfasts:

> Last night a note came to inform me that Lady Caroline and Mr. Fox and the family at Lucan would breakfast here, as they were going in a few days to England. I could not put it off, so have set all my best china in order, and prepared everything for their reception; and as they are people of taste, I honour them so far as to permit them to breakfast in the library! It has struck eleven and I hope they will not come till 12. (7 July 1750)

Nothing but the best would do for Lady Caroline Lennox, eldest daughter of the Duke of Richmond. She had eloped with the politically ambitious Henry Fox in May 1744, much to the consternation of her parents. Caroline's younger sister Emily had married the exceedingly wealthy James Fitzgerald, Earl of Kildare, in 1747; he later became the Duke of

Leinster. The Foxes were making a visit to the Fitzgerald's country seat at Carton. Delville was included on their final round of calls before returning to England.

Notice of a breakfast visit was usually sent ahead and was generally well received, but not always.

> Monday, we carried Mr. Sandford [the Dean's curate/librarian] to Mrs. Clement's Lodge in Phoenix Park, found her at breakfast, was first denied, but on hearing our names let us in. We eat a second breakfast, and walked all over her house; she very fine, and very civil, but it rained so violently we could not see her improvements abroad. Before we came away a pine-apple was brought in ready pared and cut, all served in fine old china. (22 September 1759)

The pineapple was a symbol of hospitality but, more importantly, it was a remarkable status symbol. Mrs. Clements may have produced it either to show-off or to make up for the earlier cool reception. Advanced horticultural development at the time saw heated pineapple houses go up on landed estates all over England and Ireland. Glasshouses combining pineapples and vines were called pinery vineries, and gentlemen horticulturists of the day vied with each other to produce such exotic fruit.

The Phoenix Park pineapple had further significance because Mrs. Delany considered the Clements *nouveau riche*. She had written to Anne:

> Not hear of Mr. and Mrs. Clements! Why she is finer than the finest lady in England. Dress, furniture, house, equipage – excelling all! Mr. Clements is – her husband! They set out in life very young and very humble, though both of good families; he was a favourite of Luke

Gardiner's, and has gathered together by degrees
an immense fortune, if one may judge by the
magnificence of his living; and what is quite
surprising, they are both very moderate in their
understanding ... They keep Wednesdays. (5
May 1759)

Nathaniel Clements, "her husband" who built the lodge in
the Phoenix Park, now Áras an Uachtaráin, was the park
ranger and someone who might be expected to be horti-
culturally adventurous. Mrs. Clements, for her part, probably
thought the pineapple was a good taunt for her imperious
visitors.

Mrs. Delany often had imperious visitors of her own. She
knew that entertaining such guests to breakfast was a more
economical proposition than giving a grand dinner and was a
proper demonstration of hospitality for people of their
standing.

Some day next week, if the weather is good, we
have thought of asking the Duke and Duchess
of Dorset [the Lord Lieutenant and his wife] to
breakfast. Dinners are grown such luxurious
feasts in this country that we do not pretend to
show away with such magnificence, and our
viceroy loves magnificence too well to be
pleased with our way of entertaining company.
I own I think there is a time of life as well as a
station when very gaudy entertainments are as
unbecoming as pink colour and pompadours!
(11 April 1752)

Breakfast could be a *fête-champêtre*, for the chosen few:

My garden is at present in the high glow of
beauty, my cherries ripening, roses, jessamine,

and pinks in full bloom, and the hay partly spread and partly in cocks, complete the rural scene. We have discovered a new breakfasting place under the shade of the nut-trees, impenetrable to the sun's rays, in the midst of a grove of elms, where we shall breakfast this morning; I have ordered cherries, strawberries, and nosegays to be laid on our breakfast-table and have appointed a harper to be here to play to us during our repast, who is to be hid among the trees. Mrs. Hamilton is to breakfast with us, and is to be cunningly led to this place and surprised. (Delville, 22 June 1750)

It was not to be:

Mrs. Hamilton disappointed us, and did not come till twelve; we breakfasted in our new grove at our usual time, for she knows our hours, and we are under agreement not to wait. No ceremony subsists between us; it is laid aside, though ceremony is proper to keep those at a distance that otherwise might be troublesome.

There was, however, no keeping the troublesome at bay at a free gala entertainment designed to generate interest in what is now the Rotunda Hospital in Dublin and the first lying-in hospital in Ireland or Britain. The attendance did not meet with Mrs. Delany's approval.

Went to Dr. Moss's gratis breakfast ... Dr. Moss, you must know, is the chief manager and operator of the Lying-in Hospital, and has gardens laid out for the entertainment of company in the manner of Vauxhall and Ranelagh; and in order to gather together subscribers for the next season he gave a gratis breakfast and a fine concert of music in a large room which was not opened before, and is in the gardens. The music allured us, and we went, D.D. with us, at about half an hour after eleven, the concert to begin at 12. When we came, with some difficulty we squeezed into the room, which they say is 60 ft long, and got up to the breakfast table, which had been well pillaged; but the fragments of cakes, bread and butter, silver coffee-pots, and tea-kettles without number, and all sorts of spring flowers strewed on the table, shewed it had been set out plentifully and elegantly. The company, indeed, looked as if their principal design of coming was for a breakfast. When they had satisfied their hunger the remains were taken away, and such a torrent of rude mob (for they deserved no better name) crowded in that I and my company crowded out as fast as we could, glad we escaped in whole skins, and resolving never more to add to the throng of a gratis entertainment. We got away with all speed without hearing a note of music ... The bustle and odd mixture of company (for there was from the highest to the lowest) was matter of mirth to us in the evening, when we had a little recovered our fatigue. (Delville, February 1751)

No mob but the highest in the land was entertained when King George III and Queen Charlotte came to breakfast at Bulstrode. Mrs. Delany described the occasion to her niece Mary (Dewes) Port:

> The Duchess of Portland brought her Majesty a dish of tea, roles and cakes, which she

accepted, but would carry it back herself when she had drank her tea, into the gallery, where everything proper for the time of day was prepared, tea, chocolate, etc. bread-and-butter, roles, cakes, and – on another table all sorts of fruit and ice. When the tea was done with, a cold collation took its place ... The King drank chocolate, the younger part of the company seem'd to take a good share of all the good things; as all these tables were placed near the drawing-room, the rest of the gallery was free. (12 August 1778)

The Duchess of Portland, hostess of the royal breakfast, was also the author of a very special gift to Georgina Mary Anne Port, Mrs. Delany's grand-niece. This child's introduction to fine china was promoted early. Mrs. Delany wrote with delight to her mother, Mary Port:

G.M.A. met me at the door, and made me follow her into the parlour to behold a compleat set of young Nankeen china which she had just received from the Duchess of Portland: her raptures were prodigious, and indeed they are very fine and pretty of their kind, not quite so small as for baby things, nor large eno' for grown ladies, and she insists on my telling you all this, and that there are twelve teacups and saucers, 6 coffee cups and teapot, sugar dish, milk mug, 2 bread-and-butter plates, and they have been produced for the entertainment of all my company every afternoon ... she would have written all this herself and more, but she is not allowed to write any more letters yet, and she was three days writing the last (this is her dictating). (St. James's Place, April 1779)

❀

Dinner was the most important meal of the day, and Mrs. Delany's dinners were usually eaten between two and three o'clock. As the century wore on, dinnertime was driven fashionably later and later on in the afternoon towards evening. Afternoon tea was eventually introduced to fill the gap, when dinner went to six o'clock or later. Mrs. Delany wrote, "I have had a very good second breakfast, and think now with the help of a little plum-cake I shall hold out till dinner. What a lovely day!" (11 October 1771). Tea was taken after dinner when the gentlemen joined the ladies in the drawing-room. This was when G.M.A. presided with her tea-set. Plum cake was a valued recipe in the family, and a slice or two would certainly keep hunger at bay. Anne was the master baker and she regularly dispatched cakes: "The plum-cake is come," Mrs. Delany reported from Delville on 5 January 1751, "I must cut it and write my papers to treat my young guests." On another occasion, she wrote, "I will endeavour to satisfy my dearest mama and sister, with an account of our travels. We breakfasted at Cheedle (your good cake we eat in the coach) and arrived at Trentham, where we dined" (18 June 1744).

Recipes, which they called receipts, were swapped from their receipt books where they faithfully recorded cures, household tips, cosmetic preparations, potions, lotions and food recipes. Requests flew back and forth between them: "Can you get Lady Coventry's receipt for the rose pattern cross stitch? Many thanks for that of the raisin wine" (Delville, 17 November 1750); and following shortly after, "I have made a pipe of orange wine, and next week shall make raisin wine by your receipt. This is an impertinent piece of news, is it not?"

(Delville, 12 January 1751). On her return from a stay in England, Mrs. Delany wrote, "As soon as I get my receipt-book [out of packing] I will send you the isinglass cement" (Delville, 26 May 1747). Isinglass was a gelatin obtained from fish bladders; it was used to set jellies and other moulded creams and confections, but its use here was as a binding medium for mending fine china. Isinglass appears frequently in receipts of the period. It was listed in the *Dublin Directory* of 1753 as being imported into Ireland from Denmark, Sweden, Norway and Russia, along with other exotic goods such as "Timber, Dales [deal], Fir, Train-Oyl, Iron, Copper, Stags-Horns, Hemp, Flax, Ermin, Skins, Mats and Hogs-Bristles".

The exchange of receipts continued:

> Monday and Tuesday walked in the sun in the morning; drawing, reading, prating made the time pass very well; after supper a game of cards – a new game of D.D.'s inventing called *double* commerce: if you have a mind to have it I will send you a receipt for it, if in return you will send me the *veritable receipt* of the *Irish plum cake*.
> (Mount Panther, 14 October 1752)

Sadly, the veritable receipt no longer exists, but a very fine version was published in *The Modern Cook, or Housewife's Directory*, printed by James Hoey at the Mercury in Skinner Row, Dublin, in 1766.

> The cook is directed to take six pounds of flour, six pounds of currans [currants], a pound of fine sugar sifted, twenty eggs, leave out the whites of half; a pint of new ale-yest [yeast], a full quart of very thick cream, two pounds and a half of butter, two nutmegs grated, a quarter ounce of mace beaten fine, two large spoonfuls of rose-water, four large spoonfuls of brandy,

and two large spoonfuls of orange-flower-water; melt the butter with the cream not too hot; let the eggs be well beaten, and the yest strained: a pound of almonds blanch'd with cold water, cut in small bits: Mingle the dry things together, make a hole in the middle, and put in the wet ingredients; mix them well, and beat the whole up quick with your hands; set it before the fire to rise, while the oven is heating: When tis bak'd ice it; if you like it, you may put into the Cake a pound of candy'd orange-peel and citron together.

Receipt books and ladies' directories were published as teaching aids. Hannah Glasse introduced her manual *The Art of Cookery*, 1762, by saying:

I don't pretend to teach professed Cooks, but my Design is to instruct the Ignorant (which will likewise be of great use in all private families) and in so plain and full a Manner, that the most illiterate Person, who can but read, will know how to do everything in Cookery well.

Mrs. Delany and Mrs. Dewes had no requirement for such instruction. Anne was as fully engaged with domestic life as was her sister. Mrs. Delany continued to protest its impertinence yet, from a menu enclosed with a letter written in 1745, she is not a little proud of her hospitable table:

How I could run on, but must not. I am called to range dishes on my table, which is a long one, and consequently easier to set out than a round or oval one. The table takes seven dishes in length. Here follows my bill of fare for today; is not this ridiculous? But if you *wander still unseen*, it may serve as an amusement in your retirement.

First Course.	Second Course.
Turkeys endove [endive]	Partridge
Boyled neck of mutton	Sweetbreads
Greens etc.	Collared pig
Soup	Creamed apple tart
Plum-pudding	Crabs
Roast loin of veal	Fricassee of eggs
Venison pasty	Pigeons.
	No dessert to be had.

It was customary to divide dinner into two courses of mixed sweet and savoury dishes. Instead of successive courses, one dish following another, there were two "covers" or servings of seven to twenty dishes, artfully arranged in geometric patterns and decorated with flowers, all laid on the table at one time. The first course normally contained meats: roasted, stewed, fried or, as with the neck of mutton on Mrs. Delany's bill of fare, boiled. The meats were dressed with sauces or gravies to suit. Vegetables were very often consigned to garnishes, as with Turkey Endive, though greens merit a separate inclusion on this menu. In the *Retrospections of Dorothea Herbert 1770–1806*, Dorothea frequently describes the food her family ate. Vegetables were dismissed as garden thrash (so called because vegetables came a very poor second to meat in the culinary hierarchy) but were resorted to for medicinal purposes, as she described: "We spent whole weeks in an old blue Bed under cure for the Sea Scurvy and eat such quantities of Cabbage Stumps, Celery, and Other Anti-scorbutic Thrash that we really got scorbutic disorder with worms and a Variety of Complaint."

Mrs. Delany's dining table could accommodate seven separate dishes laid lengthways. Mrs. Elizabeth Raffald, author of *The Experienced English Housekeeper* (1769), says that she knows from long experience what a troublesome task it is to make a bill of fare to be in propriety, and not to have two things of the same kind. A variety of dishes, a good balance of flavours and symmetry in the table setting were important principles. No less a person than Mrs. Delany was sufficiently authoritative to "range" her own table, which should be well covered without being crowded. Cookery books offered sample table settings, though Mrs. Delany would have scorned them. *The Modern Cook* suggests a lozenge-shaped arrangement for a course of seven main dishes. The intention was to feast the eye, tempt the appetite and provide a free-ranging tasting menu.

A closer look at some of Mrs. Delany's menus shows what was involved for the kitchen and the dining-room. Soup, if it was on the bill, was served and eaten first, and soup was a feature in Delville. D.D. had devised his own soup tureen, Mrs. Delany had drawn up the blueprint and the whole was executed in silver. A grand display of silver demonstrated wealth and status. On formal occasions, the best pieces were set up to be seen at a distance. Candlelight enhanced the effect, and from about 1700 it was fashionable to create a niche in the dining-room to contain a buffet or side-board to show off the silver.

When the soup was eaten the tureen was removed and a fish dish was put in its place. The meats were on stand-by and followed after the fish; boiled meats were usually brought in first, baked next, roasted last. Culinary writers of the day suggest removing the cold fat that swims upon the gravy in cold weather – a useful tip, as Mrs. Delany often reported freezing temperatures from Delville. Her "everyday" menu does not include a main fish dish, so not all forms necessarily applied on that particular day. The season of the year dictated the fare, and the menu, though undated, has a wintery feel about it, with pig, turkey, partridge and venison on offer. Venison pasty is an example of what was termed a "made" dish. These dishes were larder stand-bys, table fillers designed to give the hard-pressed domestics (as Mrs. Delany called them) respite in the effort to get hot meat onto the table.

Venison was plentiful at Delville.

> D.D. is raising his paddock-wall. About a fortnight ago a man got over it with three dogs and set them at our deer, but luckily the gardener saw them before mischief was done; we now have sixteen deer. We killed a doe some time ago, as *fine fat venison* as ever was eaten, but I own, though D.D. laid a plot very cleverly to deceive me, when I discovered it was one of my own deer it *took off my pleasure* of eating it, but that's a folly *I must try* to break myself of, for they breed so very fast and thrive so prodigiously, and our fields cannot well maintain above 15 or 16. (February 1751)

Breast or shoulder meat was considered most suitable for a pasty. Mrs. Raffald's recipe demonstrates just how convenient this dish could be, as it would keep for a week or more on a cool larder shelf. Her directions to the cook were:

> to bone a breast or shoulder of venison, season it well with mace, pepper and salt. Lay it in a deep pot with the best part of a neck of mutton cut in slices and laid over the venison. Pour in a large glass of red wine, put a coarse paste of flour and water over it and bake it two hours in an oven. Then lay the venison in a dish and pour the gravy over it, and put one pound of butter over it. Make a good puff paste and lay it near half an inch thick round the edge of

the dish. Roll out the lid, which must be a little thicker than the paste on the edge of the dish, and lay it on. Then roll out another lid pretty thin and cut it in flowers, leaves, or whatever form you please, and lay it on the lid. If you don't want it, it will keep in the pot that it was baked in eight or ten days, but keep the crust on to prevent the air from getting into it.

Although Mrs. Delany's venison was hidden in just such a pastry case, her squeamishness got the best of her, and this was inappropriate in the eighteenth-century kitchen or at the table.

We now associate plum pudding with Christmas dinner, but Mrs. Delany's plum pudding was less ceremonial. Her more piquant version would offset the roast veal on her bill of fare. John Nott in the *Cook's and Confectioner's Dictionary* (third edition, 1726) made plum pudding or pottage from two to three pounds of shin beef, two and a half pints of water, four ounces of fresh white breadcrumbs, mixed dried fruit (currants, raisins, dates, cooked prunes), grated nutmeg, ground mace, ground cloves, cinnamon, salt, sherry, port and the juice of one Seville orange or lemon to serve. He says to simmer the beef in the water, covered, for about two hours until tender. Strain it and keep the meat for another dish. Add the breadcrumbs to one and a half pints of the broth and soak for one hour. Then stir in the fruit, spices and salt and bring to the boil for about fifteen minutes. Add the sherry and port and simmer uncovered until the fruit is plump. Serve hot in individual bowls with the juice of the Seville orange or lemon.

Roast loin of veal was among the dishes on the first course. To appreciate the art of roasting meat in the eighteenth century, it is useful to recall every blackened-on-the-outside, raw-on-the-inside barbecued offering one has ever eaten. Cooking in Delville was done on or before an open fire. "DD, I thank God, is very well and busy," Mrs. Delany wrote. "He has laid me in such a stock of billeting and fire-fuel out of his own garden, that I shall not, I believe, want coals for the whole winter, except for the kitchen, housekeeper's room, and hall." The fire had to be stoked constantly to temperatures sufficiently high to cook a variety of foods at different rates; a partridge, for instance, would roast in twenty minutes, while a side of beef would take considerably longer. Meat was dredged with flour and basted while roasting on turnspits. Hanna Glasse desired

> the Cook to order her Fire according to what she is to dress; if anything very little or thin, then a pretty little brisk Fire, that it may be done quick and nice. If a very large Joint, then be sure a good fire laid to cake. Let it be clear at the Bottom; and when your Meat is half done, move the Dripping-pan and Spit a little from the Fire, and Stir up a good brisk Fire, for according to the goodness of your Fire, your meat will be done sooner or later.

A kitchen maid, a serving boy or even a small dog might have the repetitive task of turning the spit. Meanwhile, pans for warming sauces or making gravies would wait on trivets standing in and around the grate.

> I am just come from Holborn Bars where I have been rummaging in a fine shop for grates, and have pitched upon four! I think I will have a smoke-jack, the man says he will take care and keep it in order for nothing. I bespeak boilers, fish-kettles etc. *all of iron*, as there is an outcry against the poisonous quality of brass and copper – there is no objection to iron, only its not being so ornamental to Cinderella's apartment. (Whitehall, 10 November 1754)

When Mrs. Delany fitted out her house in Spring Gardens in London, she invested in a smoke-jack, which was a series of spits on a ratchet-and-pulley system, enabling a more efficient circulation of meats before the fire. She was always interested in scientific and technological advances and showed an early awareness of the dangers of copper cooking vessels – unlike Lord Viscount Doneraile, who built a new townhouse in Kildare Street in Dublin in the same years. Among the items from his kitchen inventory, he lists: one copper colander, three beer coppers, two copper tea-kettles, one copper drudging box and two copper ladles.

Friedrich Christian Accum, in his *Culinary Chemistry*, written early in the nineteenth century, hectored the afore-mentioned Cinderellas about the dangers of poisoning from copper. He railed that:

> stewpans and soup-kettles should be examined every time they are used; these and their covers, must be kept perfectly clean and well tinned not only on the inside, but about a couple of inches on the outside; so much mischief arises from their getting out of repair; and if, not kept nicely tinned, all your work will be in vain; the broths and soups will look green and dirty and taste bitter and poisonous, and will be spoiled both for the eye and palate, and your credit will be lost; and, as the health and even the life of the family depends upon this, the cook may be sure her employer had rather pay the tin man's bill than the doctor's.

The hot physical work of the kitchen was prodigious. Almost every morsel had to be made from source, including "katchups", which were used to flavour gravies and sauces. Salt, cheese, fruits and spices, Turkey coffee, liquorice, wheat and flour were just some of the foodstuffs imported from England and freely available from merchants in Dublin city at the time. Brandies, wines and vinegars came from France, while oranges, lemons, grapes, nuts, chestnuts, almonds, onions, sugars, aniseeds, figs, raisins and chocolate came from Spain. The feat of producing the array of dishes available to the Delville dinner table was astonishing and repeating the process daily was nothing short of heroic. Mrs. Delany decided on the bill of fare and presided over the setting of the table, but the cook and kitchen maids bore the brunt of the work. Bernard Granville's cook was known in the family as "fat Martha", a worthy woman who undoubtedly required every ounce of her strength to enable her carry out the tasks of the kitchen, such as lashing hefty joints of meat to the spits.

Mrs. Raffald had some useful tips for roasting. She directed:

> when you roast any kind of meat, it is a very good way to put a little salt and water in your dripping pan. Baste your meat a little with it, let it dry, then dust it well with flour. Baste it with fresh butter, it will make your meat a better colour. Observe always to have a brisk clear fire, it will prevent your meat from dazing and the froth from falling. Keep it a good distance from the fire, if the meat is scorched the outside is hard, and prevents the heat from penetrating into the meat, and will appear enough before it be little more than half done. Time, distance, basting often, and a clear fire, is the best method I can prescribe for roasting meat to perfection. When the steam draws near the fire it is a sign of its being enough, but you will be the best judge of that from the time you put it down.

Back in the cool refinement of the eating parlour, well away from the heat of the fire and the objectionable cooking smells, when the first course was eaten the dishes were removed. The second lighter course of meat, fish, sweet pies, puddings and tarts was then placed on the table. Mrs. Delany's partridge, sweetbreads, collared pig, apple tart, crabs and eggs fitted that bill. Little side dishes of biscuits and pickles often stayed on the table throughout the meal. After the second course the cloth was removed and dessert followed. Dessert dishes were usually jellies, creams, sweetmeats, fruit, nuts and cheese, though jellies and cheese were sometimes placed in the centre of the second course. The hiatus between courses was described in Jane Austen's novel *Emma* when the heroine explained that conversation at the Cole family dinner was interrupted: the company "were called on to share in the awkwardness of a rather long interval between courses ... but when the table was again safely covered, when every corner dish was placed exactly right ... occupation and ease were generally restored".

Sold by Patrick O'Brien at the Three Tuns in Back-Lane:

Right good Graves and Margeaux Claret, French white wine, dry Mountain Malaga, Canary Old Hock, Sherry, Right good Tent and other wines. Also neat Coniack Brandy, West India Rum, Fine Orange Shrub, Cherry Brandy, Holland Geneva, and fine Teas by wholesale and retail at the most reasonable Rates.

There was no shortage of wine. During the eighteenth century, wineglasses were not set on the table before the meal but brought to each diner on a salver or tray by a servant. When the glass was drained it was returned by the servant to the sideboard, then rinsed with water and refilled. Wines too readily to hand could give rise to temptation.

Yesterday morning sent the coach for Mrs. Hamilton, Miss Forth, etc. to Finglass; we all sat down to our different work, and the morning past away in a tranquil pleasantness. Just before dinner when I was dressed I walked into the parlour to see that all things were as I would have them, I found Master Hamilton sitting on the sofa pale as death: I took him by the hand, terrified at his looks, and found he was dirty, and looked as if he had had a fall: he could hardly speak, but would not own he had. I desired him to go and get one of the servants to clean his coat; he went stumbling along, which confirmed me he was hurt, and I desired D.D. to follow him and try if he could find out what was the matter before his mama saw him. In the meantime the ladies came down, and I was so confounded and surprised I hardly knew what I said; however, I desired them to sit down, dinner being on the table, and D.D. came in with Master H., who with difficulty seated himself. His mother instantly saw something was very wrong, ran to him imagining he had had a fall and had fractured his skull, and we ordered William our butler to take a horse and go instantly for a surgeon, for the boy could neither speak nor keep his seat, and his poor mother's agony was most affecting; but William whispered me, and said, "Madam, Master drank at one draught above a pint of claret, and I do believe he is fuddled." He had been running in the garden, came in chilled with cold, snatched

up a bottle at the side-board, put it to his
mouth, not considering the consequences of his
draught. I ran with the utmost joy to Mrs.
Hamilton, and without mincing the matter, said,
"Be easy, he is drunk." (26 January 1752)

Dinner guests were not obliged to devour everything in sight
but to partake of a little from each dish. Mrs. Hamilton and her
family, including the inebriated Master Hamilton, the Greene
family, who were relations of the Dean, the Barbers, who were
near neighbours, Letty Bushe or Sally Chapone might be of the
party at dinner on any given day. They helped themselves to
dishes within reach or asked for others to be passed round,
which all added to the conviviality of the occasion. It was
considered vulgar to eat too quickly or too slowly, which
showed you were either too hungry or you didn't like the food.
It was also considered vulgar to eat your soup with your nose in
the plate. If necessity of nature obliged you to leave the table,
you had to steal away unobserved and return without
announcing where you'd been. Chamber pots or gentlemen's
comforters were kept for the purpose in or just outside the
dining-room. Women had to make do with vessels known as
voideurs, which looked like sauce boats and required a certain
adroitness. In the Vigors family inventory, the dining-room
appointments for 25 June 1801 included two dining tables, one
"voidore", one sideboard, one dumb waiter and one night chair.

Servants cleared the table at each remove. Men and women
were placed at opposite sides of the table until late in the century
when they were arranged alternately male and female. Mrs.
Beeton pronounced this custom promiscuous. After dessert was
removed, a glass or two more of wine was drunk; the ladies
withdrew, leaving the men to their drinking and smoking. The
men later rejoined the ladies for tea, conversation and cards.

❋

On her first visit to Ireland, Mrs. Delany was impressed by the lavishness of Irish hospitality.

> We staid on the water till eight o'clock, then went to a cabin, which is such a thing as this thatched. It belongs to a gentleman of fifteen hundred pounds a year, who spends most part of his time and fortune in that place: the situation is pretty, being just by the river side, but the house is worse than I have represented. He keeps a man cook, and has given entertainments of twenty dishes of meat! The people of this country don't seem solicitous of having good dwellings or more furniture than is absolutely necessary – hardly so much, but they make it up in eating and drinking! I have not seen less than fourteen dishes of meat for dinner, and seven for supper, during my peregrination; and they not only treat us at their houses magnificently, but if we are to go to an inn, they constantly provide us with a basket crammed with good things: no people can be more hospitable or obliging, and there is not only great abundance but great order and neatness. All this is by way of digression. We went to the above-mentioned cabin, where we had tea, wine, bread and butter, and might have had supper would we have accepted of it. (Newtown Gore, 12 June 1732)

Keeping a male cook was the height of sophistication, which carried extra cachet if he was a French cook. John Loveday, an antiquarian who made a tour of the country in 1732, wrote that the Irish "are an expensive people, they live in ye most open hospitable manner continually feasting with one another". It was customary for the Irish gentry to spend lavishly on everything that brought immediate gratification – sometimes at the expense of house and grounds. There was no stint of servants, horses, cars, dogs, guns, fires, meat, wine and on foot of that, not surprisingly, guests. Yet visitors noticed that rain dripped through ceilings, windows rattled and doors hung loose on their hinges. Mrs. Delany was a fastidious housekeeper, but problems arose even in her well-regulated establishments. She reported from London:

> The house is full of workmen, and so offensive from its being laid open that she [Molly Butcher, a servant] and Bytha can neither eat nor sleep; but I hope in a few days it will be comfortable; the stopping up of the drains was occasioned by *the rats!* (Bow Window, Whitehall, 20 June 1781)

Outward show was a social imperative for the upper classes through the eighteenth century, though the drains were stopped and the butter rancid. Arthur Young, who toured Ireland in the latter years of the eighteenth century, tells us that on his first visit he spent a few days with a gentleman in County Cork and was delighted with his well-appointed table and the general air of splendour and affluence that surrounded him. But on a later visit to the neighbourhood, an auction being held in the house, he had a look into the kitchen and was horrified to find it almost completely dark and the walls as black as the inside of a chimney. He could scarcely believe that the wonderful dinners he had enjoyed on his former visit to the house had been cooked in such an apartment, and remarked, "Etna or Vesuvius might as soon have been found in England as such a kitchen."

This did not apply to Delville. When the clerical top brass were invited to dine, the kitchen was well appointed and the menu was as showy as any eighteenth-century chatelaine could wish. It followed all prescribed forms, including soup and fish and a plentiful dessert. Mrs. Delany transferred her guilty pleasure in her hospitable table and fare onto Anne.

> He (our Lord Primate) George Stone and his sister Mrs. Stone, and the Bishop of Derry, and Mrs. Barnard, dine here today. You love a bill of fare, and here it is.

FIRST COURSE.	SECOND COURSE.	
Fish.	Turkey Put.	
	Salmon.	Pick. Sal.
	Grilde. And Quails.	
Beef Rabbits.	Little Terrene Peas. Cream. Mush-	Terrene.
Steaks. Soup	and	Apple Pye.
	Onions.	
Fillet	Crab. Leveret.	Cheesecakes.
Veal.		
	Dessert.	
Blamange.	Raspberries and Cream.	Orange Butter
Cherries.	Sweetmeats and Jelly.	Currants and Gooseberries.
Dutch cheese.	Strawberries and Cream.	Almond Cream.

> I have scratched it out very awkwardly, and hope the servants will place my dinner and dessert better on the table than I have on paper. I give as little hot meat as possible, but I think there could not be less, considering the grandees that are to

> be here: the invitation was "*to beef stakes*" which we
> are famous for. (20 June 1747)

The kitchen at Delville had been modernised just before this grand dinner took place.

> Yesterday we spent the whole day (but an hour
> at dinner and that was partly) in the garden, for
> our kitchen-grate was down, and a new one
> putting up, stoves making, and a boiler placing,
> so that we could have nothing conveniently
> drest at home: we sent our mutton and chicken
> to Mr. Barber's house at the end of the garden,
> and had it drest in his kitchen, and eat it in his
> dining-room. (6 June 1747)

Providing hot meat for the table was always a challenge but some hot food was essential. The introduction of stoves to Delville meant that bread and pies could be freshly baked on site and not bought in from the pie vendors. The distances from kitchen to dining parlour, and the fashion for displaying all the dishes on the table at once at each course, meant that food went cold very quickly. Chafing dishes, which had little compartments for hot charcoal underneath the food, were used to try to keep it warm. Efforts were made to address the problem at Newbridge House, Donabate, where a "hostess trolley" made of tin and heated with charcoal was part of the dining-room furniture. Keeping food warm was an ongoing problem, but Mrs. Delany's household improvements threatened to exacerbate the situation further.

> [D.D.] has promised to build me a kitchen out
> of doors, and that which is now my kitchen to
> be turned into a room for my maids, that they
> may have no call upstairs but when they are
> about their business there. (17 June 1747)

Among the hot dishes on Mrs. Delany's bill of fare were the famous Delville beefsteaks, but we are not told how they were cooked. The excellent *Modern Cook*, which was printed in Dublin, tells us to:

> cut the Steaks off the rump, and beat them well with a roller; fry them; after they are fry'd, take them out; pour all the fat out of the pan; put in half a pint of gravy, chopt shallot, thyme and parsely, a piece of butter rubb'd in flour, and pepper and salt to your taste, toss this together till thick; lay your steaks in your dish, and pour this sauce over it: you must garnish with pickles.

In an establishment of the size of Delville, the provisioning of the house was the duty of the housekeeper. In grander houses it might be the steward, but in either case it required a shrewd eye and a sense of responsibility: purchases had to be accounted for. The author of *The Modern Cook* sounds a cautionary note on buying a Turkey-Powt (young turkey), which features on the second course of Mrs. Delany's bill of fare.

> Gentlemen, are often deceived in these fowls; for large Hen-chickens with white legs are frequently sold for them; and if scalded and trussed Turkey-fashion and Turkey-sauce made to them, it must be a good palate that can find it out, unless he had notice of it before.

Most of the dishes on Mrs. Delany's grand menu – grilled salmon, roasted quails, dishes of peas and mushrooms – had to be prepared on the day. Vegetables for the pickled salad, such as cucumbers and artichokes, were larder stand-bys and supplies were always on hand. Large quantities of cucumbers are listed in the accounts for Newbridge House. Pickling in vinegar was a common practice for keeping foods that would otherwise spoil.

For some days past I have been sending all sorts of household goods and stores for Mount Panther, and propose leaving this on Tuesday next. D.D. is finishing alterations in his garden, and giving directions for what is to be done in his absence. I am *preserving, pickling* and papering and giving directions to my maids. (15 July 1750)

Seasonings and spices were essential to flavour the soups, gravies, sauces and katchups (ketchups) that accompanied the meat and fish dishes. *The Modern Cook* instructs

Housekeepers, in the Country especially, should lay in their Groceries at best hand, and be provided with Store of Nutmegs, Cinnamon, Ginger, Cloves, Mace, Jamaica Pepper, Long Pepper, Black Pepper etc. Red Sage, Sage of Virtue, Mint, Thyme, Peny-Royal, Sweet Marjoram, etc. should be kept in paper bags for use, if not in the garden, or in season. Eschallots, Onions, dry'd Orange and Lemon Peel, Anchovies, Olives, Mushrooms, Katchup, pickled Walnuts, Mango, pickled Cucumbers, Capers etc. should likewise be always at hand.

Mrs. Delany's households were plentifully stocked. They enjoyed game, as shown in this extract, written after the dean had suffered a stroke. "We have dined on the best hare that ever was tasted. D.D. is now allowed to eat as heartily as he pleases of one thing, and his appetite, I think, is better than before his attack" (2 February 1754). Countryman John Dewes, husband of Anne, reported too on a bumper year: "We have had, and still have, the greatest plenty of woodcocks this year that I ever knew, so many that I frequently don't eat of them when they are brought to table, and no scarcity either of hares or partridges" (Welsbourn, 31 January 1773).

Rabbits and onions were on the first course of Mrs. Delany's episcopal feast, but there was more to follow. The leveret of the second course was deemed fit for a bishop, though its preparation was far less exalted. *The Modern Cook*, again, is precise in its instructions:

> A leveret, if new killed will be stiff, but if stale killed will be limber. If it be a right Leveret, it will have a small bone; if not, a knob on the outside of the fore leg near the foot; and therefore you should stroke your finger down upon the outside of the leg, near the foot; and if you feel the small bone, or knob, it is not Leveret but a Hare. When you have killed a Hare, a Leveret, a Coney, or Rabbet, you must let them be thoroughly cold before you truss them up in paniers or baskets; for if they are trussed up hot, they will turn green and stink, and spoil presently, and particularly in the Summer time. To roast a hare or leveret you must first skewer (or truss) your hare with the head upon one shoulder, the fore legs sticked into the ribs, the hind legs double. Make your pudding of the crumb of a penny loaf, a quarter pound of beef marrow or suet, and a quarter of a pound of butter; shred the liver, a sprig or two of winter savoury, a little lemon peel, one anchovy, a little Chyan [cayenne] pepper, and half a nutmeg grated. Mix them up in a light forcemeat, with a glass of red wine and two eggs, put it in the belly of your hare, sew it up. Put a quart of good milk in your dripping pan, baste your hare with it till it is reduced to half a gill; then dust and baste it

well with butter. If it be a large one it will require
an hour and a half roasting.

Cheesecakes were on the menu to balance the leveret. A
versatile, light dish, they were made in many flavours, such as
orange, almond or lemon, but a basic mixture was common to
all. Mrs. Raffald directed to:

> Set a quart of new milk near the fire with a
> spoonful of rennet, let the milk be blood warm.
> When it is broke drain the curd through a coarse
> cloth, now and then break the curd gently with
> your fingers. Rub into the curd a quarter of a
> pound of butter, a quarter of a pound of sugar,
> a nutmeg and two Naples biscuits grated, the
> yolks of four eggs and the white of one egg, one
> ounce of almonds well beat with two spoonfuls
> of rosewater and two of sack. Clean six ounces
> of currants very well, put them into your curd
> and mix them all well together.

Cheesecake continued to be a favourite long into Mrs.
Delany's old age:

> I am but just returned from a pleasant tour this
> morning with your dear child [G.M.A.]. We
> went to Lee's at Hammersmith, in search of
> flowers, from thence returned to Kensington,
> bought cheesecakes, buns etc. a whole 18
> pennyworth, bought nosegays; and are now
> came home hungry as hawks, dinner ready, and
> we must dress. (11 May 1780)

In Delville, when the cheesecakes and the second course
were finally all eaten, the cloth was removed and the dessert
was placed upon the table. It was the middle of June, the
garden was bountiful and beautiful and a lavish dessert of

fruits, creams, jellies and Dutch cheese was to be had. Not surprisingly, Mrs. Delany described herself around this time as "a *porpuss grown!*"

On another gala occasion, Mrs. Delany described the menu for the wedding of Sally Chapone to Dr. Daniel Sandford, which took place at Delville. She wrote:

Dinner at four. Here's my bill of fare:-

Turbot and Soles, remove Ham.

Force meat, etc.   2 Partridges, 2 Grouse.
        Rabbits and Onions.   Sweetbreads   Salmigundi.
Pies.   And crumbs.
                        Soup.
Boiled Chicken.   Collop Veal and Olives.   Pease.
        Cream Pudding.   Plumb Crocant.
Chine of Mutton.   Turkey in Jelly.   Hare.   Lobster Fricassee.

Desert — Nine things, six of them fruit out of our own garden, and a plate of fine Alpine strawberries.

These particulars may be impertinent, but it is doing as I would be done by; and between real friends no circumstance is ever trivial. (Delville, 6 October 1764)

❋

The Dean has now settled my allowance for housekeeping here at six hundred a-year, which I receive quarterly, and out of that pay everything but *the men's wages, the liveries, the stables, wine cellar and garden, furniture and all repairs.* (9 September 1758)

That considerable allowance enabled Mrs. Delany to provide dinners as extravagant as the next, but she strongly disapproved of excess – in others.

> We had a magnificent dinner, extremely well drest and well attended, nine and nine, and a dessert the finest I ever saw in Ireland; there were only our family and Mr. and Mrs. Ormsby, Miss Donnellan that was. The Bishop (of Elphin) lives constantly very well, and it becomes his station and fortune, but *high living is too much the fashion here.* You are not invited to dinner to any private gentleman of a £1,000 a year or less, that does not give you seven *dishes* at one course, and Burgundy and Champagne; and these dinners they give once or twice a-week, that provision is not as dear as in London. I own I am surprised *how* they manage; for we cannot afford anything like it, with a *much better* income than most of those who give these entertainments. (15 February 1752).

Conspicuous extravagance continued to be derided. "Thursday we dined at Pickerstown, about four miles off, Mr. Cavendish's and Lady Meade; we were 17 or 18 in company, and had a *vast dinner*, and *such* a *vast turbot* as I never saw for size" (16 June 1750). Hospitality became even more lavish and proved, on one occasion, a morality tale:

> Last Saturday we were invited to the Primate's to hear music ... A Perigord pie had been sent for on the occasion, to be directed to a merchant in Dublin: the pie came when the merchant was in the country, and his wife, supposing it as a present from one of her husband's correspondents

abroad, invited several of her particular friends to eat up this rare pie the very day the Primate gave his entertainment. That morning, after all the company was engaged, the Primate's *maitre d'hotel*, who had enquired often after it in vain, once more called and *got the pie*, and the poor merchant's wife looked very silly when her company came who were forced to sit down to a homespun dinner, and give up their foreign rarity. I own *I am sorry* they *did not eat it!* Such expensive rarities *do not become the table of a prelate*, who ought rather *to be given to hospitality* than to ape the fantastical luxuriances of fashionable tables. (26 January 1752)

A Perigord pie was an exceptionally rich game pie featuring truffles from the Perigord region in France.

A more subdued Mrs. Delany wrote to Anne later in the same year: she had worries about the outcome of the dean's lawsuit with the Tenisons, and retrenchment became inevitable.

Don't be uneasy about our going to the North; we have really a very pretty convenient house there, shall keep good fires, and provide ourselves with books and work, and I shall send down my harpsichord, and hope to have Mrs. Bushe with me, who has in the kindest manner offered me her company. Nor shall I want for neighbours there, and the satisfaction of doing what I think is right will make me amends for leaving Delville, and being removed further from Dublin will be another very good reason for spending the winter at Mount Panther. You'll say, suppose the decree should be in our favour, why then retire? Why? Prudence I think requires it; for we have been at great expenses without any farther demand, and it is *not so easy* to live with frugality at Delville as at Mount Panther, where every thing bears but *half price.* (14 August 1752)

And now to tell you a little of Mount Panther. To begin then: Last Sunday dined at Downpatrick (after church). Mr. and Mrs. and Miss Leonargan, Mr. Bereton, curate of Down, Mr. Trotter, agent to Mr. Southwell, dined with us; went to church again at 4 went home at 5, *two hours on the road*, and visits to Lady Anne Annesley and Mrs. Bayley and their husbands made half an hour; tired, supped, talked over the company of the day; went to bed before eleven; up next morn early; routed about the house, found many repairs wanting; sent for smith, carpenter, cowper; catching showers; peeped now and then into the garden – excellent *gooseberries, currants, potatoes,* and all the garden stuff; *fine salmon, lobster, trout, crabs,* every day at the door. Monday evening went to Dundrum, a mile off, a pleasant nest of cabins by the sea-side, where may be had kitchen chairs, French white wine, vinegar, Hungary water, and capers; *mugs* and *pigs,* of which we bought some. The French white wine is five pence per bottle – we have not yet tasted it. Tuesday, busy all the morning with carpenters. (Mount Panther, 28 July 1750)

Wines, vinegar and capers from France arrived through the nearby ports of Newry and Drogheda.

This country is famous for the goat's whey; and the season for drinking it, which is summer, a great deal of company meet for that purpose, and there are little huts built up for their reception, and they have music and balls and cards. (10 September 1744)

Mrs. Delany had noted this wholesome custom with interest on an earlier visit, but she later found that extravagant behaviour had infected the north too.

I am very sorry to find here and everywhere people *out of character*, and that *wine* and *tea* should enter where they have *no pretence to be*, and usurp the rural food of syllabub, etc. But dairymaids wear large hoops and velvet hoods instead of the round *tight petticoat* and *straw hat*, and there is as much *foppery* introduced in the *food* as in the dress – *the pure simplicity of ye country is quite lost!* (Holly Mount, 21 June 1745)

Syllabub was a frothy drink made from wine or cider, sweetened with sugar, nutmeg and lemon, to which cream or milk was forcefully added to make it bubble up. The milk was sometimes squirted into the wine straight from the cow's teat. Dairymaids, however, were far more likely to drink whey, the liquid left behind after the milk had formed curds. Regina Sexton, in her book *A Little History of Irish Food*, explained the relationship Irish people had with milk and its by-products through the centuries. Milk was the prized *bán bídh* or white food. "Bonny clobber" was a favourite way of taking milk. In this method the milk was allowed to stand for several days until "the cream came off, by taking hold of it between the fingers, like the skin of leather". This name derived from *bainne clabhair* or thick milk. *Lemnacht* or fresh milk was not nearly as popular to drink as milk in the soured state. Dorothea Herbert, in relating another anecdote of the Herbert family, wrote:

My father used to invite us all to Sup *en famille*
about his Kiln [newly built in a back kitchen]
and had always the finest white potatoes
roasted for us cooked by himself on the hot
Lime And plenty of the finest Bonny Clobber
from the Dairy.

Whey was commonly taken by rich and poor alike. The
dean liked his laced with a little sack or sherry. Goat's whey
was also taken as a restorative at Bray in Co. Wicklow. Mrs.
Delany reported, "Tomorrow we call at eight o'clock on Mrs.
F. Hamilton to go to Bray, ten miles off, to see Miss Mary
Forth, who is there drinking goat's whey, and next month goes
to Bristol" (22 May 1750). Miss Forth, a delicate girl, was
taking goat's whey to build her strength prior to travelling to
Bristol to take the waters.

This buccolic life notwithstanding, the Delany's were as
hospitable as ever. They may have been disappointed in their
northern Arcadian idyll, but the removal to Mount Panther
did enable them to live with more economy – despite the
numbers to dinner. "I had on Tuesday sixteen people here at
dinner, on Wednesday ten, on Thursday twenty-two" (17
August 1745). "Tuesday morning, had no crowd, only
fourteen to dinner" (18 July 1760).

On Thursday, at two o'clock, I was preparing
to dress for the day, when who should arrive
but my Lord Annesley and Mr. Harrison in a
post chaise, and Lady Annesley, Miss
Annesley, and Mrs. Harrison, in a coach. To
dinner, they came, but as I had no expectation
of anybody, I was not prepared for grandees,
and gave them only our dinner, which would
have done very well had not Mrs. Overall's zeal
to *make it better* made us wait for a dish of peas

till the rest of the dinner was overdone! (21
June 1760)

Sunday we went to Downpatrick; D.D. preached
as well as ever I heard him. We had a dinner, as
usual, for as many as filled a table for twelve
people. Our dinner was a boiled leg of mutton,
a sirloin of roast beef, six boiled chickens, bacon
and greens; apple-pies, a dish of potatoes – all
set on at once; time between church and church
does not allow for two courses; tea after we came
home, and talking over our company was
refreshing to us. We brought a *young cat home* with
us, but she was so cross we sent her home again
this morning, and I, alas! am catless! (8 August
1758)

When the Delanys made their visits to England, Anne
showed them every solicitude. In response to her enquiries,
Mrs. Delany wrote:

I have got now but a very indifferent cook, not
worth transporting, but am sure we shall have
no reason to wish for any other than your own.
D.D. you know, loves only roast, boiled and
broiled, and if all fails the greatest feast to him
is a fried egg and bacon, but when we are so
happy as to be under the hospitable roof of
Welsbourn we shall enjoy every delicacy the
heart can wish. (Delville, 23 January 1753)

She wrote later that year in response to another query
from Anne:

The Dean says he has no scruple about fish or
drawn gravy; the latter he seldom eats of, but it
is not from any exception to it if the creature

82

from whence it is drawn is bled sufficiently at
the time it is killed, as according to the custom
and manner of killing them they must be.
(Bulstrode, 20 November 1753)

Dr. Delany had expounded on this theme in several
pamphlets – *The Prohibition of Blood: A Temporary Precept* and *The
Doctrine of Abstinence from Blood Defended*. He first proposed his
thesis in *Revelation Examin'd with Candour*, stating that abstinence
from blood and things strangled was an indispensable duty
incumbent on the whole race of mankind to the end of the
world. He placed this duty on an equal "Foot of Necessity
with even Abstinence from Idolatry and Whoredom". That
statement was followed with a very tortured argument in-
volving the Deluge and Moses, concluding with the position
that, while eating the flesh of animals was allowed, eating the
blood was not. Anne Dewes must have been on her mettle to
feed him according to Judaic laws of butchery, which he
approved and adopted on his own whim.

When not disputing the spilling of the blood of animals,
Mrs. Delany and her circle took great delight in exploring the
hinterland. In the romantic spirit of the age, they extolled the
wonders of nature. The letters contain many reports of ex-
peditions to scenes of extraordinary natural beauty, including
the Giant's Causeway.

I am now quite at a loss to give you any idea of
it; it is so different from anything I ever saw, and
so far beyond all description. The prints you
have represent some part of it very exactly, with
the *sort of pillars* and the remarkable stones that
compose them of different angles, but there is
an infinite variety of rocks and grassy mountain
not at all described in prints, nor is it possible for
a poet or a painter, with all their art, to do

justice to the awful grandeur of the whole scene
... After gazing, wondering, and I may say
adoring the wondrous Hand that formed this
amazing work, we began to find ourselves fat-
igued. Our gentlemen found out a well-sheltered
place, where we sat very commodiously by a well
(called the Giant's Well) of as fine sweet water as
any at Calwich, and cold mutton and tongue,
refreshed us extremely after three hours' walking,
climbing and stumbling among the rocks.
(8 October 1758)

The beauties of nature, while food for the soul, were not
corporeally satisfying, and picnics were always carried to make
good this deficiency. Picnic food and food for social
gatherings were also described with relish.

Last Monday our family and Mr. Palmer's met
on a very agreeable expedition. We were in all
twenty; we left home about eleven and went four
mile in coaches and chaises, then we all mounted
our horses, and went to a place call Patrick
Down, seven mile from Killala ... I never saw
anything finer of the kind; it raised a thousand
great ideas; oh! how I wished for you there! it is
impossible to describe the oddness of the place,
the strange rocks and cavities where the sea had
forced its way. For our feast there was prepared
what here they call a *"swilled mouton,"* that is, a
sheep roasted whole in its skin, scorched like a
hog. I never eat anything better; we sat on the
grass, had a rock for our table; and though there
was a great variety of good cheer, nothing was
touched but the *mouton.* (Killala, 4 July 1732)

Luke Gernon, Second Justice of Munster, writing in the early seventeenth century, reported on the same delicacy.

> The dish which I make choice of is the swelled mutton, and it is prepared thus. They take a principal wether, and before they kill him, it is fit that he be shorn. Being killed, they singe him in his wooly skin like a bacon and roast him by joints with the skin on, and so serve it to table. They say that it makes the flesh more firm and preserves the fat. I make choice of it to avoid uncleanly dressing.

In the evenings there were house parties and dances to attend and, on one occasion, Sally Chapone, Mrs. Delany's goddaughter, came off worst at a ball in Downpatrick.

> Sally was chosen in the second set by a strange man indeed ... Such a figure, such a *no-dancer*, a *mopstick* with a brown, dirty *mophead!* And his sense (if he had any,) seemed as *stupid* as his figure and his heels, all but in the choice of his partner. (9 September 1758)

But the ball Mrs. Delany hosted herself was an altogether more satisfactory affair, and she describes it with delight.

> There were ten couple of clever dancers. Remember my room is 32 feet long; at the upper end sat the fiddlers, and at the lower end next the little parlour the lookers-on ... Tea from seven to ten; it was made in the hall, and Smith presided. When any of the dancers had a mind to rest themselves they sat in the little parlour, and tea was brought to them. They began at six and ended at ten: then went to a cold supper in

the drawing-room made of 7 dishes down the middle of different cold meats, and plates of all sorts of fruit and sweet things that could be had here, in the middle jellies: in all 21 dishes and plates. The table held twenty people; the rest had a table of their own in the little parlour, and all the dancers were together, and I at the head to take care of them; everybody seemed pleased, which gave pleasure to D.D. and myself. (21 August 1758)

The Delanys watched and approved as the young people danced. In her youth, Mrs. Delany had loved to dance and now could not resist an opportunity.

I told you I was to have a tiny ball on Monday; my company came at eleven exactly as appointed; the fiddlers here before them. They had all breakfasted, and were eager to begin, which they did *immediately*. Seven couple. I never saw a happier set of dancers. I had all ages, from twenty-one to eight years old, Miss Anne Hamilton, the eldest; and to keep her in countenance, and to *gratify ourselves*, Mrs. F. Hamilton and I made a couple for *above half* their dances. At one o'clock they found prepared for them in my dressing room green tea, and orange-tea, and cakes of all kinds. In half an hour they returned to their dancing till half an hour after two, and then rested till dinner. I had one table which held eleven, and another of eight. The two Mrs. Hamiltons and Bushe were all the company besides the dancers. At 5 o'clock the fiddlers struck up again, and for two hours more they danced as briskly as if

they had *not danced at all*. At 7 *I made them leave off*,
and gave them tea, and played to them on the
harpsichord, till they were cool enough to
venture home. (23 March 1751)

Different varieties of teas, hot chocolate, cold meats,
fruits, creams, sweetmeats, jellies and cakes, beautifully cut
and served on salvers, were the usual fare for an assembly at
home. On another scale entirely, a high-flown romantic
sensibility inspired a showpiece ball in Dublin.

The grand ball was given last Wednesday, to the
great contentment of the best company of both
sexes. The men were gallant, the ladies were
courteous! ... The musicians and singers were
dressed like Arcadian shepherds and
shepherdesses, and placed among the rocks. If
tea, coffee, or chocolate were wanting, you held
your cup to a leaf of a tree, and it was filled;
and whatever you wanted to eat or drink, was
immediately found on a rock, or on a branch, or
in the hollow of a tree. The waiters were all in
whimsical dress, and every lady as she entered
the room had a fine bouquet presented to her.
The whole was extremely well conducted; no
confusion; and the ladies say, never was there
seen so enchanting a place; but a few dissenters
have the assurance to say, it was no better than
a poppet-show. (7 February 1752)

Evening gatherings included assemblies and card parties,
where company could meet to drink tea, wine, enjoy refresh-
ments and have polite conversation.

Yesterday, we had an entertainment of another
sort, and very agreeable in its way, — an

assembly at Mrs. Butler's, a lady I have mentioned in some of my former letters, cards of all sorts; I played two pools of commerce: when that was over, at ten o'clock was placed on little tables before the company as they sat, a large Japan board with plates of all sorts of cold meat neatly cut, and sweetmeats wet and dry, with chocolate, sago, jelly, and salvers of all sorts of wine. While we were eating, fiddles were sent for. (30 March 1732)

Yesterday we spent at home, had a *petite* assembley, which we among ourselves call a "ridotto", because at ten o'clock we have a very pretty tray brought in, with chocolate, mulled wine, cakes, sweetmeats, and comfits; cold partridge, chicken, lamb, ham, tongue, – all set out prettily and ready to pick at. (Dublin, 24 January 1733)

She reported on a musical evening at home in Lower Brook Street in London.

I must tell you of a little entertainment of music I had last week; I never was *so well* entertained at *an opera!* Mr. Handel was in the best humour in the world and played lessons and accompanied Strada and all the ladies that sung from seven o' the clock till eleven. I gave them tea and coffee, and about half an hour after nine had a salver brought in of chocolate, mulled white wine and biscuits. Everybody was easy and seemed pleased, Bunny [Mrs. Delany's brother Bernard] staid with me after the company was gone, eat a cold chick with me, and we chatted till one o' the clock. (12 April 1734)

Music was very important to the entire Granville family, Mrs. Delany was a fine musician herself. They were enthusiastic operagoers and friends and patrons of Handel, who had brought the soprano Anna Strada from Naples to London as one of his leading ladies. She was reputedly so ugly she was known to audiences as "The Pig", but was not so offensive as to cause the company in Lower Brook Street to lose their appetite.

❧

Mrs. Delany was as generous as she was hospitable. Throughout her life she took great pains over the packing and dispatching of presents to family and friends. Comestible gifts on and off the hoof were very welcome. At the time the following extract was written, she was a guest of Bishop and Mrs. Clayton, on her first visit to Ireland, and Anne was given specific directions to ensure the safe passage of the treat for bishop's table.

> You are very good in getting the copple-crowned fowl: I suppose they are white ones. I writ a direction how you were to send them to the Bishop, but for fear that letter should miscarry, I will repeat it. You can, I suppose, get them conveyed to Bristol, and a bargain made for their passage thence to Dublin, but great charge must be given about them, for as the poor birds are *eatable* things, some one on board the ship may long for a tit-bit; they must be directed to Mr. Ryves, merchant in Dublin. (Killala, 28 June 1732)

She wrote to tell Anne of a most thoughtful gift given by Dean Jonathan Swift. "He is in love with Miss Kelly *at present*. He sent her some Spanish liquorish for her cold and with it a fable very prettily applied of Lycoris" (Dublin, 20 February 1733). Miss Frances Kelly died later that year of pleurisy, and Swift's gift of liquorice, described as "an excellent demulcent and decoction in catarrhal affections" was a considerate one, though not ultimately successful. With the gift he enclosed some lines ascribed to the Roman poet Gallus. Lycoris was the muse of Gallus, and the poet declared himself her love-slave. So Swift offered himself on a plate to Miss Kelly. His two great loves were already dead, Vanessa (Esther Van Homrigh) in 1723, and Stella (Esther Johnson) in 1728, so he was free to frolic. Flirting in eighteenth-century Dublin was not for amateurs and liquorice, for added conceit, was known to have aphrodisiacal properties.

Mrs. Delany's brother Bernard Granville blew hot and cold throughout his life, but he was always welcomed all the same and his approval sought. She confided in her niece Mary Dewes, taking the waters at Bristol:

> My brother came to town yesterday from Tunbridge, and to me at six o'clock, and looks much better than I expected to have seen him; He was easy and good-humoured; brought me some wheat ears and made me roast some for supper, and supped with me. Seems much satisfied that you are at Bristol, wishes you could take some asses milk, if you can't, thinks buttermilk the best thing you can take; he dines with me again to-day, and says he shall stay some days longer, and then goes directly to Calwich. He has got a new chaise. Nothing but common subjects passed between us, and he seemed in

better spirits than I expected, and does not seem to disapprove of my going to you, as soon as my business will permit me; but *wishes I was with you. How inconsistent* some men are! (Thatched House Court, 20 August 1770)

Bernard's gift of wheat ears were small game birds, famously from the Tunbridge area. Hannah Glasse has a receipt for potting them, but Bernard insisted on having them roasted directly for supper and Mrs. Delany obliged him. Bernard was a generous soul in his way, and his sister was always solicitous of him. "I am much obliged to my brother for his kind present of cheeses, ham, and pigs chaps, which would have better relish could I receive a better account of his health" (St. James's Place, 21 May 1772).

As Mrs. Delany got older and lived alone, her niece Mary and her Dewes nephews supplied her table.

Yesterday we met at chapel and she [The Duchess of Portland] said she would come and dine with me. I gave her an exquisite bit of roast pork and hashed venison. She said she never eat anything so good in her life, and it certainly proved a heartier meal than I ever saw her make, and she said, "Tell our dear Mary it relishes vastly the better for coming from Ilam [the home of her niece Mary Dewes Port]" ... The Cottingham cheeses are arrived, and are the best I ever tasted; but alas! from their richness and softness, unable to bear a rough journey, and they are sadly smashed. You will discharge my money debt, as well as for the attention and trouble Mr. Marsh has had about them. I must say again both your venison and your pork are excellent. P.S. I hope the sturgeon and anchovies

Etc. all came safe. (St. James's Place, 28 December 1771).

One month later she wrote: "My house is maintained by kind providers. Item:- Venison from Mr. Montagu; pork and turkey from Mr. Dewes; fowls and hares from Sandford; a perigot pie from Duchess of Portland on the road, and potted rabbits, all within one week!!" (St. James's Place, 27 January 1772).

Potted lampreys were a special gift that Mrs. Delany made to her friends and relations at Christmas time. Gloucester had long been famous for its lampreys. They were parasitic eel-like fish taken from the Severn and were considered a great delicacy. Lampreys appear on many of her household menus and were the subject of much correspondence:

> Six pots more lampreys for Lady Sun, if not too late. I have sent you some books of music, a dormeuse patron [pattern for a hood], a little snuff for mama, and lavender-water. (7 June 1734).

> The seal of your letter happened to blot out the price of the lampreys, and I cannot find out whether it was meant for two or ten shillings, but I suppose the latter; if so, two more pots will do until they are cheaper. If you have bespoke more they must come, and as soon as they are half-a-crown or three shillings, four pots for my Lady Sunderland. (15 March 1735)

The gift was valued, as Mrs. Boscawen's letter shows:

> My Dear Friend,
>
> I appear ungrateful, and have never thank'd you for my excellent pot of lampreys, I may venture to call it so, as it *always* is so, but I have

not eat it, because I reserved it for this day, that I have a little Christmas feast for the Countess of Rothes, Lord Lesie and other relatives, for whom I shall open my pot of lampreys, and meantime return you thanks for them. (Audley Street, 28 December 1786)

Shopping commissions were attended to with the greatest assiduity and, not surprisingly, Bernard Granville's received the most attention:

Breakfast hardly over when Court [Dewes] called to tell me how fine the Pantheon was, and shewed me a long list from Mr. Granville for *raisins, apples, and oranges, etc.* so I presume he is better and preparing for an entertainment! (27 January 1772)

"My Dear Nephew," she wrote to John Dewes on another occasion:

I wish you could have given me a better account of my dear brother's amendment. I have sent the French plumbs according to his desire, and hope they will prove good; I have also sent my brother a new fashioned cheese carver, as I know he loves *new useful* whims. I would *not venture* to pack up *Rousseau's* prints *with the plumbs,* and Mr. Weston has promised me to be very careful of it. (St. James's Place, 9 May 1772)

I have just received my dear brother's letter; my heart is full of his kindness, and I daily pray for his support and consolation. I shall send by the waggon, Bass, car. To Ashbourne, a little long box, with two flat bottles of Hungary water, 3 ounce-bottles of laudanum, a little bottle of eau de luce, Mrs. Chapone's Letters bound in one volume, and a roll of silk belonging to Mrs. Port; and I have added Lady Russel's Letters, that have given me so much satisfaction that I could not help sending them to my brother. I send the box next Monday. (I September 1773).

This list appeared in Bernard Granville's handwriting on the back of a letter addressed to his sister, then staying at Bulstrode:

Half a hundred of non parielle apples.
Ditto of golden pippins.
A dozen of Civill oranges.
A silver scoop to eat the apples, or I shall not know how to manage.
The apples must be fair and not bruised.
The apples to be of the large sort which are best for scooping.
(28 November 1774)

She endeavoured to do his bidding:

I have just sent to the Ashbourne carrier a box with a dozen Ceville oranges, half a hundred nonpareils, half a hundred golden pippins, and have taken the liberty of putting in a little bundle for Mrs. Port, as too small to send by itself. I have not been able to get your silver scoop yet, tho' I bespoke it immediately, for I could find none ready made. I would not wait for it, as I thought you might want the fruit; but I have tucked into Mrs. P's parcel an ivory one, *en attendant*. There goes also, tied on that box, a small one with superfine jarr raisins, as the confectioner, Koffin in the Haymarket, assures me; they have them now made up in those little boxes; if they are not what you like let me know sincerely, that I may mend my hand. Smith grumbles extremely that the fruiterers will not now allow *more* than 50 to the half hundred! Apples in general this year are small. There are no good French plumbs to be yet had. (22 December 1774)

I fear the Indian sweetmeats are not as tender as they should be, and the quince too sweet; but I could not meet with any better. I took the liberty of adding a pot of Smith's orange marmalade, which is tender and sharp, and to fill the box I added a few maccaroons. I hope the essence of lavender was right. (8 May 1775)

Her hospitality and kindness extended as far as the royal family. At Windsor one day when Mrs. Delany was having dinner with G.M.A., the queen, unannounced, came into the dining-room. She said she would sit down and eat with them. The dinner was a dish of veal cutlets and an orange-pudding; G.M.A. waited on the queen, who commended the cooking and said that the orange-pudding was so excellent that she wanted the receipt of it to be sent to the royal cooks, which was done; but as they never succeeded in making it as well, it was later sent up for the queen's dinner by Mrs. Delany from her own house, ready made. This orange-pudding was afterwards named "Queen Charlotte's orange-pudding".

As Mrs. Delany advanced in years, the great convivial dinners of Delville and Mount Panther shrank to solitary suppers, and she drew nearer to her fireside. Suppers were commonly leftovers from dinner. To Mary Port, she wrote, "I am just going to write a note to Mrs. Shelley. I dine alone; Mrs. Chapone could not come, so my only companion will be the Welsbourne turkey! *Worse* than a cannibal, for *they* don't devour their companion!" (15 January 1770).

Later on, she wrote, "I write this by candle-light; perhaps you'll think I write it in the dark. God bless my dear child; my best compliments to all ... I assure you I am very well, and going to eat an artichock for my supper" (3 June 1781). An account written in February 1786 listed:

> Saturday morning – We left Windsor at 11 o'clock, a fine soft day after the severe frost, got to London at half past 2 o'clock, not so much fatigued as I expected.
>
> Evening – Lady Bute, Mrs. Boscawen. A brace of partridges from Dr. Wharton.
>
> Sunday morning.- Prayers at home, had a bad night.
>
> I eat half a roasted onion for my supper, and I dreamt of hobgoblins!

The visitors had gone, the house was quiet, all the servants were in bed – except for the butler who locked up and the maid who helped her mistress retire for the night.

The domestics, so-called, were the engine of the house. Mrs. Delany was the engineer. Both strata were interdependent and in a well-ordered establishment, both ran in parallel.

This way to the servants' quarters ...

fatty john:
mrs. delany's
domestics

> I am in great concern at your being without a
> servant. There are none without multitudes of
> faults, and they will be plagues if we expect
> perfection from them. Adieu, my dearest sister.

So wrote Mrs. Delany in December 1728, and with amiable
ambivalence she ended her letter with the following:

> P.S. Poor Badge has been very ill with a cold,
> and overwhelmed with the vapours: she has
> not been able to write, and is afraid my mama
> will think her very ungrateful for not having
> herself thanked her for the favour of the
> chine, which was the best that ever was eat. (5
> December 1728)

This paradox characterised all of Mrs. Delany's relations
with her domestics. They were necessary evils, as the smooth
running of the household depended on them, but she was
concerned that Badge, her waiting woman or housekeeper, was
not well. As mistress, Mrs. Delany enveloped her domestics
within her family fold but not as full participants, more like
wayward children. She reported to Anne on her return from
Mount Panther:

> I am very glad you do *not expect me* till spring,
> for as it is impossible for me to leave this place
> before October, I think it would be *safer* and
> better not to go till April. I am come home to
> a hurry and have many things to settle in my
> household that all housekeepers are sometimes
> troubled with – servants, accusations that must
> be cleared and are very teazing, though I don't

torment myself with those affairs; but as our family is large, and consequently expensive, it requires both *my care and attention.* (17 August 1745)

Dissatisfaction with servants was a constant theme and it carried through the generations. Mrs. Delany condoled somewhat sardonically with her niece Mary Port who, as a new bride, was setting up her household at Ilam:

I rejoyce you are all so well, and congratulate you on the extraordinary circumstance that three out of four of your domestics prove to your satisfaction; but I am not surprised, tho' vext, at Pugh's proving such an ignorant useless creature. *"Well then,"* you may well say, *"my dear A.D. why encourage me to take her?"* I am now sorry I did not *discourage* you, for tho' at first I thought she seemed sensible, and I hoped capable enough for your service, latterly I suspected she would not do; but as I have no reason to depend on my sagacity I thought to object just when all was packed and ready, was giving you too great a hurry of spirits. (St. James's Place, 30 April 1774)

Domestic service was highly desirable employment for the lower classes through the eighteenth century, not least because servants were very well looked after. They received board, lodging, wages and, depending on the size of the establishment, were provided with uniform or livery. The creature comforts on offer were often in sharp contrast to the servant's own home comforts – often the corner of a mud-floored cabin or a straw pallet in the workhouse. Pay was generally low, but there were many other perquisites, including choice leftovers from the master's table, cast-off clothing from the mistress, drains from the wine casks – not to mention what was availed of surreptitiously. Rates of pay are impossible to quantify as they varied so much from town to country and house to house, but they did increase towards the end of the century with upper servants commanding substantial sums.

Along with pay, there was the possibility of considerable personal advancement. Mrs. Elizabeth Raffald (*née* Whitaker), author of *The Experienced English Housekeeper*, had worked in service for many years before taking a position as housekeeper at Arley Hall in Cheshire. There, she met and married the head gardener, John Raffald, and they set up a very successful shop and business together in Manchester. Retail was a natural progression from domestic service, and many former butlers and footmen went in that direction, Mrs. Delany wrote: "I believe I have got a footman that will do, if his character answers. Richard designs to go into the grocery business till the place comes he is in expectation of" (3 September 1769).

A tension between family and at least some of the staff was habitual in most households, though many improving tracts and sermons sought to point out exactly where duty lay. *The Compleat Servant Maid*, an early publication from 1677, directed:

> Be careful that you say your prayers morning and evening ... that you behave yourself carefully to please your Master or Mistress, be faithful, diligent and submissive to them, incline not to sloth or laze in bed ... Be careful that you waste not nor spoil your Ladies or Mistresses' goods, neither sit you up junketing at nights after your Master or Mistress be abed.

There were constant complaints about after-hours feasting and carousing in kitchens. Questions were also raised about the private discounts some housekeepers and butlers negotiated for themselves with merchants and providers. Tips or vails were another source of income, as was the selling of candle ends. Visitors were expected to make a small present of money to the footmen and the other servants who lined up expectantly as the guest took his leave. The pressure exerted to cough up became so strong that the practice had to be discontinued. One gallant footman asked, before taking a place, whether the lady of the house often had a lying-in, as in that case his potential haul of vails from the stream of caudle drinkers and well wishers would determine his decision. This practice reached such disgraceful proportions that the freeholders of the *Scots Magazine* in 1759 banded together and decreed they would neither give money nor allow their servants to accept any. Their stance was widely taken up and the practice of giving vails gradually fell into disrepute.

❧

For the servants' part, in return for board, wages and the comfort of a freezing garret, their time was wholly at the disposal of the master and mistress. They were required to work any and all hours the household demanded. The work could be very demanding physically, depending on which rung of the domestic ladder they were on. The life of a kitchen maid or scullion was one of unremitting drudgery while, at the top of the pile, the butler had all the advantages of a comfortable billet with perks and status as he glided about his duties. The housekeeper and butler, as upper servants, might also enjoy their own private rooms in the servants' quarters.

Servants were free agents and could come and go, but without a reference, which was known as a character, they had few prospects. For dishonesty, insolence or promiscuity, they could be summarily dismissed without a character. Word of mouth was an effective tool, and Mrs. Delany championed or otherwise many cases in her circle.

> George Tassener has lost his good Lady Donegal and his place. He is an honest, sober, good servant, tho' rough and unpollished. I wish any body would make a demand for Mary Butcher. She has tired me out with her temper. But alas, she had no outward charms to attract, tho' *she thinks* the shoemaker that attends her is *not* insensible. I doubt it is false fire. (St. James's Place, 25 November 1780)

Mrs. Delany was an essentially benevolent employer. Neither side of the mistress–servant equation expected equality. The eighteenth-century household had an inner core working furiously with an outer layer of leisurely order and refinement. The inhabitants of that well-oiled machine understood the premise very well and the theory worked as long as the lower orders remained grateful and did not get above themselves. Vaunting ambition, though, was a perennial problem. To her niece Mrs. Port of Ilam, Mrs. Delany wrote:

> I thought of Mrs. Jackson for you (if to be had), and spoke about her to Mrs. Sandford [formerly Sally Chapone] when she was in town. She had an intention of taking her herself, but Mrs. Viney had *set her up* on so high a footing that she took upon herself in such a manner as nobody could reasonably submit to. She expected to be one of the company at all times, and was very troublesome. There is no end of such indulgences, and all the inconveniences that attend them. These notions are as mean as their origin, which makes them *proud* of *appearing* what

they *have no pretensions to be*, and it cannot be too much guarded against. The articles agreed to when you engage with such a sort of servant should be strictly adhered to, and then any little indulgence will be an obligation, and the moment they advance too far put a check immediately. There is *no medium*: when they cease to be servants, they attempt to be mistresses. (25 November 1774)

Staff control was a constant theme. Mrs. Delany likened the subordinate position of wife to husband with that of servant to mistress. Authority conferred responsibility, and once all parties met their obligations the status quo was kept in balance:

Our Maker created us *"helps meet"* [as wives], which surely implies we are worthy of being their companions, their friends, *their advisors*, as well as *they ours*; without those privileges being our due, how could *obedience to their will be a punishment*? Our servants are *not punished* by being obedient to our will? (Delville, 14 April 1759)

However, in some cases, the servants were far from obedient. Hannah More, writer, philanthropist and bluestocking, in her old age had to be rescued from such a gang. Due to ill health she was permanently confined to her room, and her servants would send out invitations to the servants of the neighbouring families to junket nightly in her kitchen, safe in the knowledge their beleaguered mistress was helpless upstairs.

This would not have happened on Mrs. Delany's watch – she kept firm control. "Went to bed excessively tired. Got up at nine, and read a lecture to my family on the advantages of *rising early!* For want of the *usual* bell that used to call them up they are *later* and *later*" (The Thatched Cottage, 15 January 1770). Encompassing the domestics within the broad family network conferred a childlike dependence on them, evident in an incident reported to the Rev. John Dewes when Mrs. Delany was seventy-two. Her sang-froid and leadership were admirable.

> I felt two shocks [five powder mills were blown up at Hounslow, 5 January 1772], but was not alarmed, taking it for a sudden rising of the wind, when my maids knocked at my chamber-door, looking like spectres, and said the house was coming down. I immediately thought I had had rogues of workmen, and that my house was actually falling. I put on my warmest capuchin [hooded cloak], called my servants to follow me, and walked to the street-door, where I was assured it was an earthquake. It was a con-solation to find it was not an earthquake, and I not a little comforted to find my own house staunch ... I am very comfortably settled in my new house, which is warm, airy and convenient. At present my head is confused with calling in my bills and making up my accounts, for I think nothing my own till all is paid for. (St. James's Place, 7 January 1772)

❀

At Delville, the household was complicated by the employment of relatives of the dean. This was a common practice in Ireland, harking back to the Irish idea of tamhlacht, where extended family were retained around the chieftain's hearth. These relatives were installed before the couple married, so Mrs. Delany inherited them, whether she liked it or not. On the occasion of her first visit to Ireland, the then Mrs. Pendarves took George, who was a niece of Dr. Delany's, to train up as a personal maid. This George, who was known only by her surname, spent some years with Mrs. Pendarves in England, and this young woman was the subject of much interest when Dr. Delany wrote in 1735:

> I am very glad to find from your account of George that one of my nieces has found the way to my esteem. I beg to assure you madam and I beg you to assure her that her good behaviour to you will not only recommend but endear her to me. Your goodness to her is beyond all acknowledgement. (8 February 1735)

Four years later, Dr. Delany wrote again concerning George:

> The poor of this city and country are in a miserable condition and though more than usual charity exerts itself in their favour, I am afraid many thousands will perish ... I mention this partly as an apology for not sending the fifty pound I promised her [George] which however I will not fail to remit with interest as soon as I am able and I beg you will assure her with my best wishes that your regard for her has greatly endeared her to me. (26 January 1739)

Mrs. Delany became very fond of some of her servants, especially those who worked closest to her. In the case of waiting women, like George, Badge and later Smith, who acted somewhat in the role of personal secretary, she was deeply concerned with their welfare. George died in her service, and

Mrs. Delany complained in a letter to Anne that an eminent London physician had "seen her off". Perhaps to compensate somewhat to the family for her loss, she tried to place her brother as a valet.

> I have had the good fortune (I hope) to provide for a brother of my poor George's, a very ingenious clever young man; as the Bishop of Clogher has lately lost his gentleman, and upon my recommendation has taken Mr. George, who will have a very happy life, for they are very good to all their family, and it is a profitable place. (28 February 1746)

"Be not served with kinsmen or friends for they expect much and do little," the Earl of Derby warned his son, but Dr. Delany took no notice; his relations continued to be retained about the house and lands at Delville.

> Did I tell you of another wedding in hand here? A nephew of D.D.'s, who is a kind of steward to us, and a sober good sort of young man bred up to farming affairs. He is going to be married to a clever girl, bred up in the same way − a niece of Mrs. Barber's; the Dean gives them a very comfortable farm about twelve miles off, and they are to supply us with all farming affairs. When this is done the Dean has not a relation left that he has not portioned or settled in some comfortable way; and if I were to tell you all the particulars of his benevolence and his goodness towards them you would be astonished that his fortune had answered so well the beneficence of his heart, but these are the things for which he has been blest. (31 January 1745)

Another niece, a Miss Delany, helped to manage the house, and her marriage to Mr. Green was reported.

> I gave you a short account of our wedding-day, which passed off as well as such things generally do. They are still in the house with us, and will stay till the beginning of May that we go to the North. Mr. Green is an agreeable man to have in the house, as he is very well bred and easy, conversable, and reads to us whilst we work in the evenings, so that we spend our time very pleasantly. The Councellor Green has three brothers, the two eldest great sugar-bakers, and one of them made a present to the Bride of a bill of fifty pounds the day after she was married. (Delville, 2 March 1745)

The Greens, now part of the Delany family and living at Delville, were closely connected to the trade of sugar baking. Elaborate sugar-paste table decorations were extremely fashionable, and supplying them for table settings was a highly profitable and skilful business. These confections were sometimes so elaborate they were hired for special occasions. This association with trade, however, coupled with the fact that a niece of the dean's had formerly been maid to Mrs. Delany, may have added to Bernard Granville's towering distaste of his sister's match. Social mobility was a two-way street. For the Greens and sundry Delany relations, proximity to the very well-bred Mrs. Delany was highly advantageous and a step closer to gentility itself. To Bernard Granville, such proximity was a step away. The danger of the family descent, however, did not exercise him to take on a well-bred, wealthy wife himself, a cause Mrs. Delany despaired of:

> I find his [domestics] *are not right yet*, nor can they ever be in good order till he has a wife to manage

them, for *men* are *no judges of domestic affairs*; we were designed for *that purpose*, and *have* the talents that are *fit for the purpose.* (Holly Mount, 10 August 1745)

By the middle of the nineteenth century, the mistress of the house had evolved into a china-doll-like figure, stationed in the parlour, far removed from kitchen or household mechanics. This separation had come about slowly, as gentility came to be equated with idleness. Mrs. Delany had scant tolerance for such foolishness. She called herself housekeeper and was very proud of her skills. "I think the knowledge of houswifery *is very necessary to every body, let their station be what it will*, but I am afraid my Pauline got cold with her mince-pie making" (29 December 1757). She and her sister were practitioners who passed on their skills to the next generation, albeit in confectionery and in the arts of the still room (a room originally used to distill cordials and perfumes). Mrs. Delany wrote: "I shall send you some oranges for orange wine as soon as they are good, I give you notice now that you may have your sugar and vessel ready" (4 December 1749), and in the same letter, "Miss Hamilton is my confectioner today, and is at this time making *orange-flower bread* of my *own orange flowers*, of which I am not a little proud; I am called to assist." Much later, at a time when London society was in thrall to the vice of gambling, she commented wryly: "Of *old* the *greatest ladies* in their land *fed their sheep* and *milk'd their goats*; but the *bon tons* have other ways of killing old father Time; happy *if* as innocently!" (9 August 1779).

With her hands-on experience and commanding position, Mrs. Delany supervised her domestics with some authority. Housekeepers, waiting women, personal maids, stewards, night-watchmen, bodyguards, butlers, cooks, cooks' maids, tutors, postillions, governesses and footmen come in for mention at various times through the correspondence. The numbers of staff varied from house to house, according to her needs, and the domestics themselves changed situation frequently. Some went walkabout:

> Pray have you heard anything of Will Cull since he left us? I am much afraid he is gone astray. I charged him to go directly to Gloucester, but as you have not mentioned him in any of your letters I suppose he has taken some other road. (28 February 1746)

> I beg you will be careful how you trust to the floods, and don't venture to cross them in rainy weather, since they are so soon swelled. I hope you have got a good coachman, – I believe we have; Will Vaughan, the wild colt I brought from England, has left us; he was a slovenly, sullen fellow, and proved very ungrateful; after having been nearly a year useless to us, and a great expense, as soon as he was well he gave us warning – no loss. I have got a pretty little boy I am training up, but *there's not much encouragement* for such undertakings; he has been well brought up, and I hope may prove more grateful, but never had the small-pox, which will make me afraid of carrying him with us to England. (Delville, 26 January 1753)

❧

Mrs. Delany's households were relatively modest, so duties were not as strictly demarcated as in very grand establishments like Bulstrode, the home of the Duchess of Portland. A footman might perform the duties of postillion or bodyguard or butler. Jonathan Swift in his *Directions to Servants* had scant regard for such compliance. Mrs. Delany informed Anne: "There is just published a humorous pamphlet of Swift's, I think called 'Advice to Servants'; it is said to be below his genius, but comical – I have not yet seen it" (16 November 1745). Swift's advice to the novice footman was:

> Never submit to stir a finger in any business but that for which you are particularly hired … if the corner of the hanging wants a single nail to fasten it, and the footman be directed to tack it up, he may say he does not understand that sort of work, but his honour may send for the upholsterer.

Footmen feature regularly in Mrs. Delany's dispatches – most of them called John. References to them were sprinkled into her letters: "Then I called for my tea-table, sent John of a Howdee to my Aunt Stanley, and at his return he brought me a letter from my dear sister" (19 November 1728). Was it the same John she later complained of? "John King is with me, and grows fatter and fatter" (3 February 1732). This same John may well have provided the model for Swift's footman, who is advised thus:

> It often happens that servants sent on messages are apt to stay out somewhat longer than the message requires; perhaps two, four, six, or eight hours, or some such trifle … When you return, the master storms, the lady scolds … But here you ought to be provided with a set of excuses, enough to serve on all occasions: for instance, your uncle came fourscore miles to town this morning on purpose to see you … you went to see a brother footman going to be hanged … some nastiness was thrown on you out of a garret

window, and you were ashamed to come home
before you were cleaned ...

Whether Mrs. Delany's servants delayed on messages,
whether they were over-fed or under-worked, they were all
over-weight. "Some way or other all domestics are bewitched;
my poor fatty John is very ill of a pleurisy, and Mrs. R.'s
innocent young man, Thomas, is gone to St. Bartholomew's!"
(4 February 1771). A year later she reported:

> Fat John will no more *rowl* off Mr. Marsh's grey
> horse, or weigh down the Ilam mule, no more
> snore by the great kitchen fire, or tope
> Staffordshire ale! But don't be alarmed, *he is alive*,
> and alive like to be, but is gone home to his
> Zantipe, and I have got a bonny Scot in his room
> that has a very good character for essentials, and
> seems a ready servant, really able to defend me at
> home and abroad (29–30 January 1772).

John's wife was dubbed Zantipe after the shrewish wife of
Socrates. It seems Mrs. Delany was not very confident of
Fatty John's prospects of marital harmony.

The footman or under-butler role in Mrs. Delany's
households could encompass anything from delivering and
returning messages to accompanying the master or mistress to
the playhouse or on visits. He would fetch and carry parcels;
he would announce guests:

> Thursday we walked in the garden and fed the
> robbins, – several of them eat out of D.D.'s
> hand. Whilst we were enjoying the fresh air
> Michael (my new footman) came running out of
> breath. "Madam, *Mrs. Clayton* and Mrs. Barnard
> the younger are come." We wished them at St.
> Woolstans. (24 March 1759)

He might be required to serve tea and coffee to the ladies:

> Last Friday morning I had a hurley burley visit
> from the Marchioness, just as my own breakfast
> was over, with her vegetables in her pocket to
> compose her tea (sage, baume, and ground ivy).
> After twenty fiddle faddles that worried my
> man Josiah almost as much as they worried me,
> two toasts round the loaf, neither too thick nor
> too thin, too hard or too soft were made. (St.
> James's Place, 21 March 1780)

The footman would be required to clean the shoes, light and tend the fires, call for a coach, light and trim the candles and, in the absence of a valet, brush the master's hat and coat. The butler was his superior. He had the heavy responsibility of the master's wine cellar, the care of his valuable plate and glass and the supervision of the male servants. The real theatre of operations for the butler and footmen was the eating parlour or dining-room.

Thomas Cosnett published a most useful guide, *The Footman's Directory*, in 1823. Cosnett's instructions on all aspects of the footman and butler's duties are minute and exacting; so much so, they instruct on which part of the foot – toe, ball or heel – the footman should lean when handing a plate to a diner. Though published early in the nineteenth century, Cosnett's method of dinner service evolves from and is consistent with eighteenth-century service. In a much-abbreviated form, the following treatment describes how they pirouetted about the dining-room.

> In putting on the cloth, let the table be dusted,
> and the green [baize] one put on first, then take
> the linen one, observing to have it the right side
> outermost: this you may easily know by the

hemming and the fold of it. If there be mats to put under the dishes, let them be put even in their proper places. Then lay the knives and forks at proper distances from each other; Next put on the water-bottles and glasses.

If the family dines by candlelight, the candles are in general put in the centre of the table. If there be many changes, you should have six large plates for each person, with pudding and cheese plates, and as many knives and forks; Have three wine glasses for each, and at least two rummers.

In setting out your side-board and side-table, you must study convenience, neatness and grandeur, as you cannot think that ladies and gentlemen have splendid and costly things without wishing them to be seen or set out to best advantage ... On the side-table the cold plates, cheese-plates, and dessert-plates are put; also the salad, vegetables, and cold meat; the steel knives and forks and the silver forks. Let these, as well as the rest of the things, be so arranged as to be handy, and also to look ornamental. Do not bring the cheese into the room till wanted, as the smell of it may be disagreeable to some of the company.

Having got most of your things ready, I shall now consider the dinner ordered. It in general takes the cook half an hour to dish it up, which gives you time to get the rest of your things into the room, and do what would not be proper to have been done before; such as cutting the bread and putting it round; placing the plate and dish-warmers, lighting the lamps and candles, and having proper lights in the passages; that you may see how to go on, and not knock the tray against the wall in carrying it up, which often causes the gravy to be spilt, or the things to be broken. Let the soup, or any other dish which is likely to slop over, be carried up by hand. In carrying up and putting on, you must be quick as possible, that the dinner may not get cold before the company sit down ... By casting your eye up and down the table, you will soon discover whether the dishes are set in a proper line and at equal distances from each other; if they are not, those who sit at the top and bottom will perceive it in an instant.

As the first course is put on the table before the company come into the room, you will be able to arrange it properly, which will be a guide to you in the after courses; as there will be an impression on the cloth where the dishes have been removed ... Notice the different ways in which different persons carve particular joints. Let the heads of fish be put to the left hand of the carver, and also the heads of hares, rabbits, and roasting pigs: Turkies, geese, ducks, fowls, pheasants, woodcocks, snipes, partridges, and all sorts of game, are put with the heads towards the right hand, as they are best to carve this way.

When you have put the plates round, and the dishes are on the table, see if you have the sauce-boats with the gravy and sauces in them, the vegetables, salad, and cold meat, if any, and if every thing be in its proper place. When all is quite ready, go up as quick as possible to announce dinner; do not, however, just go to the room door and there bawl out, "Dinner is ready, Sir," or "Ma'am;" but, if the room be large, go a little way towards your master and mistress, and say, *"The dinner is served, Sir;"* speak in an audible manner, but do not bawl aloud.

While waiting at dinner never pick your nose, or scratch your head, or any other part of your body; neither blow your nose in the room; if you have a cold and cannot help doing it, do it on the outside of the door: But do not sound your nose like a trumpet, that all the house may hear when you blow it; still it is better to blow your nose when it requires, than to be picking it and snuffing up the *mucus*, which is a disgusting habit. Do not yawn or gape, or even sneeze, if you can avoid it; and as to hawking and spitting, the name of such a thing is enough to forbid it, without a command. When you are standing behind a person, to be ready to change the plates etc. do not put your hands on the back of the chair, as it is very improper; though I have seen some not only do so, but even beat a kind of tune upon it with their fingers. Let your demeanour be such as becomes the situation which you are in. Be well dressed, and have light shoes that make no noise, your face and hands well washed, your finger-nails cut short and kept quite clean underneath; have a nail-brush for that purpose, as it is a disgusting thing to see black dirt under the nails.

As soon as the removes are put on the table, uncover all the dishes. When you have handed the meat, be as quick as possible in handing the vegetables and sauceboats round, as it too often happens that the sauces are forgotten. Do not wait to be asked for every thing by the company, as you may see when they want bread, vegetables, and sauce, and likewise what may be wanted on particular occasions; such as mustard to duck and goose, fish-sauce to the fish, mint-sauce to the lamb, bread-sauce to fowls, etc. etc. Keep your eyes on the table also, to see when the plates require changing. Be deaf to all the conversation of the company, and attentive only to their *wants*. When you change the plates, put them gently into the plate-basket, that you may not break them; and the knives and forks into the separate trays allotted for them, making at all times as little noise as possible.

The first course is put on in general before the company come into the room, but the other must necessarily be put on afterwards ...

When you perceive that the company do not seem inclined to eat of the dishes on the table, you must keep your eye on your master or mistress, to receive the signal when to remove the first course; and you must, previously to your going to wait at dinner, arrange with the cook, that you will let her know a little before you begin, that she may be ready with the second: be very particular not to forget this; if you do the cook cannot be ready, and the company will be kept waiting through your neglect.

As soon as you receive the signal for removing the first course take all the carving-knives, forks, and spoons which have been used, from off all the dishes ... begin removing the dishes from off the table in the same way that you did the knives, forks, etc; ... in taking off and putting on, you should lose no time, not be running backwards and forwards any more than you can help. Let your dishes be taken off and put on in systematic order, so that you make no bustle and confusion in the room; be *quick*, but *quiet* in your movements. As you take off the dishes, put them into a large tray, which of course you will have ready ... empty your tray as quick as possible, and put the second course on it; not in too great a hurry, as you may spill the gravy, or break the dishes, but be no longer than you can help in carrying the things up and down.

It sometimes happens, when there have been only four dishes for the first course, there have been six for the second; be particular in putting them on; have the bill of fare [written plan] in the tray, or on the side-board, then you will be able to look at it, and avoid mistakes; as it is reasonable to suppose that ladies and gentlemen like to have the dishes put on the way which they have contrived for the things to answer each other.

As soon as the company have done with the cheese, remove it from the table; then take all the things quite off, both dirty and clean; have a spoon (if there is not a proper table-brush) with a plate, and take off all the bits of bread, then with a clean glass-cloth and another plate, brush all the crumbs off the cloth: as soon as this is done, put round the finger-glasses, one to each person. As soon as the finger-glasses are done with, remove them; then take off the cloth with the green one also, and put them out of the room at once, otherwise it is very likely in your haste you may fall over them. When you have removed the cloths, if the hot dishes have drawn out the damp, take a cloth and wipe it off, but do not do it with a dirty cloth ... the tables may have been cleaned with oil, or wax, which will come off on the cloth; therefore have a neat cloth for this purpose, and do not use it for anything else.

As soon as you have wiped the table, put the dessert on ... Observe the same rule in putting on the dessert as the other courses. When they are all put on, then put on the sugar-basin and the water-jug, between the top and bottom dishes ... Let four table-spoons be laid to serve the dessert with, and if there be a cake, let a knife be put with it ... The sooner you leave the room after the dessert is put on, the better; never loiter about the room when the company are drinking their wine. Some servants whom I know, will be rattling the knives and forks, and removing all the clean glasses, etc. etc. from the dining-room before they leave it, but this is quite unnecessary, and appears disrespectful.

It is unlikely that Cosnett's paragon of virtue would take Swift's advice; he suggested:

If you are a young, sprightly fellow, whenever you whisper your mistress at the table, run your nose full in her cheek, or if your breath be good, breathe full in her face; this I have known to have had very good consequences in some families.

❧

Male servants generally slept in attic rooms, while the females were housed in basement garrets. Jane Fenlon in *Goods & Chattels: A Survey of Early Household Inventories in Ireland*, 2003, catalogues Corofin House, Co. Clare, which belonged to the O'Briens of Dromoland. A household inventory of 1717 shows the appointments of a garret room where at least four servants slept. Listed were:

> 4 beds, 2 of them small flock beds, 2 Old broken Caddows [woollen coverings or coverlets], 1 Old Rag, 4 Bedsteads with short feet, 1 Close Stool Box [a hinged wooden cabinet or seat containing a chamber pot], 1 Child's Cradle with a Bed & Quilt, 1 Stand, 3 Grates, 3 Fenders, 20 Small pieces belonging to ye fires, 2 pairs of Tongs, 4 Proackors (Pokers) and 1 Fire Shovel.

This garret was clearly used for storage as well as dormitory accommodation.

Doneraile House, 45 Kildare Street in Dublin, the townhouse of Lord Doneraile, was furnished in the period from 1746 to 1750. The inventory for the servants' hall shows:

> 1 table, 2 racks for liveries (made by Jno. Dowling 1749, 2s. 3d), 2 forms, 1 knife board, 2 settle beds (made by Richard Reilly 1749, £3.00), 2 feather beds and 1 mattress in them, 2 pairs of blankets, 2 rugs, 2 mats, 1 wig block and stand, 1 wooden bowl and knives and forks.

The household linen inventory of 15 April 1762 lists:

> 15 pair of servants' sheets, 5 pr of them new marked, a pair taken for China cloths quite old not fit for use, 3 pair of pillow cases, 3 white

Manchester quilts, 3 white Frenchwork quilts, 8 house napkins, 2 pr of fieldbed sheets, 8 oyster rubbers and 4 dishing cloths.

Mrs. Delany's domestics probably also slept between cast-off sheets, and her solicitude of them did not end there:

I have been acting as surgeon, as poor John cut a terrible gash in the fleshy part of the inside of his hand. I washed it well with arquebuzade [a distilled water made from aromatic plants such as rosemary] and put on the black plaster, and in a few hours it was easy, and I hope will be soon well; it bled very much, and frightened our poor Welshman to a great degree; and the constern-ation of the house was as great as if his head had been cut off. (Mount Panther, 8 August 1758)

Mrs. Delany and Anne condoled with one another over the health of their domestics, but their own convenience was very much at the root of their concern.

I am very sorry poor Frank has been so much out of order, I mean had so bad an accident as burning his hand; a clever faithful servant is truly a treasure. Smith has been much out of order but is better. (Delville, 27 March 1752)

Yesterday I was put into a sad fuss by my housekeeper being taken very ill; she is fat and short-necked and complained so violently of her head that I feared an apoplexy; but Dr. Barber had her bled and vomited immediately, and she is now in a fair way of doing well. She would have been a great loss to me, as she is I think an excellent servant, and one that I may

trust with the care of my house in my absence.
(5 April 1746)

A good housekeeper was a valuable servant and she
enjoyed considerable status. In the journal of her visit to
Bulstrode, Miss Mary Hamilton, niece of Sir William
Hamilton, ambassador to the court of Naples, gave an insight
into the significance of the housekeeper and the *modus operandi*
of a great house. She wrote:

> Mrs. Delany came and invited me to go with
> her and sit in the drawing-room. She brought
> the papers, I read a few paragraphs to her. She
> then left me, said she hoped to meet me in the
> drawing-room. Mrs. Woodward, the house-
> keeper, then came and invited me to see her
> room and her store rooms, and I followed her.
> She showed me her rooms, her china closets, her
> linnen presses, her stores etc. etc. offered me
> anything I chose to eat of cakes or sweetmeats,
> etc. I took some orange cakes to please her. She
> gave me flowers, and a peacock's feather to keep
> and use as a mark in a book to remember her
> by; she said a thousand civil things to me. I saw
> also the steward's room, which is large, and here
> the upper servants dine; it appeared to be hung
> round with pictures, but I did not stay to
> examine them. Went to the drawing-room,
> where dear Mrs. Delany was; she had her
> spinning wheel and her table, and I my little
> table and fringe knotting etc. (Bulstrode, 5
> December 1783)

> Soon after the Duchess left me Mrs. D. came;
> she told me as I was not dress'd she would order

the servants to bring the oysters (which she eats at 2 o'clock) to be brought in my room. She said many kind things to Betty [Miss Hamilton's maid]. As the upper servants dine at 2, Betty left me soon after the servants brought the oysters and laid the napkin in my dressing-room. I was obliged to receive Mrs. Delany *en robe de chambre*, and after we had finished our goute [snack] she left me. I finished dressing, and I remained in my room till the dinner-bell rung ...

We went to dinner; the common chit chat of the great world was the conversation ... Mrs. Delany came to me a quarter of an hour before 7. At 7 Mr. Keys (the groom of the chambers) told us tea was ready; we had each our little table, our candles, and work; conversed upon the news of the day – fashions, dress etc. etc. a quarter to ten came to my room to leave the ladies at liberty to talk without any restraint ... about quarter past ten the groom of the chambers came and told me supper was ready. (Bulstrode, 6 December 1783)

Dinner at Bulstrode was now eaten fashionably late, around four or five o'clock in the afternoon; oysters instead of plum cake now filled those between-meal gaps. Betty ate her dinner at two o'clock with the upper servants in the steward's room. The servants had their dinner first, and when it was out of the way they were ready to wait on the family dinner. A greater number of male servants to females demonstrated status, and Bulstrode's male retinue went so far as to include Mr. Keys, the groom of chambers, who patrolled the rooms and ushered the visitors to tea or supper.

Patricia McCarthy, in her article "Vails and Travails: How

Lord Kildare Kept His Household in Order" (in *Irish Architectural and Decorative Studies: The Journal of the Irish Georgian Society*, Volume VI, 2003), gives us a good idea of what the servants ate in a large, well-appointed establishment: They fared very well indeed. The upper servants (i.e. steward, housekeeper, butler, clerk of the kitchen, personal maids and valets) dined in the steward's hall at 4 p.m. on

> "Mutton and Broth, Mutton Chops, Harrico or Hashed, Roast or boiled Pork with Pease Pudding and Garden things or, Stakes, Roast, or boiled Veal with Garden things when Veal is killed at Carton". Once a week they had mutton or beef pie, and each Sunday, roast beef and plum pudding. Leftover meat from this meal was to be eaten for supper and breakfast, "adding some Potatoes or any kind of Garden Stuff, Cheese or Eggs". In the servants' hall they fared almost as well, dining at 1 p.m. on "boiled Beef, Cabbage and Roots, every Sunday to have a Piece of Beef Roasted and Plumb Pudding, or any other kind of Pudding".

These dinners were good approximations of the family dinner, and Mrs. Delany's domestics, most of whom she dubbed fat, were probably just as well fed as Lord Kildare's.

❧

In her more modest sphere, Mrs. Delany's Smith became a combination of housekeeper and waiting woman, as Badge had been:

> You are very kind in inquiring after Smith; she was very sick at sea, but well again as soon as

landed; she is much delighted with Delville, and (as much as she has seen) with Ireland. *She* and *my housekeeper* take to one another extremely; and I hope I am now settled with honest quiet domestics. Fribble behaves himself very well, and Thomas will make I believe, in time, a very good butler. (6 June 1747)

In a bachelor establishment, such as Bernard Granville's, a housekeeper might reign supreme. In a great house like Bulstrode, while still important, the housekeeper, Mrs. Woodward, was not top of the tree – a house steward controlled the finances the house and estates. Mrs. Delany herself held the reins in her households, but there was considerable overlap with her housekeeper and waiting woman. She supervised the packing up of the house herself prior to going north:

I have a great deal of business on my hands; for I must see all my fine furniture and pictures well papered, and I have a new inventory to make of my household goods, and two drawers of papers to look over and separate in order. I hope my housekeeper is one I can trust; she is a sober woman and does everything required of her extremely well, and I shall take Betty Woodal and Margaret with me. (22 March 1746)

Superior servants, such as the lady's maid or waiting woman or governess, were answerable to the mistress only. The housekeeper kept the upper and lower housemaids, kitchen maids, dairymaids, laundresses and sundry others busy, sweeping, scrubbing, scouring, lighting fires, dusting, beating carpets, fetching water and whatever else was called for. She supervised the rotation of household linen, sheets and blankets and kept them in order. She provisioned the house; she assessed and bought in the fish, oysters, tripe, lemons, woodcocks, lobsters and chickens from the travelling vendors who came to the kitchen door, and she gave a faithful account to her mistress. This was usually an imprest account – the cash was given in advance and accounted for at the end of the month. She kept her store cupboards of provisions, spices, nuts, dried fruits, flour and sugar and tea under lock and key and monitored the stocks with an eye to economy or not, depending on her integrity.

Keeping a rein on accounts was central to the house-keeper's role. In setting out for Ireland for the first time, the then Mrs. Pendarves put her house in order: "Last Friday I dined at Mr. Wesley's ... After dinner I came home to settle accounts with Mrs. Badge, and order the packing up of the box; when that was done I returned to my company" (13 July 1731). As a much older woman, setting up home anew in St. James's Place, accounts still had to be settled:

> London is eno' to turn the brains of old as well as young. What with Smith's long lists of what is wanted, household accounts during my absence, visits morning, noon, and night, I have hardly time left me to scratch a few lines to my dearest Mary. (St. James's Place, 23 December 1777)

Eighteen months later, Smith's health was failing, and Mrs. Delany's erratic letter shows how disturbed she was.

> I thank God, I am pure well, but much perplexed about Smith, convinced it is quite necessary for me to have a servant; and as necessary that she, poor creature, shall be free from all care but "the one thing needful" ... Smith has lived with me 34 years, and baiting, human frailties, which no one is without, has been a *most excellent servant*, and loves me most sincerely ... There is a person, I

believe, you saw (Mrs. Rea) recommended by Mrs. Sandford, who I wanted to be with G.M.A. when she was with me, that were she disengaged I should wish to have, and, by all accounts, is just what I want; and I heard she was going to quit her place: so I shall enquire after her, for I am very unwilling to take a perfect stranger about me ... I have got Mary Butcher here; the Dss made me send for her last Thursday to assist Smith to pack up. (Bulstrode, 9 August 1779)

A thought has just come into my head that if I can bring it about will make me easier about Smith. Mrs. Blackburn (now very infirm) but well eno' to be a comfort to Smith, has a good house in the Haymarket with a very good sort of woman, who has more lodgers. They furnish their own rooms, and provide themselves with food and give £8 a year. If there is a spare room, and Smith will settle in it, I will make her income up to twenty pounds a year, and give her things towards furnishing her room. She shall still be my servant, and make my caps, and do any work she can should it please God she should grow better; she is very bad, but suffers with great patience. (Bulstrode, 9 August 1779)

Mrs. Delany's provision for Smith did her great credit, as the problem of indigent housekeepers was a perennial one. The *Dublin Daily Advertiser* ran the following advertisement:

For the Benefit of an Alms-House now erecting in St. Warborough's Parish for the Reception of reduced House-keepers. At the Theatre-Royal in Smock-Alley on Thursday 28 of this Instant,

October, will be acted a play called Henry the Fourth; and the Humours of Sir John Falstaff. N.B. It is to be humbly hoped that all well Disposed Persons will contribute to so Useful and Necessary a Charity. (21 October 1736)

Mrs. Delany's charity was not required for long.

I am sure you wish to know how I do after the shock of losing my old and faithful servant; for such it was, tho' expected, and rather to be wished for than not. There is a natural gratitude in the human mind, that makes one for a time recollect the good we have received, and rises above any inconveniences that might have sometimes mixed with many useful qualities; but I find I have suffered for some time past more on her account than my own, for now that her sufferings are over, and I have had some days' recollection, I find I am much relieved and more composed than for some months past. Poor Smith was buried last Monday; it was her request to be buried as near as possible to her sister Hawkins. I could not propose to her in her last illness giving up her accounts or keys; and therefore it is necessary for me to go to town before I go to Bulstrode ... Burchel is an excellent attendant as far as I have experienced, and tho' not altogether the servant I want is a very agreeable servant. I wrote you word I had engaged Lydia Rea. (Bill Hill, 2 September 1779)

There was no end to demands and Mrs. Delany's purse was tried again.

You overrate my poor tokens; poor little specimens of what I wish were in my power to do! But every year brings some new expense, and clips the wings of beneficence; the last year was an expensive one, and my lawyer's merciless bill is unpaid. Court thinks the demand on me for Smith's funeral I *ought* not pay, as she left *so much money*; but I fear I have made it unavoidable, by giving the executor reason to think I would; but I will not do more than honestly I ought to do; this is by way of excuse for the poverty of your Christmas boxes. (St. James's Place, 18 January 1780)

Losing a jewel of a housekeeper was something Mrs. Delany's great correspondent Mrs. Boscawen could sympathise with.

My dear friend, I think it is the time for these losses. I was complaining to our friend the Dean of Gloster of the great one *I had had*; he answered it "could not have been more irreparable than his," in a housekeeper lately dead of a fever, who had liv'd with him twenty years, and was the worthiest, best, faithfullest servant imaginable, knowing all his ways, all his friends, and providing everything so cleverly, with so much capacity, activity; in short, he is *undone* – as *I am* for poor Sleeve, (whom I see methinks and hear at every corner of this cottage). (Glan Villa, I September 1779)

Mrs. Delany found a suitable replacement. "I believe I have already told you how well pleased I am so far with Rea; and indeed she promises me much comfort, and seems so happy to be with me, that it adds to my satisfaction" (Bulstrode, 29 October 1779). Lydia Rea's role like Smith's before her was a combination of lady's maid, waiting woman and housekeeper. In a grand house the waiting woman would command the lady's maid, but such strict definitions did not apply in Mrs. Delany's household. The lady's maid functioned in a highly personal capacity, assisting at her mistress's toilette, the morning and evening dressing and undressing; arranging her head, hairdressing being an important skill; caring for and mending and altering her clothes; making her caps and aprons. The lady's maid would see to her mistress's bed and the cleanliness and tidiness of her chamber. She would supervise the bringing of water for washing and removal of all slops or would do this work herself if there was no underling. Her work was light compared to the other household maids', and perks could include the odd cast-off.

A person engaged in the capacity of waiting woman was of different calibre. Accomplished in her own right, she might be a widow or a down-at-heel gentlewoman or the daughter of a clergyman. She would be expected to be literate, to entertain her mistress with reading aloud and good conversation. She should be an able needlewoman, a mistress of fine work and capable of supervising plain work. She would travel with her mistress as her companion and pack and care for her belongings on the journey. She would act as secretary and be entrusted with correspondence.

Astley was one such servant. She was a clergyman's daughter and was in Mrs. Delany's service at the time of her death. Mrs. Delany wrote to Mary about her arrival and gave an account of her looks:

> Mrs. Astley is come, tired to death with travelling all night; she is going to drink some tea and go to bed. She appears to me to be just what I want; about Molly B's. size (but holds her head up better); not handsome, but nothing

disagreeable in her appearance, which is all I can
see at present; tomorrow we shall settle to
business; today it would have been rather too
much. (St. James's Place, 11 July 1782)

Years afterwards, when Astley was quite an old woman, Lady
Augusta Llanover, great-grand-niece of Mrs. Delany, who edited
her letters for publication, sought her out in her retirement.

Mrs. Delany had become quite famous in her latter years
in London. She was courted for her accomplishments, her
gentility and her conversation. She was particularly admired
by the younger Blue Stocking set, who were gratified by her
attendance at their soirées, though Mrs. Delany herself cast a
wry eye on proceedings.

I dined yesterday with our *little plump Montague*
and her son; you were much enquired after, and
your health drank. From thence I went by
invitation to Mrs. M., *the witty* and *the lean*, and
found a formidable circle! I had *a whisper* with
Mrs. Boscawen, another with Lady Bute, and a
wink from the Duchess of Portland – *poor diet*
for one who loves a plentiful meal of social
friendship. (The Thatched Cottage, February
1769)

Fanny Burney, author of *Evelina* (1778), was one of the
young protégées who worshipped at Mrs. Delany's feet. Mrs.
Delany encouraged her, as she had encouraged the artist and
printmaker William Gilpin, the portraitist and history painter
John Opie and many others she believed worthy of promotion. To aid Fanny Burney, financially hard-pressed at the
time, Mrs. Delany canvassed for an appointment at court and
secured her a position as dresser to the queen. In her later
published diaries, Fanny Burney, by now Madame D'Arblay,

asserted that Mrs. Delany was the object of charitable donation from the Duchess of Portland and others. This charge greatly offended Lady Llanover. She asked Astley to clarify the matter, and Astley was unambiguous in her response:

> Except for a small basket of vegetables once a week, not anything once in a month was ever sent by the Duchess of Portland, who never had company at her own house. She drank tea in St. James's Place all the winter, when Mrs. Delany invited those who the Duchess liked to meet. I had to make tea at many different times (and a pound of fine tea, at 16s. a pound, was gone in no time), with cakes, and etcs. As to money, I am certain not even the present of the least trifle did the Duchess ever give Mrs. Delany; but her spending the Summer at Bulstrode ...

Fanny Burney overstated her intimacy with Mrs. Delany and implied a knowledge of her private correspondence, which further upset Lady Llanover, but Astley was there as eye-witness.

> As to Madame D'Arblay's looking over Mrs. Delany's letters and papers, I doubt the truth of it, with good reason, for more than a fortnight before we left St. James's Pl. I was employed upon them every morning in examining and burning a large box of letters, which grieved me to destroy, as some of them were written by the first people in the world; but *I was obliged to obey*, and observed at the time that the box of letters (containing hundreds) would have been a fortune to anybody were they published. "*That is what I want to prevent*" was the answer.

Manuals and directories for servants of the day advised discretion. Private family business or family secrets should not be discussed in kitchens. Most particularly, private family matters should not be broadcast further afield, but they undoubtedly were. However, the tables could be turned and the servants could provide entertainment for the family. Lady Llanover published the following extract in good faith. She believed it to be from the hand of a loyal retainer, but it seems much more like a parody by Mrs. Delany, where she impersonated "A.G.", a former housekeeper of Bernard Granville's, writing to the incumbent, Martha.

> Indeed, my good friend Martha, it has been a deadly while I have taken to answer your kind letter, but what can a body do with one eye, and that a very bad one ... You are capering about in your cardinals, and things, like a girl of twenty. I suppose you are about getting a young husband. I was told so, and much good may it doe you, if he give you a hearty thrashing now and then. I wish you would tell me who he is; write me word what his name is. But I hope this affair do not make you forget the dear piggs, and turkeys, and geese, and ducks; send me word if they be in good heart and thriving. And what is master doing? Is he smothered amongs the lime and bricks? Or has he got his work done ... How has the season been with you? Have you got any fruit? We have not as much as curans fitt to make a little wine with. Well, I wish you wou'd let me know what master is doing! Had he finished his house, done all he has to doe, and got rid of his workmen? Surely, I thought, he wou'd have been in London before now, and have got a new gown on purpose ...

When not lampooning the domestics, Mrs. Delany was watchful of propriety. She reminded Mary of her manners. "I am quite happy about your nurse," she wrote to her niece, Mary Port:

> as to your housekeeper, if honest, sober, and careful, something else must be overlooked, as there is no perfection in mortals even of a higher rank ... I am glad you got the brawn. I not only every day feast on my Cottingham Cheese, but have been so generous as to bestow a whole one on the Duchess of Portland; by-the-bye, should you not thank her for the rose-trees, as well as wishing her a happy new year? (St. James's Place, 31 December 1771)

❧

Particular attention was paid to the recruitment of servants for the children of the family. They were required to be models of decorum, but this good example was set from the top. Children required a battalion of domestics, from wet-nurse to governess and all points in between. The governess was a being apart. She was usually quite a young woman, accomplished and educated. She ranked well above the lower servants but had to remain aloof from the upper servants to guard her lofty status. She ideally came from a respectable family, and she should have a good appearance – such attributes might give her entrée to family gatherings. Hovering about the perimeters, she had a delicate high-wire act of superiority to her fellow servants and deference to her employers to perform. She was placed in a lonely no man's land. Her principle duty was the instruction of the children, but first the babes were nursed and weaned.

Wet-nursing was the usual practice in upper-class families, though maternal breast-feeding had been advocated for the child's benefit from the late seventeenth century. The Granville women were unconvinced, remaining unsentimental about babies. Sometimes the wet-nurse came to the home of the infant, but more often she took the child to her own much humbler home and nursed it along with her own brood. So for many infants, the first experience of nurture came from a surrogate mother. The biological parent, when the child was eventually handed over, was a relative stranger. The mother may not have seen their child's first steps or heard their first words.

Mrs. Delany was involved in choosing a nurse for Court Dewes:

> I am as much perplexed for you as you can be for yourself in regard to my godson, but I think if you can be reconciled to the nurse's house, that the story you have heard can be no great objection, but will rather for the future make her more careful, as she seems to be a good sort of woman. A deaf nurse is not to be endured; the poor dear may make his little moans, and have a thousand uneasinesses that she will hear nothing of. (Clarges Street, 12 November 1742)

We can only speculate as to what horror took place in the nurse's house. Swift's satirical direction to the wet-nursing profession in his *Directions to Servants* was:

> If you happen to let the child fall and lame it, be sure never to confess it; and if it dies, all is safe. Contrive to be with child as soon as you can, while you are giving suck, that you may be ready for another service when the child you nurse dies, or is weaned.

Fosterage from home could last for a couple of years, if the child survived. This next extract is a rare fragment from Mrs. Granville, mother of Mrs. Delany and Anne, following a visit from her grandson Bernard Dewes, who was Anne's second child.

> Yesterday I had the pleasure of seeing my little Banny who is the fairest thing I ever saw, and very lively; he was with me by nine o'clock, and staid till five, eat *buttered turnips* for *his dinner* heartily, and a mess of milk and bread before he set out again. In my opinion he is not like father, mother, or brother, but the picture of your poor brother Bevil; he is but a small child but tall and well-proportioned, the finest skin I ever saw, and of his hair I shall enclose a lock for you to see. Mrs. Peters and the nurse send their duty, and the former says she (and her husband) *dread the time* of your taking him away from them.

It is astonishing to our sensibility that a mother should require a detailed description of her own child and a lock of his hair. Though the letter is undated, little Banny was probably about two years old and almost ready to leave his foster family and return home. When a child survived what the Georgians deemed the animal state of babyhood, full attention was turned to his or her education, and very tender care was taken. The Dewes family grew and thrived, and as Mary Dewes came into her girlhood, a suitable governess was engaged:

> I am very glad you have got Miss Hine with you; she seems to be a good kind of young woman. If she knows how the *crokand* sugar

[candied sugar like a honeycomb] used to be done at Mrs. Norcliff's, I wish you would prevail on her to teach Sally [Chapone] how to do it. (Bulstrode, 10 December 1749)

Miss Hine was employed as governess, but her accomplishments included the making of confectionery, something both Mrs. Delany and Anne enjoyed. The more skills a young woman had at her command, the more desirable she was to a family. Regardless of her cooking talents, a good command of French was essential. French had been the language of the English court at the time of Charles II, and fluency was a signal of gentility. A governess would instruct her young female pupils in their letters, grammar, simple arithmetic, history, geography, French and fancy needlework to the level of her own attainment. Extra masters could be drafted in for dancing, painting or music as needed. The boys of the family would be tutored in the classics, Latin and Greek, mathematics, possibly the sciences, if available, and history and geography. Private tutors at home, a good public school, university and the grand tour polished off the young men of the Granville class, though not all attained a university education. Far less emphasis was placed on formal education for girls: they were prepared for the marriage market, and their education was designed to produce the next generation of wives, mothers, hostesses and housekeepers.

Young Mary Dewes' travelling arrangements were of great concern when she made a visit to her aunt Delany in London. The retinue, which included the Dewes' family nanny, a personal maid and a footman, was to accompany a child of ten:

I am greatly obliged to you and Mr. Dewes for his being so willing to trust me with so great a charge as your little daughter. It would indeed be a higher obligation if he would come himself

and bring you with him. I will do my best to
spirit up Mrs. Emily, and I will engage what
masters you please for Mary, and will endeavour
to treat her in every respect as you would wish
... A post chaise and Nanny Ward to take care
of her, and Mrs. Emily and Frank to escort
them, I hope will bring her safely; and as soon as
you can send her I am ready for her. Nanny
Ward will return in the chaise, as I don't
apprehend her staying in town for a week will be
of any use to Mary, and you may want her.
(Spring Gardens, February 1756)

This visit followed in a long tradition of Granville aunts
introducing their young nieces into society. Aunt Stanley had
taken Mary Granville (later Mrs. Delany) into her London
home at eight years of age. Mary was received there as a
cuckoo in the nest by Miss Tellier, who was appointed her
personal maid, governess and companion. Old family ties and
grace and favour appointments had complicated the delicate
position of this unhappy young woman. She was the daughter
of a governess who had lived with Aunt Stanley. After some
years, bad health forced the governess to leave her position,
but before she left, she strategically placed her daughter, Miss
Tellier, under Aunt Stanley's protection. Miss Tellier, for good
measure, was goddaughter to Aunt Stanley. Mrs. Delany wrote
in the autobiography of her early years:

> The girl was then fifteen, about three years
> before my aunt took me from school, at which
> time I was eight years old. Miss Tellier was
> sensible, ingenious, and very well in her
> appearance; perfectly mistress of French, and
> she behaved herself with great affection towards
> her benefactress, whose great partiality and

> indulgence to her made her expect more than
> she had a right to claim. She soon grew jealous
> of the increasing kindness *I* met with ... Miss
> Tellier fell into an ill state of health, and
> attributed it to a blow I had given her upon her
> breast, which might have happened in my sleep,
> as I was always her bed-fellow, but I am sure not
> intentionally, as I was not of a revengeful nature.

Miss Tellier, drawing on all the cunning of her dependent position, sought to have her rival removed, a situation doubtless made more uncomfortable by the forced intimacy of the shared bed.

Nearly a century later, G.M.A. Port made her treasured visits to her Aunt Delany in London. The Port family was growing apace with the addition of brothers and sisters, John, George, Bernard, Harriet and Louisa. Mary Port also had the care of her husband's young relation Miss Sparrow; so along with her growing family her staff problems expanded.

> The good account you give of yourself laid such
> a foundation of good-humour, that I bore with
> tolerable composure the surprising account of
> Susan's [maid of Mary Dewes Port at Ilam]
> ingratitude towards you. I own it was unex-
> pected, and let her say what she will there must
> be some hidden reason for her behaving in so
> unaccountable a manner; She was too young and
> too little acquainted with service to be a com-
> fortable servant to you in your present situation;
> when you were more disengaged you had leisure
> both to direct and correct, but now you require
> a servant, who knows her business, And whose
> attention must have you principally in view.
> "All this is true, my dear A.D.; but where

shall I find her?" I wish I could find such a one for you my dear M.

I told Smith the affair, and did not find her so much surprised as I expected, but very sorry it so happens. I have only heard of Mrs. Faulkener's niece, who lives with Mrs. Montagu, but have not seen her, though I intend it; she is about thirty, has not been at service, was bred up by an aunt (now dead) who kept a warehouse for hats and cloaks, etc. and no doubt would be happy to come to you; but the great objection is not having been at service, for having known what it is to serve, only can make them know the value of a good mistress. (4 February 1771)

Personal referral and testimonial was the preferred route for domestic staff recruitment, but if that method failed an employer could advertise or go to a Register Office and hire a servant. Mrs. Elizabeth Raffald had set up her own Register Office in Manchester, a place where servants seeking work were introduced to employers. Her perfectly respectable intention was misconstrued by low individuals who treated the office as a "pimp's clearing house", and Mrs. Raffald was obliged to clarify the matter in an advertisement: "As several of Mrs. Raffald's friends in the country have mistook her Terms and Designs of her Register Office she begs leave to inform them that she supplies Families with Servants, for any place, at ONE shilling each."

The problem of servants and their hire continued well into the next century. The Dublin Society set up their own Register Office for the Improvement and Encouragement of Servants, and the annual report of 1825 gives the reason for setting up the office: "The general acknowledgement of the inconveniences and evils felt from the want of trustworthy and competent servants, together with a desire to benefit in various ways that useful class of persons." The report goes on to say that one of the chief difficulties of the Committee

> has been that arising from the inconsideration
> (not to use stronger terms) of Masters and Mis-
> tresses granting more favourable certificates of
> character to Servants, than on private enquiry
> they have deserved. In some instances this may
> be the result of mistaken kindness.

Support for the venture was slow, again possibly through misunderstanding:

> It is right that the Committee should state their
> belief that their efforts have also been retarded
> and subscriptions less generally made, for the
> public not fully discriminating between the
> objects of this benevolent Institution, and those
> Registries in various parts of the city, which
> however respectable and convenient some of
> them may be, are of quite a different nature
> from this Society: and it is well known that
> there are others, which so far from being careful,
> do not in any wise bear a respectable character.

Mrs. Delany stayed with the time-honoured personal-referral method and travelled in hope.

> This morning I have had a person with me
> recommended to you by Mrs. Sandford [Sally
> Chapone]. Her appearance and manner decent,
> civil, staid, about forty or more; has a healthy
> look, and says she is healthy. She expresses her-
> self in very good language, and speaks French

as fluently, having been used to it from her infancy. I thought she might not submit to some rules necessary in a private family, but she said she should submit to any rules in whatever family she entered, and that she always drank water, and no malt liquor. She seems to be the very person you wished for, when we talked over the affair at Ilam. I mentioned to her that you would have a niece under your care; that she must also have attention, which she is willing to do, and any sort of work she can do, and will do to the utmost of her power. In short, if she answers to her character and appearance, she will be a treasure to you in your nursery, and to that I should devote her. She is about my size. She immediately entered into the necessity of a constant attention and proper decorum toward children. She will not come under £15 a-year. Her name is Hand. Her brother keeps a French school of reputation at Bristol; her mother lives there, and her niece Mrs. Sandford has just taken into her family. (14 October 1773)

Hand was not a success because two years later Mrs. Delany was in quest again.

Miss Vrankin (but if she comes to you pray let her be called Mrs.) is a sort of servant so much sought after, that they raise their demands *very high*. I am convinced sixteen pounds a year is as much as you *ought* prudently to give, but if she only boggles at that, and twenty will content her, I will make it up to her if on tryal you approve of her. (19 January 1775)

Miss Vrankin, or Mrs. Vrankin to pay her proper respect, may have been a little too young or too pretty, as Mrs. Delany anxiously hovers on the sidelines.

> I am impatient to hear again how you approve of Mrs. V. on further acquaintance, but *don't* let your liking of her and natural indulgence lead you to make her *too familiar*, and to forget the station she is in, as that will give her *less* consequence with the young people, I know P.'s [Mr. Port's] good humour and comicality will lead him to *joke* with her sometimes, but *his judgement* will correct that, as *he knows* there is a great difference between *civility* and *familiarity*; the *one* will teach her what is *due* to *him*, the other would be *toute au contraire*; and tho' she seems very steady, knowing, and prudent for age, you must consider she is very young, and may learn a great deal from your advice. I think when you have any company it would be best for her to dine above stairs with G.M.A., and use her to it *at first*, or she may think it hard afterwards. (27 April 1775)

Sadly, we have no account of Miss Hand or Mrs. Vrankin's experiences, flirtatious or otherwise. The governess's perspective, however, can be seen in the experiences of Mary Wollstonecraft, author of *A Vindication of the Rights of Women* (1792) – a most unlikely governess. She took the position of governess to the daughters of Robert and Caroline King, Lord and Lady Kingsborough, at their residence, Mitchelstown Castle, in County Cork. The King family was very wealthy and had vast estates locally. Janet Todd, in her biography *Mary Wollstonecraft: A Revolutionary Life*, 2000, gives a detailed description of Mary's time there.

Mary Wollstonecraft took the job at a time of great personal disadvantage. She had published *Thoughts on the Education of Daughters* in 1787, but she had mounting debts and a failed school enterprise behind her. To be governess to the Kingsborough girls was a very good appointment but one more suited to a French speaker, which she decidedly was not. Mary Wollstonecraft's own education had been somewhat patchy. For £40 a year she was engaged to take charge of three of the five daughters of Lord and Lady Kingsborough. This was a large sum, which might help discharge some of her debts. She hoped she had not been over-sold by enthusiastic friends or creditors. She began frantically brushing up her French and smartening her appearance; though she lacked money for clothes, she would have to do.

She wrote:

> From what I can gather – Lady K. must be a good kind of woman – and not a very happy one – for his Lordship has been very extravagant – and the children neglected and left to the management of the servants – Lady K. says that those who hitherto had the care of them neglected their minds and only attended to the ornamental part of their education, which she thinks ought ever to be a secondary consideration – These sentiments prejudice me in her favour – more than any thing I have heard of her – for I cannot venture to depend on the opinion of people who are dazzled by her superior station in life.

This sentiment was expressed before she met Lady Kingsborough, and she was disappointed:

> Lady K. is a shrewd clever woman a great talker – I have not seen much of her as she is confined

to her room by a sore throat – but I have seen
half dozen of her companions – I mean not her
children, but her dogs – To see a woman
without any softness in her manners caressing
animals and using infantine expressions – is as
you may conceive very absurd and ludicrous –
but a fine Lady is new species to me of animals.

The children didn't fare any better. She found them disagreeable
on first sight, wild, uneducated and "not very pleasing".

Despite her disdain, Mary Wollstonecraft was treated very
well at Mitchelstown – "like a gentlewoman". Castle guests
and relations hearing about this famous author–governess
wanted to meet her. This did not mean social acceptance: she
was called on as a curiosity or a trophy or to make up the
numbers in the drawing-room. Mary struggled very hard with
these social slights.

If my vanity could be flattered, by the respect
of people, whose judgement I do not care a fig
for – why in this place it has sufficient food –
though rather of the grosser kind; but I hate to
talk all myself, and only make the ignorant
wonder and admire … His Lordship, I have had
little conversation with – but his countenance
does not promise much more than good
humour, and a little *fun* not refined.

Her feelings towards the children improved. The tall, plain
fourteen-year-old Margaret was a "sweet girl".

She has a wonderful capacity … and in all probability will be lost in a heap of rubbish miss-
called accomplishments. I am grieved at being
obliged to continue so wrong a system – She is
very much afraid of her mother – that such a

creature should be ruled with a rod of iron, when
tenderness would lead her anywhere ...

Mary Wollstonecraft hated "conversations with nothing in
them" and rituals of dress that consumed time:

I see Ladies put on rouge without any *mauvais
honte* – and make up their faces for the day – five
hours, and who could do it in less in – do many
– I assure you, spend in dressing – without
including preparations for bed washing with
Milk of roses etc. etc.

She thought matters might improve with the remove to
town for the season. She was sent ahead to the Kings' fine
townhouse, 15/16 Henrietta Street, in Dublin. The street
housed the grandest grandees in the country, bishops, dukes
and earls, and was a hive of activity during the Dublin season.
There, she had a fine schoolroom, the use of one of the
drawing-rooms and a parlour to receive male visitors in. Mary
had hoped to see less of Lady Kingsborough in Dublin, to
have more "quietness in my own apartments", but instead she
was caught up in the bustle and confusion of town life, the
preparation of dresses and wreaths of roses for balls and
masquerades, which "the whole house from the kitchen maid
to the GOVERNESS are obliged to assist, and the children
forced to neglect their employments".

Mary Wollstonecraft's social inferiority caused her many
problems. She wrote to her sister:

Indeed, she [Lady Kingsborough] behaved so
improperly to me once, or twice, in the
Drawing room, I determined never to go in to
it again. I could not bear to stalk in to be stared
at, and her proud condescension added to my
embarrassment, I begged to be excused in a civil

way – but she would not allow me to absent myself.

When she did comply and came to the drawing-room with bad grace, she was surprised that the ladies tried to get rid of her before the gentlemen arrived, although this withdrawal was normal procedure for a governess. "Nay would you believe it, she used several arts to get me out of the room before the gentlemen came up ..." Her dignity was ruffled in other ways too. She complained that the expense of hairdressing and clothing fit for genteel company would have exceeded the sum she had to spend on such things, at which point Lady Kingsborough offered her a present of a poplin gown and petticoat. Mary angrily refused the gift, though it was common practice for mistresses to offer clothes to their maids and this was generally taken as a mark of great favour. Mary Wollstonecraft, who needed dresses badly, took it as an affront. Not surprisingly her employment was terminated after one year.

During this very strained year with the Kingsborough family, Mary Wollstonecraft's maternal tenderness had been awakened temporarily when the children fell sick with fever – even her ladyship was moved to abandon her dogs and visit her own children. Attendance in the sickroom was a fundamental requirement in a century where fevers, agues and disease arrived suddenly and unpredictably. There was little recourse but to home nursing. The mistress of the house had a repository of cures in her receipt book and nursekeeping was a key role.

Mrs. Delany wrote:

> This is the eighth day. Mrs. Hamilton lies in a little bed in the dressing-room next to Sally, and will not suffer me to sit up beyond my usual hour. As she is very watchful, and never goes to

bed when at home and alone before two o'clock, it makes me comply easily. The nursekeeper also is a very sober, good sort of woman, and used to tend in the small pox, but it is too critical a distemper to trust entirely to any nursekeeper till after the turn. I gained some experience with the Lady Bentincks. (18 July 1759)

Mrs. Delany was writing about Sally Chapone, daughter of her childhood friend Sarah Kirkham and god-daughter to Mrs. Delany and Anne. Sally had contracted the deadly smallpox.

This way to the sickroom …

3

rotten
apple
water:
mrs. delany's
medicines

My Dear Cousin,

I have the favour of yours of the 4th instant, and likewise the bacon (as you call it), but before I eat it it shall be a ham. Your direction on the basket was *quite wrong*; you must direct for me, in Holles Street near Cavendish Square, or at the Smyrna Coffee House in Pall Mall. I am exceedingly sorry I cannot have the pleasure of seeing my dear aunt [Mrs. Granville], but I hope I shall have that satisfaction before I die. I am full of ailments, and withal so weak, that I cannot get into nor out of bed without help; and to complete all, either by a strain or other accident, I have got a contraction of the nerves of my right thigh, with a lump at the upper end, not at all agreeable. If this should continue I am afraid my intended journey into Warwickshire will be defeated, for I can hardly bear the coach a mile. Tell my aunt that I use oil of earthworms with opodeldoc to endeavour to dispel the lump, but hitherto without any visible effect, and that if she knows of anything that will do to let me know it. I am afraid I have tried you sufficiently with my impertinence, for which I heartily ask your pardon, and am

My dear cousin's
Most affectionate humble servant,
Westcomb. (17 August, believed to be 1746)

This letter was from Sir Anthony Westcomb, Mama Granville's nephew, to Anne. His complaints were well entertained if for no other reason than the unmarried Sir Anthony had made Anne's son John his heir. The morbid attention to the minutiae of health among the Georgians was engendered, though, by very real fear. Death from fevers, infections, accidents or childbirth swept lives away at very short notice, and Mrs. Delany and her contemporaries lived daily with that crude reality. This partly accounts for their obsessive interest in their own health, and our perception of their fear as rampant hypochondria is misplaced to some degree. However, it may also be true to say that among certain members of the Granville family the tendency was something of a fetish. Sir Anthony was a connoisseur.

Another fine relation, the Countess Granville, called "the dragon", rallied sufficiently to write from her sick bed:

> I hope you have not so good a reason for your silence as I have had for mine; I have been dying this three months, have not stirred out of my apartment or been able to write to anybody ... I confess I am in your debt one letter, which I did not think worth answering, since it was only compliments, I wrote immediately as kind a letter as I was well able to word it to you and your brother, which you did not think fit to take any notice of till a month after, so that I concluded it had miscarried; and ordered my servant to write to the post office to enquire of the letter carrier if he had delivered such a letter, which enquiry produced me the letter I have not done myself the honour to thank you for ... I shall make no excuse for my blots and mistakes, for I think it is almost a miracle that as ill as I am, I have been able to write so long a letter.

Anne sent detailed accounts of her own health, her husband John's and the state of health of the children. The domestics might be included if they were unwell and also the horses, dogs, cats or cattle. The former Mrs. Pendarves, seemingly an authority on everything, responding to an enquiry about Anne's favourite mare, wrote:

> I grieve for Madam Jenny's eye; enclosed, my Lady Sunderland has sent you some Portugal snuff; if Jenny has any film over her eye, let some of it be blown once a day through a quill – it is infallible; if a humour, lapis caliminaris pulverized and put into rose-water, is excellent, but my brother recommends a rowell under her jaw, which Mr. Foley's groom understands to be sure how it is to be done. (17 August 1736)

Reciprocal news was expected, and no detail was too "impertinent" to include. A letter arriving at Delville confirmed the health of the beloved Dewes family. This was a comfort and a cause for rejoicing. Mrs. Delany could rest assured all was well until the next crisis, at which point she would consult first with her friends and then provide all the assistance her arsenal could provide – receipts, cures or counsel.

A contraction of the nerves of the right thigh might well concentrate the minds of Sir Anthony's careful relations in the short term, but they had many more serious ailments and illnesses to engage them. One of the deadliest of these was smallpox, the spectre of which caused great alarm. News of friends or relatives stricken with smallpox was circulated with trepidation. Mrs. Delany engaged in the great debate of the day: whether to inoculate against it or not. Smallpox was a highly contagious disease, and about one in five to one in seven died from it. Rank was no safeguard, and the young were particularly vulnerable, as they were vulnerable to tuber-culosis.

Mrs. Delany's god-daughter Sally Chapone recovered from smallpox, but her health was compromised afterwards. Mrs. Delany had experienced the nursing of smallpox at first hand with the daughters of the Duchess of Portland, Elizabeth, Margaret and Harriet, the Ladies Bentinck. They fell like ninepins after their brother Edward contracted the disease. Anne Dewes had already safely nursed her children through, and the family at Bulstrode now depended on her notes. Mrs. Delany chronicled the steady march.

> Lord Edward complained of excessive weari-ness, and had no appetite, at night the Duchess ordered him some Gascoign's powder and small negus, but it would not stay on his stomach: he fell asleep and the next morning was a little feverish, the apothecary sat up with him. Doctor Hays from Windsor was sent for, and all symptoms made them suspect it would prove the small-pox. We were yesterday greatly alarm-ed; the child was excessively ill, Dr. Heberden is here; he finds the child in as good a way as can be expected in the beginning of such a disorder, for it proves the small-pox. The doctor seems to think it will be a middling sort, neither the best nor the worst. I have sent Smith away, as she has not had the small-pox, and shall have a young woman come down to me tomorrow who I had hired as a housemaid. The Duchess's spirits are more composed; She has given the young ladies *their choice* to stay in the house or go to Whitehall; and they have so much fortitude that all *begged to stay*, and say they shall be

miserable to leave her. *Next* to your own children *they are* what I am most anxious about: I think in all probability the young ladies will catch it. (Bulstrode, 25 December 1754)

The variola viruses, major and minor, caused smallpox. The confluent or "worst sort" brought on a dangerously high fever and extensive putrid rash. Variola minor was a less severe form with much lower death rates. Transmission was face-to-face, which endangered all who came in contact with the victim during the contagious phase. The disease could also be contracted through the clothing or bedding of the affected person, so great care was needed in the management of the sickroom.

Mrs. Delany was well acquainted with the most advanced medical practitioners of the day. She mentions them in her letters. Doctor Richard Mead was one such, a Fellow of the College of Physicians and of the Royal Society. He had been physician to Queen Anne and George II and to the Duchess of Portland. In his lifetime he had encouraged inoculation against smallpox and preached against the contemporary practice of hot, closed sickrooms in *Medical Precepts and Cautions*. He promoted the radical notion of cool, clean chambers washed with water and vinegar. This, he wrote, was contrary to what "Modern Authors mostly advise, which is to make Fumes with hot Things, as Benzoin, Frankincense, Assa Foetida, Storax, etc. from which I see no reason to expect any Virtue to destroy the Matter of Infection". Perfumes, resins and balsams such as benzoin and frankincense, which were burned in sickrooms, did, however, mask the foulness, because the smell from the smallpox victim was almost unbearable.

The disease itself conferred immunity, and Mrs. Delany's close attendance on the Bulstrode sickroom suggests she was an earlier survivor. The incubation period normally averaged twelve to fourteen days, during which time the victim felt perfectly well and was not contagious. Time scales were impossible to judge, though, as incubation periods varied. Once the disease was confirmed in one member of a family, nurses kept anxious watch for signs in the others. Lord Edward went down with the classic early onset symptoms of fever and general malaise, headache, backache and vomiting. The negus, which was a hot drink of port, sugar, lemon and spice, "would not stay on his stomach".

When the small red spots with a central depression appeared on the tongue and in the mouth the diagnosis was confirmed. The spots developed into infected sores, which then opened and exploded large amounts of virus into the mouth and throat. The patient was then at his most ill and most contagious. The rash progressed and spread to all parts of the body, and this often brought a welcome lowering of temperature. The disease "turned", which was the term used by Mrs. Delany and her contemporaries. The victim began to feel a bit better. Three days later the rash developed into pustules. These felt like pellets under the skin. In about three weeks the pustules scabbed over and fell off. The patient was then free of contagion but was often left with a potent reminder.

> Thank God Lord Edward is quite out of danger of his late distemper – he has had a better sort than at first was apprehended; it turned before the ninth day: he is the patientest little creature I ever saw. The young ladies still hold up heroically; they have been taught to depend on Providence, and they credit their good teachers. It will be extraordinary if the young ladies escape the infection, for though

they do not go into the child's room, they see everybody that come immediately from him; they are prepared no otherwise than by taking Cheltenham water, which they have done twice, and are to take it once more; they eat no meat for supper, and take care not to catch cold. How long was it between your children's taking it of one another? Tell me very exactly; the Duchess keeps up her spirits charmingly, and when we are not in the room with the dear child (in which we take our turns), our works go on; our main work is a carpet in double cross-stitch for the Duchess's Gothic cell. (Bulstrode, 1 January 1755).

Cheltenham water, a chalybeate mineral water bearing iron salts, was, according to local advertisement, useful for constipation, rheumatism, gout, scrofulous affections, exudations and worms, but its efficacy against smallpox was doubtful. Received wisdom had it that fevers and distempers were inflamed by animal foods, such as red meat, and red wine but reduced by a low diet, including foods such as milk and chicken. These methods and avoiding direct contact with the infected person were the only bulwarks against smallpox available. Dr. Mead wrote with sound sense:

a Specific Preservative from Small-Pox is impossible, the most that can be done, will be to keep the Body in such Order, that it may suffer as little as possible. The first Step towards which, is to maintain a good state of Health, in which we are always least liable to suffer by any external Injuries; and not to weaken the Body by Evacuation. The next is, to guard against all Dejections of Spirits, and immoderate Passions; for these we daily observe do expose Persons to the more common *Contagion* of the Small-Pox. These Ends will be best answered by living with Temperance upon a good generous Diet, and avoiding Fastings, Watchings, extreme Weariness, etc. Another Defence is, to use whatever Means are proper to keep the Blood from Inflaming. This, if it does not secure from *Contracting Infection*, will at least make the Effects of it less violent.

Despite the low diet and avoiding red meat, the next victim fell.

Last Monday at dinner Lady Margaret Bentinck was taken ill: everybody imagined all infection over. Lady Margaret continued faint and cold, but recovered herself so well as to drink tea with us: but yesterday morning she complained of giddiness in her head, and great pain in her back. The doctor was instantly sent for from Windsor, but the apothecary who was in the house felt her pulse, and saying it was absolutely necessary *to bleed her* without staying for the doctor, she was let blood. The doctor came in the evening and thought the symptoms would end in the small-pox, which is this day confirmed. She says she "is very glad" (when she can speak), that she "has got the small-pox". Her sisters are determined *not to leave her*, unless the Duchess forbids them, but she is silent on that point, so that in all probability here will be the same succession as was in your family, and I hope in God as favourably! The

Duchess has got your paper of observations, and looks it over every day. Lady Margaret has fallen ill, just at the same time Court did after Banny's taking to his bed, which I think was twenty-one days ...

I will let you know every day ... you may believe I cannot think of leaving this place ... Lord Edward is quite well again. (Bulstrode, 15 January 1755)

❋

By the middle of the century, the medical profession had evolved a formidable armoury to combat the array of human disease that faced it. Bloodletting, emetics and purges were key treatments, and these were used across the board for a variety of diseases including inflammatory fevers, coughs, headaches, rheumatism, abscesses and even some forms of heart disease. These treatments were tried on the smallpox patients in Bulstrode.

Medical thinking of the day considered the human body "as composed of tubulous fibres that constitute hydraulic machines and solid matter". This was the theory proposed by Herman Boerhaave, who was regarded as the founder of clinical teaching and the most influential medical teacher of the age. The tubes contained fluids that were moved around the body by the action of the solids and the solids were in turn "nourished, preserved and restored" by the fluids.

Although the fluids went under the traditional name of humours, they were not the blood, phlegm, yellow and black bile of Hippocrates and Galen. The fluids were the alimentary juice or chyle, blood, lymph, oil and secreted humours. The fluids or humours had to be kept in balance, but to further complicate matters they were influenced by the so-called non-naturals. These were air, motion and rest, sleep and waking, things taken in – food and drink – things excreted and, most importantly, passions and emotions. The individual could exercise some control over the non-naturals and had a duty of care to do so.

The juggling act involved in maintaining the balance kept the responsible citizen constantly supervising his bowel movements. Stools and urine were the primary diagnostic tools of the medical profession and changes in either could be interpreted as a portent of disease or a change in the course of a disease. Regular evacuation was a cornerstone of good health, and Mrs. Delany insisted on various occasions that Mary Dewes and G.M.A. take rhubarb. This was medicinal rhubarb, Polygonaceae, the rhizome of which was sliced and ground and used as a remedy for constipation.

Diagnosis of any disease was rarely straightforward. It was believed that humours could shift and diseases metamorphose and move from one part of the body to another. One exotic example of this was flying gout. Physical evidence of fevers, rashes or diarrhoea gave clues, but diagnosis was often guess-work.

Once a diagnosis was made, the treatment was often harrowing and of dubious value. In bloodletting, doctors had various means to remove blood. They could slice small cuts into the flesh, usually of the arm, by means of a lancet and allow the blood to drain off into a bowl. Leeches could be put on to suck the blood away or a scarifier, which was a small box-like instrument of spring-loaded blades, could be run along the surface of the skin to make a series of cuts. A warmed cup was placed over the scarified area to form a vacuum to bring the blood to the surface. This bloodletting was also performed as a preventative, almost recreational measure. Mead had long campaigned for hygiene, but the crude bleeding methods virtually guaranteed infection. Mrs. Delany sent this report to Anne:

> Mrs. Tichborne has had an ugly accident from bleeding with a leech, one of her fingers was swelled, and she fancied if she bled it with a leech it would abate: she bled about two ounces, and was very well after it, but the next day her hand and arm swelled to such a monstrous size as if it had been poisoned. (27 November 1736)

Modern medicine suggests that certain levels of blood loss triggered the adrenal glands and appeared to revive the patient, so empirical evidence showed an improvement. Mrs. Delany's correspondence is littered with bleedings and blisterings, and she clearly approved of them: "A thousand thanks for the particular account you give me of yourself. I am very glad you have been blooded, for with so much bustle as you must go through the blood cannot but be a little heated" (Delville, 26 July 1744). On another occasion she flew to the bedside of her cousin:

> It was half an hour after three before I got to Mrs. Foley's ... The physician that now attends her has had her blooded, and blistered on the arm and the pit of her stomach, and with all these operations she has not lost her strength, which gives me hopes that her youth will at last get the better of her complaints. (Bulstrode, 17 December 1749)

There was very little understanding of the cause of infectious disease, but bringing infection to the surface and out of the body was regarded as an urgent requirement. Blisters were artificial lesions intended as exit points for harmful matter. There are many receipts for raising blisters, but cantharides, a powder of dried beetle mixed with various media and applied by plaster, was very commonly used. The effect was caustic and irritant, causing a vesicle of infected matter to form at the site of the plaster. The unnecessary pain, however, inflicted on the already weak, was appalling. The young Lady Weymouth had just given birth, and Mrs. Delany wrote in some distress:

> [She] continues extremely ill, she has not had since this day se'nnight three hours' sleep; her fever is very high and she has been the greater part of that time delirious: she has had *nine* blisters, but to *no purpose but to torment her,* for they have *injured her much!* (24 December 1736)

Lady Weymouth died shortly afterwards, probably from puerperal fever compounded by the application of blisters and other untold hardships.

This was the range of treatments available to the smallpox patients in Bulstrode, where Lady Betty was the next victim.

> The small-pox is come out very favourably with Lady Margaret. Lady Betty was taken in the night on Tuesday, no bad symptoms appear; the doctor thinks her in as good a way as she can be at present. We are in daily expectation of Lady H.; she continues well, but will not quit her sister's rooms all day. (Bulstrode, 17 January 1755)

> Lady Betty rested very well last night (natural rest). Lady Margaret I fear has not a very good kind; I don't believe it will turn before the 11th or 12th day; she bears it with great composure, but her throat is very sore, and her eyes close up. Our Duchess bears up as well as she can, but her anxious state you can much easier imagine, than

most people. Dear Lady Harriet still holds out, but certainly if she is ever to have it can hardly now escape. She is (or at least appears to be) in very good spirits, and prepared to receive it whenever it comes; the poor Duchess looks every moment with affectionate and examining eyes for some alteration in her. (Bulstrode, 20 January 1755)

Lady Harriet did not escape.

Lady Betty and Lady Margaret are, thank God, out of danger. Lady Harriet I hope is in a good way, but it is early days with her, and we must have some days of anxiety before we can know what we are to expect. This very sharp weather is a disadvantage to us; the dear Duchess is as well as her present situation will allow. (Bulstrode, 27 January 1755)

I hope in God Lady Harriet will do well, but we have had an alarm by a violent bleeding at her nose, which has already bled 15 or 16 ounces: it is at present stopped by Eaton's Stiptic. The Duchess is truly to be pitied, her apprehensions are very great. (Bulstrode, 29 January 1755)

The Duchess's apprehensions were well founded: smallpox cut swathes through communities. Robert Goodbody, who was born into a Quaker family at Mountmellick, Co. Offaly, in 1781, recorded his experience. His four-and-a-half-year-old brother had already died.

In the fall of the year 1788 I had the small-pox naturally [not by inoculation], one brother and two sisters. My brother Thomas took it first, when he was better my sister Sarah and I were down, lying in two beds in the same room. We were both very ill, I was covered over in all parts of my body with confluent pock and was blind for many days, with a very sore throat. I don't think I ever was stout for many years after, and I lost my eye-lashes, never having them good to this day ... My sister Ann had but a few spots, but made more noises crying than us all: she was then about two years old. All the rest of us were very badly marked, and I was a long time very red after it, and was annoyed by the boys calling me frosty face.

In the ninth month of 1793 my brother Samuel, a handsome child died of the small-pox, about three years old. I was fond of him and felt very much seeing him, for perhaps 12 hours dying in convulsions. My sister Jane was then about 5 months old, and had it very bad. My mother was nursing her. She was frightfully swelled in her face, near the size of two infants. I well recollect the care my mother paid to her, night and day, holding her on her lap, and trying to keep her nourished at the breast although a loathsome object as well as offensive, but she recovered. (Michael Byrne, *Memoirs of Robert Goodbody, of Mountmellick, Clara and Tullamore, 1781–1860*)

In Bulstrode, the children continued sick and Mrs. Delany continued her journal.

> I write, I thank God, to my dearest sister with some comfort today. I hope the worst is over

with Lady Harriet; she is indeed a sweet creature; so patient under her pains, so cheerful, so thankful for the least amendment. I always thought the Duchess blest in her children, but I did not know their full worth (nor I may say hers) till this trial. She says I have been a great support to her, and she would not have liked to have anybody but myself, and I am sure it was necessary she should have somebody, for the Duke has been too much affected to command himself enough to be a comforter. (Bulstrode, 31 January 1755)

Dear Lady Harriet goes on as well as can be expected considering she has not a good sort. She has vast resolution in bearing her present most miserable condition for surely there cannot be anything more terrible to bear for the time it lasts? Between whiles she tries to make comical jokes upon her own figure, and keeps up everybody's spirits with her good-humour. Lady Betty is as fair almost as ever, her eyes as sparkling, and in charming spirits; she has not known the danger her darling sister has been in. I hope, in a few days she will be able to come into the Duchess's dressing-room. Lady Margaret comes on slowly, and her spirits are but indifferent at the best. The Duchess has been for some days much out of order; she has not been able to go to them for three days, which has helped to sink her spirits. (Bulstrode, 3 February 1755)

Lovely Lady Harriet is in a fair way of recovery, which *I could not say till now*. The Duchess is better. I was under great apprehensions for her a few days ago; she had all the symptoms of a fever, but they are gone off. Lady Betty is so well that if to-morrow is a fine day, she is to come up into the Duchess's dressing-room. Lady Margaret is slower in gathering strength. As to their fare faces, I fear Lady Margaret will suffer a little and Lady Harriet a great deal, but we are at present so glad to have her *alive*, that we are not yet mortified about it. The Duchess has ordered the rotten apples to be distilled, and is much obliged to you for your kind attention. (Bulstrode, 5 February 1755)

Many years earlier, the then Mrs. Pendarves had dispatched a receipt to Anne:

As for the rotten-apple water, I sent Mrs. Badge to Mrs. Clark about it, and she says it is wonderful the quick effect of it and very safe; and that if you use it at all, you should do it night and morning. It must be the rottenest apples that can be had, put into a cold still, and so distilled, without anything besides. But I am under no apprehensions of your being marked, and I dare say your complexion will be better than ever it was. (10 February 1729)

In the manner of all receipts for foods, medicines and household needs, Anne copied this receipt into her book and retrieved it years later for the young ladies at Bulstrode. Dr. Mead, too, had advised, "the repeated Use of Acid Fruits, as Pomegranates, Sevil Oranges, Lemons, tart Apples, etc." Survivors commonly carried "frosty faces" and permanent scars, and many sorry examples are cited in the correspondence.

Saturday we staid at home the greatest part of the day. I eloped for an hour or two to make a visit to a young lady [Letitia Bushe] who is just recovered of the small-pox. I think I never saw a prettier creature than she was before that malicious distemper seized her – a gay, good-humoured, innocent girl, without the least conceit of her beauty ... All the men were dying whilst she was *in danger*, but, notwithstanding their admiration of her ... she is divested of those charms that occasioned their devotion. (25 November 1731)

Reports from Bulstrode continued favourable.

Lady Harriet has had a good night, and says she "could almost dance a jig." I have got the harpsichord removed into her bed-chamber, and wish I may be able to charm away the evil spirit of pain, but I fear it is not powerful enough even to lull it for a moment. (Bulstrode, 16 February 1755)

The Duchess is much better: Lady Betty, I believe, will not be marked at all, and Lady Margaret not so much as we apprehended at first: I can't say what Lady Harriet will be yet ... The last time I was at Lady Harriet's bed-side she desired me to say she "shall shew you a pure spotted face" when she has the pleasure of seeing you in town. (Bulstrode, 19 February 1755)

Blindness was a common legacy of smallpox; deformity and impotence were others. Mead urged "leaving the Place infected is the surest Preservative, so the next to it, is to avoid, as much as may be, the near Approach to the Sick", but decamping could be difficult, as Mrs. Delany's friend Lady Andover found. She did not quit her son, Master Howard,

> night or day till some time *after they were out* [the spots], and then with some violence was dragged from him to go Fisherwick across the river almost opposite to their own house; the daughters remain in the house, and Lady Andover continues well. (Bulstrode, 2 January 1756)

❧

Inoculation against smallpox was championed in England by Lady Mary Wortley Montagu (1689–1762). A formidable character, she had contracted the disease as a child, and her only brother had died from it. She carried the marks into adulthood, being "deprived her of very fine eye-lashes". As a young woman, Mary, to the great consternation of her father, the Earl of Kingston, eloped to marry Edward Wortley Montagu. When he was stationed as Ambassador to Turkey in 1716 she accompanied him and observed inoculation practised there. She wrote an account of it to Mrs. S.C. Adrianople, on 1 April (thought to be 1717):

> *A propos* of distempers, I am going to tell you a thing that will make you wish yourself here ... the old woman comes with a nut-shell full of the matter of the best sort of small-pox, and asks what vein you please to have opened. She immediately rips open that you offer to her with a large needle (which gives you no more pain than a common scratch), and puts into the vein as much matter as can lye upon the head of her needle, and after that binds up the little wound with a hollow bit of shell; and in this manner

opens four or five veins ... The children or young patients play together all the rest of the day, and are in perfect health to the eighth. Then the fever begins to seize them, and they keep to their beds two days, very seldom three. They have very rarely above twenty or thirty in their faces, which never mark; and in eight days' time they are as well as before their illness. Where they are wounded, there remain running sores during the distemper, which I don't doubt is a great relief to it ... There is no example of any one that has died in it; and you may believe I am well satisfied of the safety of this experiment, since I intend to try it on my dear little son.

The inoculation as described by Lady Wortley Montagu was the injection of infected matter directly from a pustule. Vaccination, pioneered by Edward Jenner later in the century, was matter taken from a cow suffering with cowpox, a disease related to smallpox. Inoculation produced a mild form of the disease and was infectious, a fact that gave rise to the fear and consternation of those considering having it performed. The Dowager-Countess Gower informed Mrs. Delany somewhat balefully: "the letting of the inoculated people walk abroad has spread the small pox all over this country" (6 September 1775). Both inoculation and vaccination elicited the manufacture of antibodies but vaccination was not infectious.

The first inoculation of a known individual in England was Lady Mary Wortley Montagu's daughter, also called Mary, who later became Lady Bute. The operation was performed in London in April 1721, and Lady Montagu was reviled as an unnatural mother for putting her daughter at such risk. The medical profession denounced her, and the Church railed against her. Mrs. Delany was a close friend of Lady Mary Bute and was well aware of all sides of the debate.

The question was a delicate one: to inoculate or not to inoculate. Death rates for inoculation were about one in ten. "For parents are tender and fearful, not without hope their children may escape this disease," wrote the Reverend J. Hough in 1737, "or have it favourably, whereas, in the way of art, should it prove fatal, they could never forgive themselves: for this reason, nobody dares to advise in the case." Mrs. Delany was equally cautious when she wrote to Viscountess Andover: "If the inoculation scheme takes effect ... I am quite in your ladyship's way of thinking about it – that it is too nice a point to give one's opinion either way" (Delville, 2 April 1767).

Risk notwithstanding, it is difficult to understand why the very progressive Duchess of Portland had not had her children inoculated when other friends of Mrs. Delany's had ventured theirs. "Mrs. Forth Hamilton is now under an anxiety," she wrote, "I am sure you will feel for – her two children were inoculated last Friday morning. I hope they will do well" (Delville, 26 May 1747). Mrs. Delany also reported to Mary Dewes in March 1780 that Lady Stamford, who was the former Harriet Bentinck of the "pure spotted face", had inoculated her own daughter Louisa and two of her sons. Harriet ensured her own children would not bear the marks.

❃

Fevers and agues were another large group of diseases that engaged Mrs. Delany. They are constantly reported in the letters. Fevers brought fear and dread in their broad ungovernable sweeps. The young, enfeebled and old were particularly vulnerable. The immune systems of the population in general appear to have been quite low. Contemporary accounts are full of people being confined for weeks with colds or by apparently trivial accidents rapidly taking a near-fatal turn. Earache, sore eyes and bad teeth were extremely debilitating and are frequently reported. In *Patients, Potions and Physicians: A Social History of Medicine in Ireland*, Tony Farmar explains that life expectancy at birth in England actually fell between 1720 and 1750. Many children died at birth or in infancy, but those who did survive seem to have been weakened. The cumulative effect of poor nutrition and not-quite-cured ailments meant that small bruises and injuries took a long time to repair. Add to this the "lowering" diets children were put on to prevent fevers, and they had an uphill battle to achieve adulthood. The Bentinck family, already debilitated from the smallpox, fell prey again to another killer disease of the eighteenth century, scarlet fever. Mrs. Delany reported from Spring Gardens in London:

> Lady Betty is very well again; Lady Harriet recovered of her fever, but extremely sunk with it; but Lord Titchfield [eldest son] is *now* in the beginning of the fever and it is impossible not to be alarmed about him, and that dear innocent Lady Margaret *is an angel*, I think one may venture to pronounce that. *She died yesterday about noon!* The Duke and Duchess's distress is really not to be described. (24 April 1756)

Fever covered a multitude of symptoms, including parched throats, headaches, sweating, blotches and rashes, faintness, exhaustion, vomiting, diarrhoea, convulsions, confusion and coma. Fevers came on fast, and the treatments were often as debilitating as the disease. Mrs. Delany reported on her relation:

> Lady Carteret is very much out of order with a feverish disorder, which has not yet intermitted enough to give the bark, but she has been blooded and blistered; she was something better yesterday; Dr. Hollins attends her, and proposed giving her the bark last night. She

holds up pretty well all day, but has very bad
nights, though she does not keep her bed.
(13 February 1739)

Ague was a family of lesser, non-fatal malarial types of
fever frequently reported in the correspondence. It was one of
the few afflictions for which a specific treatment existed: the
aforementioned bark. The bark was given in the lull between
waves of fever and was often recommended by Mrs. Delany. It
was the dried bark or stem of Cinchona Succirubra or Red
Cinchona bark, a plant that grew in South America, mostly in
Peru. It was also known as Peruvian bark or Jesuit's bark, as the
Jesuit order was credited with bringing it to Europe. We know
it today as quinine, the primary treatment for malaria through
three centuries. It was the society physician, entrepreneur and
collector Sir Hans Sloane who acquired a stock of quinine and
dispensed it in England. He became known for his
popularisation of this very expensive treatment for agues.

The very unpredictability of fevers and agues caused great
alarm, and so their progress was noted with forensic precision.
The Honourable Robert Boyle, son of Richard Boyle, Earl of
Cork, and founder member of the Royal Society, was a
considerable authority. In the preface to his *Medicinal
Experiments or a Collection of Choice Remedies for the Most Part Simple
and Easily Prepared*, he offered his personal experience as his
credentials. He wrote:

> For the grand Original of the Mischiefs that
> have for many Years afflicted me was a fall from
> an unruly Horse into a deep place, by which I
> was so bruised, that I feel the bad effects of it
> to this day. For this Mischance happening in
> *Ireland* and I being forced to take a long
> Journey, before I was well recovered, that bad
> weather I met with and the as bad Accom-

modation in *Irish* Inns, and the mistake of an unskilful or drunken Guide, who made me wander almost all Night upon some Wild Mountains, put me into a Fever and a Dropsie, (viz. an Anafarca:) For a compleat Cure of which I past into *England*, and came to *London* but in so unlucky a time, that an ill-conditioned Fever rag'd there, and seiz'd on me among many others; and this through God's goodness, I at length recovered, yet left me exceeding weak for a great while after; and then for a farewell, it cast me into a violent Quotidian or double Tertian Ague, with a sense of decay in my Eyes, which during my long Sickness I had exercis'd too much upon Critical Books stuft with *Hebrew* ...

"Poor Mary had two fever fits on the road," Mrs. Delany wrote about her maid. "She has a medicine given her of bark and snakeroot that I believe stopped it. Pray what is your receipt of bark and snakeroot?" (Clarges Street, 10 November 1743). Snakeroot or Black Cohosh was given in nervous diseases; it was also used to "assist the expulsive action of the uterus". William Buchan, writing about "Intermitting Fevers, or Agues" in his *Domestic Medicine* (1760), recommended a smart purge that:

has been known to cure an obstinate ague after the Peruvian bark and other medicines have been used in vain. The first thing to be done in the cure of an intermitting fever is to cleanse the stomach and bowels ... Vomits are therefore to be administered before the patient takes any other medicine.

However unpleasant the vomitings, purgings and expulsions might have been for poor Mary, she was a healthy young woman and survived the treatment, but babies and young children frequently did not. Buchan guessed in 1769 that of all children born in England, half of those under twelve years of age perished. These young deaths were regarded as a natural phenomenon. Mrs. Delany, writing about the son of their childhood friend, told Anne:

> Master Sutton is dead at last, after a very terrible fever of above a fortnight; I was with poor Lady Sunderland at the time he died, and she was much shocked with it and had suffered a great deal with seeing him endure so much, and is out of order in her own health; but I hope when she comes to consider calmly, and that the natural affection a mother must feel at first for the loss of a child gives way to reason, she will be reconciled to this stroke, for such a child is really no loss. (Bulstrode, 27 November 1743)

Mrs. Delany was far less complacent about her own nephew, Court Dewes, who was Anne's eldest child.

> I am very much concerned for my dear godson, but hope before this reaches you that his ague will have left him. Two *infallible receipts* I must insert before I proceed further.
>
> 1st. Pounded ginger, made into a paste with brandy, spread on a sheep's leather, and a plaister of it laid over the navel.
>
> 2ndly. A spider put into a goose-quill, well sealed and secured, and hung about the child's neck as low as the pit of his stomach. Either of these I am assured will ease.

Probatum est. (Clarges Street, 1 March 1744)

Five days later she wrote:

> It is impossible for me not to be uneasy, when I
> know my dear little godson is ill, and what you
> and my mother must suffer when he is so,
> though an ague is so common to little children,
> and not of dangerous consequence. I hope
> before this arrives he will have lost every
> symptom of complaint, if not, it is best to give
> him bark in the only way children can take it,
> which very seldom fails. I have sent a
> prescription from Mrs. Montague and Mr.
> Clark. Everybody agrees you should give the
> child meat now; he may eat meat three times a
> week, and pudding or panada the other days.
> Sometimes sheep's trotters, which are both
> innocent and nourishing; and make him to be
> jumbled about a good deal for fear of falling
> into the rickets, and throw away his wormwood
> draughts, for they *signify nothing* for an ague.
> Have an attention to him about worms, which
> are the cause of most children's illness; pray
> God bless the dear boy, and send you many
> years of joy and comfort with him! (Clarges
> Street, 6 March 1744)

When Aunt Delany urged the bark "in the only way
children can take it", she intended wrist plasters. She also
recommended them for Mary Dewes: "I bless God that my
dear little girl has missed her ague; I suppose you will repeat
the bark plasters to Mary's wrists before the usual time of
the ague's returning, which is generally in eight days" (St.

James's Place, 20 February 1750). The bark, in quills or shavings or powdered form, was shaped into small parcels and strapped to the wrist. These were worn at intervals during the course of the ague. Wrist plasters, however, were the least of Court's treatments. In the belief that animal foods overheated the blood, his meat intake was reduced. On his fasting days pudding or panada, which was a mush of bread and milk, was recommended for him. The panada could be made sweet or savoury and fortified with a little medicinal sack and was certainly a more attractive option than sheep's trotters. Mrs. Rundell, author of *Domestic Cookery, by a Lady* (1806), has an appetising receipt for a broth of sheep's trotters in her chapter "Cookery for the Sick and for the Poor". She directs to:

> Simmer six sheep's trotters, two blades of mace, a little cinnamon, lemon-peel, a few hartshorn shavings, and a little isinglass, in two quarts of water, to one; when cold, take off the fat, and give near half a pint twice a-day, warming with it a little new milk.

The inventory of treatments shows that Court's ague swung from chills to sweats and fever and all points in between. The child was clearly bedridden for some time and his muscle tone weakened, so Mrs. Delany's solution was to jumble him or drive him about in a light chaise or some such vehicle for exercise. His wormwood draughts were to be discontinued. Wormwood was absinthe and, made into a cooling drink, it had tonic and fever-reducing properties. It was commonly used for agues, despite Mrs. Delany's rejection of it.

Worms proper were next on the menu, and Mrs. Delany's medical knowledge on the subject came from all sources, the highest and the lowest. Throughout her correspondence she quotes, on the one hand, from the most eminent physicians in the land and, on the other, old wives' tales. The following receipt sent for Bunny is an example of the latter:

> I hope Bunny will find benefit from the elixir; it is a very good thing. I am told by a very wise woman, that quick-silver-water is the most effectual remedy for worms that can be taken, and must be continued constantly for a year together, and the elixir may be taken at times. *A pound of quick-silver boiled in a gallon of water till half the water is consumed away to be constantly drank at his meals, or whenever he is dry.* (Delville, 7 November 1751)

Quicksilver was liquid mercury, commonly used in the treatment of syphilis.

It fell to Court's lot, as the first born, to be the guinea pig for his mother and aunt. Anne Dewes, an anxious mother, wrote to their mutual friend and relation Lady Sarah Cowper:

> Three weeks since I was riding out with my eldest son [Court] for a little air, he is eight years old, and had rode a little horse several months, which now threw him; his foot hung in the stirrup, and he was dragged a hundred and forty yards: the footman took him up *for dead*. He was senseless, but, thank God, not a broken bone or sprain; and his bruises (*which were bad*) are now quite well, and he has not the least inconvenience remaining, but jumps and runs as much and as well as ever, and that is perpetually! How I kept my senses and did not fall off my horse I don't know. The cares of a nursery *are incessant*; my two youngest children have very bad hooping-coughs. I have brought them to this

place (a house of Mr. Dewes' ten miles from our constant dwelling) to try change of air, but they are not yet better; I wish I had more agreeable subjects to write upon. (Mapleburrough Green, 23 August 1750)

Anne's fright about Court was valid: riding accidents and accidents with horses were common occurrences and sometimes fatal. Mrs. Delany reported to Anne:

I was much vexed not to be able to write to my dearest sister last Thursday and by that means you will be a post longer than usual without hearing from me; but I was hurried with people of business all the morning, and a little discomposed with an accident that has happened to a nephew of the Dean's. He was thrown off his horse on Saturday, and though his skull was not fractured, the shock was so great as to deprive him of his senses ... On Wednesday they thought him better, but on Thursday his brother came to me in such grief about him it was impossible not to be touched by it. Yesterday he was trepanned and Dr. Barber, who has just been with me, says he thinks there is now more hope for him than there was. Poor young man! He unfortunately rode a vicious horse. (17 March 1753)

Trepanning involved boring through the skull to remove bone, an operation carried out while the patient was conscious. Alcohol was used as a sedative and for pain relief:

Poor Ramsay George [a brother of Mrs. Delany's maid George], after great sufferings, being twice trepanned, and several painful operations, is by this time released from his misery, and I hope happy. In his intervals of sense, which were very short, he seemed sensible of his condition, and prayed fervently. (24 March 1753)

When Court's medications were over, Mrs. Delany's preoccupation with the health of the family turned to Mary Dewes, who had whooping cough or, as it was commonly known at the time, chin cough. This was another extremely distressing, infectious and dangerous disease. Mrs. Delany, on stand-by as always, consulted her friends and drew from their stock of receipts for Mary's cough. "The Duchess of Portland's receipt for a hooping or any nervous cough," she wrote, "is rubbing the palms of the hands, soles of the feet, and pit of the stomach with oil of amber and hartshorn, an equal quantity, night and morning, and the back-bone with rum" (17 January 1758). Some days later, she added, "The Duchess of Portland is a great friend to ground ivy tea for a cough – a quarter of a pint at breakfast, and as much going to bed" (Spring Gardens, 19 January 1758).

Mrs. Delany recognised that some discretion might be needed for her next great idea. "Does Mary cough in the night?" she enquired.

Two or three snails boiled in her barley-water, or tea-water, or whatever she drinks, might be of great service to her; taken in time they have done *wonderful cures*. *She* must know nothing of it – they give no manner of taste. It would be best nobody should know it but yourself, and I should imagine *six or eight* boiled in a quart of water strained off and put into a bottle, would be a good way, adding a spoonful or two of that to *every liquid* she takes. They must be fresh

done every two or three days, otherwise they
grow too thick. (Spring Gardens, 21 January
1758)

Mrs. Delany was not alone in this. Dr. Mead had a very
similar receipt for "Snail Water" in his *Pharmacopoeia Pauperum*
of 1718.

❋

That Anne's children survived infusions of mercury,
decoctions of snails and rhubarb grains for regularity of the
bowels is a tribute to their constitutions. It is not surprising,
though, to find that Court Dewes later travelled the spas of
Europe in search of health. He lost his teeth early, a very
common occurrence at the period, but liquid mercury
probably accelerated the process. As an adult, he wrote to his
brother John:

> I am very sorry my sister is tormented with the
> toothach. In the long experience I have had of
> that disorder I have never found but one thing of
> service to me, and that is, an oz. of juniper
> berries boiled in a pint of vinegar till it comes to
> half a pint, and to wash the mouth with it as hot
> as you can bear it; but I have never used it unless
> when I was *very bad*, as it is apt to take the skin off
> the inside of the mouth. I think I am almost
> passed having the tooth ach now, and must
> comfort myself as well as I can, that what I have
> *lost* in *beauty* I have got in *ease!* (Welsbourn,
> 27 October 1778)

It is, of course, no surprise to discover that Bernard
Granville was a trying patient. Mrs. Delany danced attendance
on him during one of her London visits.

I left my brother last night between nine and
ten; he takes wormwood draughts every six
hours, and lives upon slops; I go to him at 12,
stay till 3, after dinner at six, and stay till nearly
ten: so that I have not seen anybody else ...
Since my writing this I have made my brother
two visits. I found him up at one o'clock; he had
eaten bread and butter and rusks, drank tea and
almond milk, his fever much abated ... I have
prevailed on him to have a nurse-keeper, and
have got one that nursed Lady Dartmouth.
(Spring Gardens, 14 January 1758)

Illness motivated Bernard Granville where other appeals to
fraternal ties and affection manifestly failed. He scribbled this
cheerful note at the bottom of a letter to Anne:

I think so good an opportunity of going with
Mrs. Delany to Cheltenham and Bath should
not be lost, as it is very likely to establish your
health. You might excuse yourself to any engagement that might prevent you, and I think
no friend can take anything ill of that kind, for
health is the first thing to be thought of, and
the sooner any disorder is quelled the better
chance there is of passing the latter end of one's
life easy. (3 July 1755)

Anne's health was a constant worry. Mrs. Delany wrote:
"Your cough not gone yet? *That I don't like*; I beg you will drink
asses milk and ground ivy tea" (Lower Brook Street, 2 April
1734). On another occasion she held consultations with her
London physician on Anne's behalf:

Dr. Bamber was with me yesterday, I sent for him
to ask him about your lameness, (for I am, thank

God, very well); he says it will be of no bad consequence, and if you had immediately applied vinegar, and kept your bed one week, it would have saved you a great deal of trouble; that the swelling is nothing but the effect of weakness, and is very common after such an accident: he advises one ounce of Castille soap dissolved in half a pint of camphorated spirits of wine, rub your ancle very well with it in the morning, and roll it with a gentle bandage, not too tight; and you must not walk nor keep your leg down so long as the swelling continues. He recommends rest more than any application, and lying abed long in the morning – a prescription *well suited to this weather*, and easily followed. Dr. Bamber desires his compliments to my brother and you. (Clarges Street, 28 January 1744)

Over years and distance, Mrs. Delany maintained her careful watch:

I received my dearest sister's letter dated the 26 July the day before I left Clogher, which gave me an account of your not having been well; but hope your next letter will give me the satisaction of knowing you are quite well. If upon bleeding you found your blood was thick, I wish you would take hartshorn for some time every day, and take care of yourself. (13 August 1748).

If you find your disorder not entirely removed, or have any reason to apprehend a return, you must submit to going again to the Bath. I know how uneasy a thing it is for you to leave your family, but by this time I suppose you may send your two eldest boys to school, and Jacky and

Mary might go with you. I am sure Dr. Burgh will be for the Bath, as it did you so much service the last time you were there; but I know I need not entreat you to take care of so precious a life. (Delville, 19 September 1752)

The cause of Anne's final illness is unknown, but some years before Mrs. Delany had written:

Donnellan sends her kind compliments, and begs you will drink lime-water, about a pint a day; you may make two or three draughts of it, and drink it at any time, adding to each glass a quarter part of very warm milk. (November 1753)

William Buchan also recommended lime-water for when "the menstrual flux may be too great". If Anne was suffering from a gynaecological disorder with profuse bleeding, the frequent therapeutic bleedings she underwent can only have served to vanquish her entirely.

Mama Granville's health was not neglected. She suffered lingering coughs, and the former Mrs. Pendarves wrote to Anne:

Your account of my dear mama has revived our spirits. My brother was here this morning before eight, to know if I had had any account of her? ... I forgot whether asses' milk used to agree with my mother; if it does, and she has any remains of a cough, I wish she would take it, 'tis a sovereign remedy, and the greatest sweetner of the blood in the world. (13 February 1739).

She enquired again a short time later:

You are very good in giving me so constant an account of my mother; did I not know your truth is to be depended on, I should be excessively uneasy about her, but you seem to assure me so sincerely of her being better that I believe you. Can't she take *turnip broth*? If it is a little disagreeable at first a little use will make it tolerable; I *actually love it better* than any soup, it is very good for a cough, and cured mine. (Park Street, 17 February 1739)

When Mama was diagnosed with that most aristocratic complaint, gout, Mrs. Delany proved ever resourceful:

Though I cannot hear of my dearest mama's suffering pain without feeling it myself, I hope and believe this fit of the gout will be a blessing to us all, by prolonging her life; for where there is a disposition towards it, it is safest when it gives pain in the limbs: pray God keep it from her stomach! If she could take the Rawleigh Cordial, it is the best thing to prevent its coming into her stomach, and to give her rest. (Clarges Street, 3 April 1744)

A fortnight later, Mama was no better: "My dear mama's pain I feel at this distance; the sickness I believe proceeds from the pain: cannot you prevail with her to take palsy drops? She used to do that, and they are very proper" (Clarges Street, 17 April 1744).

Gout occurs with great regularity in Mrs. Delany's correspondence. William Buchan wrote in his *Domestic Medicine* that "excess and idleness are the true sources from whence it originally sprung" but, despite this mortifying judgement, gout had a certain cachet. It was a disease only the rich could afford. Gout meant an abnormally high concentration of uric acid in the blood, causing deposits or crystals of sodium urate to settle in the joints of the extremities, classically the big toe.

A sufferer, Sydney Smith, described this extremely painful condition; it felt, he said, "like walking on my eyeballs".

Wrapping the foot in soft flannel, fur or wool to drive out the gouty matter by perspiration was one remedy. The Earl of Guilford, a correspondent of Mrs. Delany's, wrote:

> I have had a little gout in my foot without much pain. It obliged me to wear a great laced shoe for some days, and I have still some flannel in my own shoes. I think it has been a great relief to my nerves and spirits, which stood very much in need of it, and I am, I thank God, pure well. (Waldershare, 30 October 1785).

The Earl believed his fit of gout saw off the nervous disorder. Mrs. Delany worried that Mama's gout might settle in her stomach. This phenomenon of flying or wandering gout assailed a visitor to Bulstrode:

> Mr. Monck has kept his bed two days past with a feverish cold – *a panic*, least a fit of the gout should seize him here ... Mr. Monck very bad, has been bled today; they think his complaint the gout on his lungs. (Bulstrode, 21 September 1768)

Physicians and patients alike believed that gout could flow, almost at will, around the body. George Cheyne (1671–1743) in his definitive guide to gout, *The English Malady* (1733), wrote, "The *Nervous* or Flying *Gout* ... is owing to the Weakness, Softness, or Relaxation of the *Nerves* of those Persons who labour under it." He went on to explain that it was only the élite whose nervous systems were sufficiently refined to be susceptible to nervous complaints. In the event of gout fixing on stomach or lungs or another internal part, it should be recalled immediately, like an unruly pup to heel.

William Buchan directed:

> When the gout attacks the head or lungs, every
> method must be taken to fix it in the feet. They
> must be frequently bathed in warm water, and
> acrid cataplasms applied to the soles. Blistering-
> plasters ought likewise to be applied to the ancles
> or calves of the legs. Bleeding in the feet or ancles
> is also necessary, and warm stomachic purges.

The watch over family health continued and dispatches
went back and forth. Mrs. Delany wrote:

> We had such sharp piercing winds in Passion-
> week that it demolished us all. The Dean has
> had a cold; I have no complaint now but want
> of voice, and that I hope will soon be better. I
> am in good spirits, no headache, sleep at nights,
> eat chicken broth and gruel. I tell you exactly
> the truth, as I depend on your doing the same
> by me. (Delville, 7 April 1752)

Dr. Delany was watched over in turn:

> I am come home to take care of my dear D.D.
> who is not well; he complains very much of his
> head, and is just going to take hartshorn and sack
> whey, and go to bed; I hope a good night's rest
> will cure him. (Clarges Street, 26 April 1744)

The hartshorn, taken with great regularity in Mrs. Delany's
correspondence, was hart antler, used as a source of
ammonia in smelling salts. Age was catching up on Dr.
Delany, and matters took a turn for the worse when they
were in London.

> On Saturday the Dean was perfectly well, only
> complained of a weakness and watering in his

left eye ... On my return the Dean was just as I had left him, and in the morning went to St. James's early prayers; when I met him at breakfast, his left eyelid was much fallen, and his mouth drawn a little awry. I immediately apprehended what it was, but as *he did not perceive it himself* I was loath to take notice of it, and as he had promised to read prayers to Mrs. Donnellan I sent to Dr. Heberden to meet us *there*. The Dean read prayers very well, but his voice was not so clear, which he took notice of himself; and on looking in the glass saw what indeed had terrified me to such a degree that I hardly knew what I did. I thank God no bad symptom has increased; he was cupped on Sunday night, and had a perpetual blister laid on, and takes valerian and other mixtures. It is undoubtedly an attack of the palsy, but everybody assures me it was *as slight* as such an attack can be, and that by such early care I need not doubt his recovering. (Suffolk Street, 29 January 1754)

A few days later she wrote:

My dear D.D. is no worse; I cannot say he is better. The doctor today on his complaining of a pain behind his ear, has ordered him a blister in that place also; he continues nervous draughts and hicra picra, but his mouth continues in the same way, and so does his eye; it is impossible to see that alteration without a *terror* of what may happen. (January 1754)

Hicra picra or hiera picra was a purgative compound of bitter aloes and other ingredients, made to a Granville family receipt.

The Georgians believed that people brought their ailments on themselves, by sin or, at the very least, by excess worry or by neglecting regular evacuations, diet, proper air, exercise or sleep. Mechanical and analytical ideas began to affect the way people thought about the body and sickness as the century advanced, but Mrs. Delany upheld the orthodoxy when she pronounced on Lord Chesterfield:

> It is generally thought the anxious life he has led among gamesters has occasioned this stroke. Whatever effect it may have had on his constitution, it is a severe reproach and blemish to his character as a man possessed of superior talents ... Is it not strange that he should at last fall a sacrifice to that desperate vice, gaming? It can be accounted for but in one way – the want of religion: without which there is no ballast to keep the vessel steady. (New Street, Spring Gardens, 31 January 1756)

Nothing of that kind could be imputed to Dr. Delany: he was blameless and his first stroke of palsy through God's providence (as Mrs. Delany saw it) was not fatal. The blisters and other frightful remedies of the day, however, undoubtedly diminished the quality of his remaining years. Ten years on, he was declining rapidly, and Mrs. Delany opened her heart in a rare exposition to her friend Lady Andover.

> I have been sadly anxious for some time past for my dear D.D., he has been *very ill*, and reduced very low, which, to a man of his years, must give cruel apprehensions; however, I thank God his good constitution has at present got the better, and he is as well as he has been for some months past ... my hand feels tired; for my

nerves have been more shocked than I thought them capable of, for though *my heart has felt extreme sorrow*, I cannot say my nerves were ever so affected before. Why should I tell you this? It was unawares. And yet, why should I not? A sigh relieves an oppressed mind, and it is not more than that; and the communications of friendship give that relief which nothing else can. (Delville, 18 November 1766)

Mrs. Delany's own health was exceptional. The life expectancy at birth of a gentlewoman born in 1700 was about thirty-seven years. Mrs. Delany exceeded that by over fifty years, which gave rise to considerable admiration in her own lifetime. She was remarkably fortunate in her strong constitution and also in the fact that her illnesses, ailments and accidents appeared to be relatively minor. Crucially, pregnancy or childbirth never threatened her health. She had had a fall or some mishap at Bulstrode when she sent this account:

> I hope my dear friends at Calwich will make themselves quite easy on my account, for I am as well as it is possible for me to be under my present circumstances; indeed much better than I imagined anybody could be after my accident, as you may conclude from my being allowed to write this letter, which I do with perfect ease to myself. Saturday I got up to dinner and eat boiled chicken very heartily, and yesterday eat roasted chicken; and this morning have sate an hour in the dressing-room, whilst the bedchamber was airing. (9 January 1743)

The dean fussed over her every bit as much as she fussed over him, and he reported progress to Anne:

I am set down my dear sister, with the worst
pen and ink in the world, but the best good
will to write to you, and to inform you that *the
Pearl* is, I thank God, as fair and *much more
precious* than ever. She has actually forbidden me
to say one word of vapours or hysteric
headachs; but I am tied to truth, and therefore
must own to you that she has had, both
yesterday and to-day, complaints of that kind,
but without the least symptom of anything
that deserves more attention than the inevitable
concern … She is at this moment in high
mirth with the Duchess; she eat her dinner
with a good relish, has just drunk a cup of
caudle, and I think she is well disposed for her
supper, and gives hopes of a good night.
(Bulstrode, 11 January 1744)

A report of Mrs. Delany being seriously ill reached the
ears of Bernard Granville, and the dean's tone in response to
him was defensive.

The truth is I thank God, she never was in
danger, nor attended by more than one
physician, Dr. Barber. To him I added a surgeon
… yet I thought that so valuable a life should
rest upon the most solid supports that skill
could supply and therefore I ordered them to
hold a consultation with Dr. Robson and Dr.
Barry which I suppose gave occasion to the
report of her being attended by four physicians,
these perfectly agreed in the method in which
Dr. Barber had treated her, and therefore I chose
not to alarm her by the appearance of those
strange physicians. I thank God she is now well,

and I trust in God will long continue so.
(Delville, 27 May 1746)

Her ailments were occasionally self-inflicted. After a visit
to Mr. Preston of Swainton, she wrote: "Lord Mornington's
(Dangen) is six miles from them where I was to have gone last
Wednesday, but a little disorder, occasioned by eating too
many cherries, obliged me to come home" (Delville, 20
August 1748).

*

In Mrs. Delany's correspondence, colds, chills and damps
were taken very seriously as harbingers of worse to come, but
with due diligence they could be avoided. Circumstances
sometimes defeated the best intentions:

> I got a cold by a succession of company last
> Sunday, who drank tea in my garden; the last
> company was the Duchess of Manchester, Lady
> Arabella Denny, Mrs. Fitzmorris, who staid till
> very late, and the wind north-east. I was taken
> ill that night with a pain in my head and sore
> throat, and was blooded on Monday, took
> physic on Tuesday, repeat the same tomorrow,
> and shall not attempt writing. (Delville,
> 29 May 1750)

She reported again with some impatience:

> I have had a slight cold, but am quite well again:
> I got it last Monday in a cold shop staring at my
> Lord Lieutenant's parading – a custom always
> observed the 4th November, King William's
> birthday, whose memory is *idolized* here almost to
> superstition. (7 November 1751)

Headaches are regularly reported, and one bout neces-
sitated postponing the annual trip north.

> Here we are instead of Mount Panther, the
> weather too bad to think of such a journey, and
> Dr. Barber thought as I had of late complained
> of the headache, that it was proper for me to be
> blooded, which I was on Monday sen'night, but
> got cold the latter end of the week, and was a
> little feverish on Sunday last. D.D. sent for Dr.
> Barber, who had me blooded again, kept me in
> bed on slops and juleps three days, and the day
> before yesterday I came down stairs, and find no
> bad remains but a little cough; but Dr. Barber
> absolutely insists on my not going into the
> North, and I believe D.D. will go the week after
> next without me. (Delville, 31 March 1754)

The following year the dean and Mrs. Delany were in
England when their departure for Ireland was delayed by
another illness. Bernard Granville, galvanised by the drama of
it all, proved masterful. He wrote to Anne:

> My sister [Mrs. Delany] wanted to tell you she
> had a very good night, but I snatched the pen
> out of her hand to tell you so myself, and if you
> have any confidence in my truth I think her so
> much better that I have not any more uneasiness
> about her, and hope you will not have any
> either. If you have any skill, she should take
> Bath in her way to Ireland, not that I think she
> will have any immediate occasion, but it is
> always good after a cholic. (Spring Gardens,
> June 1755)

Mrs. Delany was pathetically grateful:

I have not yet ventured down-stairs, as the weather has been damp and cold, and my brother's kind attention is such that he will not suffer me to run any hazard. It seems a determined thing my going to Cheltenham, and then to the Bath; the time not yet fixed. (3 July 1755)

I dined below stairs yesterday, and this morning had the comfort of joining with my family in prayers. I cannot express to you the comfort and the support my brother's tenderness has been to me. As to the Dean's staying in England, it is what he wanted no solicitation about ... My brother has been so good to stay in town on my account, and has not named a time for going ... I hope it will not be thought necessary for me to go to Cheltenham till the middle of August. I pleaded hard for drinking the waters at home, but Dr. Heberden will not hear of it. (Spring Gardens, 5 July 1755)

The Granville–Delany–Dewes clans were regular visitors to the spa towns of England, Bath, Bristol, Cheltenham and Tunbridge Wells. There was a social side to illness and nervous disorder. A jaunt to the waters provided not only restoration for wearied nerves but also an excuse for a family gathering. Mrs. Delany wrote inviting Anne to come to Cheltenham:

The road to Mickleton was most terrible, and bad enough to foil the best horses in England; but all that is over; we have got a charming lodging and a room at your service, if you will make us a visit, at Mrs. Hughes's near the well. I begin with one glass tomorrow morning. (Cheltenham, 9 August 1755)

Taking houses or lodgings in local houses was the common practice in the spa towns. Visiting the spas had become very fashionable, and all classes and types who could afford it did, which meant, of course, the mix was more democratic than might usually be found in Mrs. Delany's circle.

Betsy Sheridan, younger sister of playwright Richard Brinsley Sheridan, accompanied her father, Thomas Sheridan, to Tunbridge Wells in August 1785, and she reported to her sister, Alicia Le Fanu, in Dublin on the company at their boarding house:

> Yesterday we had new Ladies — Quakers — one about six foot high, large in proportion. They quietly took their seats beside each other at the foot of the table and I would not have met your eyes for an hundred pounds, indeed it was a universal effort to refrain from laughing.

She went on to talk about her father's aversion to frightful women and added:

> my Father's dislike to our primitive Christians has risen to such a height that he declared to me he could not digest his dinner in such company and so we withdrew from the boarding table. I am not glad of it as a little society was better than none but to say the truth those Women are too much in the Cook Maid stile. (*Betsy Sheridan's Journal, Letters from Sheridan's Sister 1784–1786 & 1788–1790*, edited by William Lefanu)

Mrs. Delany hardly fared better. "Here are swarms of Hibernians," she wrote.

> I thought a Parliament winter, and a new Lord and Lady Lieutenant would have kept them at

> home. I must go to the Rooms (which begin on
> Monday) *for privacy*, for if I stay at home I may
> have a drum every night.

In the same letter, she reported, "After dinner came two Irish
ladies, Mrs. Greene, her fair daughter, Lady Falkland and
Miss Leake ... Lady Falkland is as ugly and as unpromising
of anything either good or agreeable as any human creature I
ever saw" (4 September 1757).

The ugly, the vapourish, the sick, the lame, the
hypochondriac and the louche had taken the waters at Bath for
years on the site of the original Roman baths. Bath had the
only true thermal waters in England. The therapeutic content
was considered particularly beneficial for chronic rheumatism,
gout and paralysis. The centre of activity and the place to see
and be seen was the famous Pump Room, where the warm
mineral water was sold by the glass. The itinerant Bath population sipped the water, promenaded, gossiped and gaped.
Mrs. Delany wrote, "Henshaw thinks I have drank the waters
long enough. I find them very apt to heat me, and cannot
venture on more than two glasses a day" (23 November 1755).

Proximity to diseased persons with swollen, smelly limbs
or to the "demi-gentry", as Mrs. Delany called them, did not
deter the Delany–Granville party. Their social life in Bath
proceeded elegantly. "My brother," she wrote,

> likes his room up two pair of stairs, so I have
> given up your apartment to Mrs. Masters, and
> have brought the harpsichord up stairs: it stands
> very well at the end of the room, and I have
> placed the screen behind the chair for the
> harpsichord, which does very well. I have not
> yet made my public appearance; I was a little
> tired with my journey yesterday, and sent Sally
> to the ball with Mrs. Thomas. My brother

engaged to the cribbage party in the rooms.
(Bath, 8 November 1755)

Bath and other spa towns, as well as being therapeutic centres, served as marriage marts. Sally Chapone, young and pretty, accompanying the Delanys, received her first proposal there. The warm, relaxed atmosphere clearly encouraged connubial thoughts, and Mrs. Delany reported breathlessly:

> He [Mr. Granville] gave us tea last Friday at the
> ball ... But what do you think? The poor sailor
> [Mr. Smith] is in *earnest smitten*, and has prevailed
> on his mother to mention his wishes, which she
> did to me on Friday last, that we all breakfasted
> there. (17 November 1755)

Mr. Smith was not encouraged and Sally, after a long wait, finally married Dr. Delany's curate and librarian, Dr. Daniel Sandford, in 1764. Many imprudent alliances, however, were made in the heady atmosphere of Bath.

Mrs. Delany wrote, "Tomorrow Sally and I *swim together*." This was in the King's Bath, a giant communal cistern situated beneath the windows of the Pump Room, where strollers could stare down at the patrons and invalids wallowing in a large bath, up to their necks in hot water. The men wore brown linen habits and the women camouflaging petticoats and jackets of the same fabric. It was steamy enough to melt the hardest heart of the most resolute chaperone, but not Mrs. Delany's. She regarded masquerades, pleasure gardens and such places as morally dubious, and the Bath was hardly much better. Moral probity and physical health were two sides of the same coin, and propriety in all things was her guiding principle.

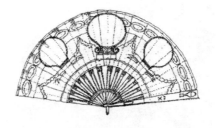

4

miss dolly mode:
mrs. delany's
manners

The following letter accompanied a doll that Mrs. Delany had bought and dressed for her grand-niece Georgina Mary Anne Port, daughter of her beloved niece Mary Dewes Port. The doll, named Miss Dolly Mode, was a model of propriety, just as she hoped G.M.A. would be. The frisseur, or hairdresser, had dropped Miss Dolly while teasing her hair into a suitable style and had broken her nose, but because Mrs. Delany had already made the doll's beautiful clothes with her usual painstaking precision, she was dispatched with her disfigurement.

> Miss Dolly Mode's box just pack'd up to go to the carrier next Friday, containing – *imprimis*: a lady à la mode in accoutrements – but in every other respect *toute au contraire*, for she can neither rouge, nor giggle, nor run away; she is nailed down to her good behaviour, and when you set her at liberty, the nails must be carefully drawn out before Miss Dolly can gain her liberty; then the thin paper that wraps her up to be unpinn'd, which will discover a broad blue ribbon that fastens her down (round the waist) to the box, ditto across her legs. I leave the rest of the unpacking to your delicate fingers. I hope to hear she arrives unrumpled – feathers and all. A box with Miss Dolly's things, a parcel with pamphlets, and the copy of a countenance sent to you by Bernard, and also from him a book of musick you desir'd him to get, and if I could have packed in everything I wish to send to Ilam it would have been a rich box, but I, alas! Have nought but love. (St. James's Place, 28 May 1776)

G.M.A.'s training in propriety was to start early. Miss Dolly Mode was dispatched when she was five years old, and Mrs. Delany sent her a considerable essay on the subject the following year. Another homily was sent when she was nine:

> I don't doubt but you will do everything in your power to make your dear papa and mama happy, and nothing can make them more so than seeing you properly behaved in every respect. Don't neglect *"Mrs. Propriety"* who we used to talk of so frequently, and I promise you the better you are acquainted with her the better you will like her. (Bulstrode, 9 July 1780)

Aunt Delany left nothing to chance.

Propriety was one of her constant themes and governed everything. Mrs. Delany was a model of decorum in her day and was regularly applied to by friends and relations, titled and otherwise, for direction. The politician and orator Edmund Burke, who met her at Bulstrode, confirmed her reputation by describing her as the best-bred woman in the world.

Propriety related closely to virtue and religion. Mrs. Delany gave wholehearted allegiance to the tenets of the established Church of England, to the extent of marrying a clergyman, but she was sincere and devout in her practice, unlike many who viewed the Church as merely a living and a possible route to preferment. Propriety, which she deemed feminine, governed education, recreation, conversation, deportment, decorum, dress, manners, civility and all social intercourse. The smooth running of the status quo in society depended on it being observed, so she was class conscious and knew her place in the pecking order. "Mrs. Propriety" set the tone but religion was the cornerstone, as Mrs. Delany reminded the six-year-old G.M.A. in the unfinished essay.

Your dear Mama has carefully attended to your childhood, and laid that foundation which alone is worth building upon, by forming your religious principles ... I only mean to recommend to your intimate acquaintance a lady. This friend I present to your regard, is never presuming, pert, or conceited, but humble, modest, and unaffected, attentive to everything that can improve her understanding or polish her manners. She never takes the place she ought not, or is at a loss to know what belongs to her. She never gives her opinion but from a desire of further information ... Her name is *Propriety.* To define her exactly is difficult, and the pleasure and honour of her company must be diligently sought for; and never for one moment neglected, for if once lost she is very rarely regain'd.

This impressive essay offered some very high-flown notions but thankfully went on to secular subjects such as fashion and dress. The great towering hairstyles then made fashionable by Georgiana, Duchess of Devonshire, and the bon ton were often ridiculed by Mrs. Delany and her friends. She wrote:

The fashion, if you chance to live with the beau monde, must be complied with; but sense forbids it should be to any extremity, and, indeed, in my youth it was reckon'd *very vulgar* to be *extravagantly* in the fashion: but the fair lady who I hope will be your constant companion, when she finds you are upon the point of being seduced by her enemies *Vanity* or *Assurance,* will give you a twitch and save you. In the country nothing is more absurd than to dress fantastically, and turn the brains of your humble neighbours; who will pique themselves in apeing *the squire's* daughter! And believe me this *can't be innocently done*, as [such an example] will certainly interfere with their station of life, and make them less willing to submit to the duties of it. Dress ought always to be suited to the situation and circumstances of the person. The friend at your elbow (Lady Propriety) is the best frisseur in the world, and the most reasonable. She understands every part of dress to admiration. She will never suffer you to wear your hat with *one edge* to touch your *nose*, and the other edge perpendicularly in the air! With long streamers dangling like a poor mad woman, who I remember lived in a hollow-tree and a toad was her companion; she used to beg ribbons to dress herself with, but yet was *not* so mad as to wear her head-dress *too* high to go *under the arch of her hollow-tree!* Fashions are fluctuating, by the time you wear lappets of a womanly dress it may be less lofty, but whatever it is bear in mind that *moderation* is always genteel. (Bulstrode, 3 August 1777)

Mrs. Delany's crusade had started decades before with her sister, Anne Granville, G.M.A.'s grandmother. Mrs. Pendarves, as she then was, monitored Anne's progress in every area, it seemed. Fluency in French was a polite accomplishment. Formerly the language of court, it served as a code, separating the wheat from the chaff in society and Anne's education in French had been neglected. She hadn't had the advantage of the French-speaking governess Miss Tellier at Aunt Stanley's.

Mrs. Pendarves determined this deficiency should be made good. She wrote:

> The sense of your French paragraph is very well to be understood, though not properly wrote; however that must not discourage you, for many an Englishman born and bred at school does not write English better than you now do French, that learned but three months; read constantly, and set yourself every day a task out of the grammar, and I am sure, without any assistance besides your own industry, you will conquer all the difficulties of it. (New Bond Street, 5 August 1731)

Anne was also instructed in the flirting arts. Mouldering away with her French grammar in Gloucester, she received the following command from Kilalla, Co. Mayo, where Mrs. Pendarves was enjoying the best entertainment the county could produce to entertain her: "Do *display your fan*, my dear sister, never spare it, and make those wretches tremble that would make you a slave were you in their clutches" (6 September 1732). The late Mr. Pendarves was possibly in her thoughts at the time. The language of the fan was eloquent and subtle and its clever use as articulate as any plain speaking. A fan was normally held closed between the thumb and first finger of the right hand. A fan closed, tip to lips, indicated the conversation was being overheard. A fan closed, tip to right cheek, meant yes and, on the opposite cheek, no. Covering the left ear with a closed fan meant keep our secret. Displaying the fan wide and lowering it pointing towards the ground indicated severe distaste and seems to have been the recommended flourish. The innocent young men at the Gloucester assemblies no doubt got the message.

Mrs. Delany's tuition in *les graces* (as she called them) really came into its own after Anne's marriage to Mr. John Dewes in 1740. The training-up of children was work requiring the utmost vigilance and propriety. The birth of Mary Dewes in 1746 gave Aunt Delany, as she was called, fertile ground to work on. Anne's three sons had arrived before Mary, first Court, the eldest, then Bernard, sometimes called Bunny or Banny, and then John, called Jacky. Mrs. Delany's attitude to the boys was cautious; her methodology of child rearing was preventative measures first and corrective measures later. The small detail of her not having any children herself and no experience whatsoever was absolutely no deterrent. She wrote to Anne, a nervous first-time mother, regarding Court:

> My love and blessing to the dear, happy boy, that
> flourishes under your care; I don't apprehend you
> will be too indulgent, and you know the way to
> save yourself pain is to have *a thorough command of*
> *your children* when they are very young. (Delville,
> 28 June 1744)

Court found favour with his aunt, and she commended him a little later:

> I was much amused with your account of dear
> little Court's gallantry; I am very glad he shows
> already so much politeness: *politeness is the polish of*
> *virtue*, and it ought not to be neglected. Is not
> three years old *very young* for breeches? I know it
> is the *fashion*, but I should imagine the spring a
> better time for changing his dress than the
> latter end of the year. (Delville, 24 August
> 1745)

Little boys and girls at this time were dressed alike until the boys were "breeched", somewhere between four and seven; putting boys into trousers launched them into the man's world.

Aunt Delany was not squeamish about corporal punishment, when it was considered necessary. "I think you have exerted the motherly authority very heroically," she wrote, "and I don't doubt but that he will bless you in time for the *little smart*" (Delville, 30 November 1745). Lady Augusta Llanover, great-grand-niece of Mrs. Delany, who edited her letters for publication, added a footnote to this piece, wholeheartedly applauding Anne's course of action. She wrote that the use of

> that wholesome instrument a *real birch rod* in the hands of judicious parents had sadly fallen into disuse from maudlin sentiment. This was under the mistaken idea that the reasoning faculties of children can be exercised before they are formed, and that the instantaneous and efficacious, though harmless, smart of a few twigs of birch was beneath the dignity of a mother to apply or a descendant of Adam to receive.

Sally Chapone, daughter of Mrs. Delany's girlhood friend Sarah Kirkham, was the shared godchild of Mrs. Delany and Anne. Sarah Kirkham had been a high-spirited, forthright young girl, disapproved of by Mrs. Delany's father, and her daughter Sally appeared to have inherited some of her outspokenness. Mrs. Delany wrote:

> I am glad you have got our little god-daughter Sally; I hope she will improve from your advice, and by *all means curb her* if she is *too forward* in giving *her opinions*; a conceited man or woman is *abominable*, but a conceited girl is *insupportable*. Conceit or opinionativeness becomes no sex or age: those that know the world *most* make a bad figure with it, those that have *not* had an

opportunity of seeing the world *are ridiculous with it*. It ought to be *rooted out betimes*; it is a weed that otherwise will choke the most delicate qualities of the mind. (19 January, probably 1742)

The focus changed with the arrival of Miss Mary Dewes in February 1746.

> I am more obliged to my friends at Gloucester than I can express for the good news they have constantly sent me of my dearest sister's being so well, and as little can I express how happy and thankful it makes me. I have this moment received a letter from Mrs. Viney, dated the 19th instant (which I think was your ninth day); she tells me you are better than you have ever been yet, and that my niece eats pap purely. It will save some trouble *if you can* bring her up by hand, and since she is naturally so stout *I believe it may perhaps be done*. Feed her and dance her well. (Delville, 28 February 1746)

Pap was baby or invalid food made usually of bread and water with local variations. Mrs. Delany herself had thrived on pap, or so she declared to Anne by way of encouragement. Years later when the infant in question, Mary Dewes, had her own first baby, G.M.A., pap was in demand again, and the receipt was supplied by Countess Spencer, mother of the famous Georgiana, Duchess of Devonshire, who wrote:

> Dear Madam,
>
> Lady Cowper [godmother to Mary and G.M.A. and mother in law to Countess Spencer] commissioned me to send you the inclosed receipt for children's pap. I am glad of this or

any opportunity I can have of enquiring after your health …

Take a white halfpenny-roll, such as are sold at *country* Bakers, piqued at each end, and let all the crust be pared off very thin (that is the outward crust of all), then put the rest of the roll into a pint of *very fine spring-water*, which must boil till it looks like a jelly, it must then be strained into a *China* or *earthen* bowl through a lawn sieve. This, if rightly done, will be of the consistency of a jelly when it is cold; it is to be taken out in small quantities as wanted, to be warmed and mixed with a *little* milk, and the milk should be mixed into each cup-full, when it is warmed, and not into the whole quantity. (Brighthelmstone, 5 September 1771)

Mary flourished and Mrs. Delany and Anne pledged to lay their "wise heads together about her many and many an hour". This child, dubbed Pauline, became a beloved surrogate daughter to her aunt in Ireland.

I am most truly thankful that you are so well, and have a little female infant to exercise your own good judgement on; which will want little assistance, for I think you are guarded against the errors of *mistaken fondness* towards your children. I thank you for the *right* you have given me over my *"Pauline"*. (Delville, 5 April 1746)

The following letter comes from Anne, concerning her sons' education. She wrote:

Mr. Dewes, I am sure, as well as myself, shall always think ourselves obliged by the kind notice and advice you give in regard to our children, but I fear he will not consent to a public school, he is so fearful of the bad ways and vices they have there to encounter: and besides, he is really afraid of the hardships and severity they are to undergoe *much more than I am*, for I own I am ambitious to have them excel and make a figure ...

Does not the Dean think it will be better to have them at different schools? I have a notion that going together, as they are so much of the same age, whichever excels may raise an em-ulation, and prevent the love I wish to subsist between them; now when they meet as strangers at breaking-up times at home they will naturally be fond of each other. But this is a point I can't well determine upon, the Dean can better advise us; Bunny is fully as quick in learning as Court, but does not love it, and is very *heedless*, and he has a naturall artfulness that is generally *com-mended* in children, but I take great pains to break him of it. Pauline is not yet so genteel as Jacky because she is very fat, but she bridles very well. (Welsbourne, 10 February 1748)

Mary was probably fat and waddled as a result of her pap. As to "bridling", Lady Llanover explained in her footnote that one of the first lessons in deportment at the period was to hold up the head on entering a room and to keep the chin in, the term for which was bridling, and then, having curtsyed at the door:

> to advance deliberately towards the person who had the first claim to the greeting, to *sink* low gradually, and to rise slowly and grace-fully. Girls were always made to curtsey in the

first *position*, because if there was any unsteadiness in the knees and ancles, it would be immediately detected, – the hands were folded and *kept to themselves*, and *butting* and *bobbing*, and rushing about with outstretched palms was unknown.

Mary was two at the time.

Mrs. Delany, who generally delighted in children, was occasionally appalled by their behaviour. The Dewes children were the exception to this rule, of course. She wrote:

> Sir J. Meade is heir to a great estate, a child of six years old, most *unreasonably indulged* – a fine sensible boy, but under *no sort of command*. I had 20 frights for my china, shells and books: his little fingers seized everything with such impetuosity that I was ready to box him; had I been his mama I should have been *most heartily ashamed of him*. With pleasure I recollected that my little nephews would have been much scandalised by his behaviour, and wished them here to set a good example. His sister, a girl about ten, is already a fine affected lady, knows everything, and pretends to ridicule, such airs! Well, thought I, my Pauline will not be such a forward, pert thing! That's my comfort!

"Lady Meade," she continued "is a well-behaved, handsome woman, *not* bred up with *elegant politeness*, but *civil*, and does not want for understanding: so it is not amazing she cannot see the wrong behaviour of her children and how insupportably troublesome they are?" (Mount Panther, 28 July 1750).

❀

Recreation was important and bound by strict propriety. Reading was an important pastime, both for instruction and entertainment, and the Delany and Dewes households were very well read, as befitted their social standing and intellectual curiosity. They discussed their books in detail. There are many references in the correspondence to afternoons and evenings spent, work in hand, listening to the chosen volume being read aloud to the company. Mrs. Delany considered it her Christian duty to avoid any material that might contaminate the purity of her mind. History books were suitable, as were biographies, works of philosophy and collections of sermons. Novels were generally suspect, but there were some exceptions – notably the works of Samuel Richardson. Samuel Richardson had become the publishing rage of the day, and Mrs. Delany and Anne were devotees. They entered into a rapturous correspondence concerning his immense novel *Clarissa*, published serially through 1747 and 1748.

His first work, *The Apprentice's Vade Mecum*, written in 1733, was a conduct manual responding to the "epidemick Evils of the present Age", and this subject was guaranteed to enlist Mrs. Delany's sympathy. He followed this in 1740 with *Pamela: Or, Virtue Rewarded*, an epistolary novel about a young servant girl's physical and moral struggle against the advances of her conniving master. The success of *Pamela* was a publishing phenomenon. It was considered so edifying it was even preached from the pulpit. *Pamela* had her detractors too – chief among them Henry Fielding, who satirised her unmercifully in *Shamela* as a scheming, manipulative minx – but Richardson had found his lodestar. Pamela's reward was on earth, but his next heroine, Clarissa, got hers in heaven, and delayed gratification answered Mrs. Delany's code perfectly.

The heroine, Clarissa Harlowe, with whom Mrs. Delany closely identified, is a beautiful young girl of high intelligence, scrupulous moral judgement, strong resolution and warm humanity. She becomes the victim of her greedy family who try to force her to marry Roger Solmes, whom she detests; and she becomes attracted to the handsome, intelligent, debonair Robert Lovelace, whom she deludes herself into thinking may be rescued from his life of debauchery. He uses her innocence cruelly: she is inveigled out of her family home, imprisoned in a brothel, escapes, but is lured back to captivity, drugged and raped. She escapes only to die a harrowing death.

Mrs. Delany wrote:

> I am now as deeply engaged with "Clarissa" as when I was first acquainted with her, and admire her more and more; I am astonished at the author: his invention, his fine sentiments, strong sense, lively wit, and above all his exalted piety and *excellent design* in the whole. I find many beauties escaped me in my first reading; I was so much interested and run away with by the story, that I did not give due attention to many delightful passages. I am just got to her triumph after his villany: how poor, and despicable a figure does he make upon their first meeting, and how noble and angelic is her appearance and behaviour! The contrast of flagrant guilt and injured though unconquered innocence is most judiciously and beautifully drawn. My heart was almost broke with her frenzy, but that scene afterwards composed and revived my spirits, and made me almost rejoice in her distress; this, and making up my shell-lustre, has taken up every home hour that has not been interrupted by company; I will not lay by either till I have finished them. (Delville, 6 October 1750)

Dr. Johnson reputedly remarked of this lurid romp, spun out over a staggering fifteen hundred pages, "Why, Sir, if you were to read Richardson for the story, your impatience would be so much fretted that you would hang yourself." Mrs. Delany's engagement was not with story alone but with the novel's vast and tortured sensibility, and she was quick to jump her paragon's defence. She wrote to Anne:

> You had better have told me who called Clarissa "*fool*", for I have laid it to the charge of several, by turns, and only one is guilty! I hope it was *not* Mrs. Dobson. To call Clarissa *fool*, argues a *weak* judgement in the *criticiser*. (30 June 1750, Delville)

Samuel Richardson was known to Mrs. Delany's circle. She corresponded with him, as did Anne. He encouraged a coterie of highly refined, educated women to exchange views on *Clarissa* as it was being written. They were sent drafts as the novel progressed, and Hester Mulso Chapone, sister-in-law to Sally Chapone, was chief among Richardson's correspondents. She was also the author of *Letters on the Improvement of the Mind* (1772), a work later championed by Mrs. Delany. Hester Chapone is credited with being a model for some of Richardson's heroines. She represented to him the epitome of feminine delicacy and breeding. Mrs. Delany and Anne were not quite so sure: their highly tuned sensibility and superior radar registered some social nuances and infelicities in the otherwise excellent Hester/Clarissa. They gossiped about it between themselves:

> I gave you an account of a letter I had written to Mr. Richardson of the books D.D. ordered him to send you ... as you read Clarissa, when you object to any particular expressions *let me*

know the page and the *line*. (Delville, 2 June 1750)

Mr. Richardson's novels, with all faults, passed inspection, but ten years later, Laurence Sterne's tour de force *Tristram Shandy* did not:

> The Dean is indeed very angry with the author of Tristram … and those who do not condemn the work as it deserves; it *has not* and *will not* enter this house, especially now your account is added to a very bad one we had heard before. We were upon the brink of having it read among us; Mr. Sandford heard Faulkener, the printer, cry it up so much, and say it had had a great run in England. (Delville, 24 April 1760)

The overwhelming reaction to *Tristram Shandy*'s publication was delight; even Georgina, Countess Cowper, Mary Dewes' other godmother, had read and enjoyed it. However, Mrs. Delany's fine sensibility tolerated the insidious prurience of Richardson but rejected the comic bawdiness of Sterne.

Meanwhile, safe from the contagion of bad books, the careful watch over the education and morals of the Dewes children was as vigilant as ever. Mrs. Delany gave free rein to her considerable grasp of child psychology.

> I don't fear your prudence in the management of your children. Love, coupled with fear, are the bands that must confine them to what is right. A wrong and over-indulgent conduct of parents to children is the *greatest cruelty* to them; for if they never meet with contradiction till they are of age to engage in the great concerns of life, how will they be able to sustain the contradictions, disappointments, and mortifications they must

encounter in this world? But a perverse, injudicious manner of contradicting and thwarting them, and very severe corrections for trifles, does them I believe almost as much harm as a universal indulgence. (Delville, 24 November 1750)

Mrs. Delany's concerns repeated themselves down the generations. She was anxious that Mary should have a good command of French. She wrote to Anne;

I am sorry you have been disappointed of the French woman, as beginning French very young, gives a freer and better pronunciation than can be learned when they are older, but as this is an *embellishment* more than any *material* accomplishment, and if (which you can do very well) you teach her the grammar, and how to read, that will do for some years, and when you meet with a servant to your mind, that can save you some part of the attention you now have, take her by all means, for it is too much for you to have the whole care of so many upon your spirits; I hope the boys will be so well next year, that you may put the two eldest to school. (Delville, 30 November 1750)

Propriety was also brought to bear on the children's recreation:

I think it prudent in a moderate degree to encourage in young people an inclination to any innocent amusement, and am happy when I find they have a turn for any art or science; the mind is active, and cannot always bend to deep study and business, and too often bad company and bad ways are the relaxations sought; to guard against that nothing is so likely as any amusement that will not tire, and that requires application to bring to any perfection, and of course must prevent that idleness which *at best* makes them *very insignificant*. I agree with Mr. Dewes, that an immoderate love to music may draw young people into many inconveniences: I would therefore confine it as much as I could to an amusement, and never allow it to be their business. Painting has *fewer objections*, and generally *leads people into much better company*. I have not many fears for *our Mary*, the good education and constant good example she is blessed with, I hope, will make her another sort of thing than the generality of the young girls. (30 December 1752)

❄

Mrs. Delany's preoccupation was chiefly with Mary: "that child takes up much of my thoughts," she wrote in November 1750. When Mary was barely a year and a half old, Mrs. Delany wrote:

I thank you, my dear, for your good accounts of *Pauline*, but I am better pleased to hear of her sense and sprightliness than of her *beauty*; though I hope she will not want as much of that as is necessary to give a *pleasing impression* — not a rapturous one, for that may prove more to her *unhappiness* than *happiness*. (Believed to be 11 July 1747)

She warned again, when Mary was five years old, that beauty was superficial and a snare:

> If Pauline proves handsome, which *indeed* I think she *bids fair for*, it is in vain to hope that she *can be kept ignorant of it*; all that the wisest friend can do for her is to teach her of how little value beauty is – how few years it lasts – how liable to be tarnished, and if it has its advantage, what a train of inconveniences also attend it; I do not wish our Pauline *blind* to her own perfections; but rather have her *so far* sensible of them, as never to do anything that can make the advantages Providence has bestowed upon her a reproach, but an incitement to do honour to herself and her family. I wish you had the opportunity of having her learn to dance: I make it my request to you, if you have, that you will not lose it; her cousin Granville, who is one of the best dancers I ever saw, danced a minuet very prettily at five years of age; it is not only an advantage in giving a graceful air to the person, but it *gives strength* to the limbs, and is the *best sort of exercise she can use.*
> (Delville, 16 March 1751)

Mrs. Delany was determined Mary should make a figure:

> I *cannot* think it necessary for the accomplishment of a young lady that she should be *early* and *frequently* produced in public, and I should rather see a little awkward bashfulness, than a *daring and forward genteelness!* Good company and good conversation I should wish my niece introduced into as soon as she can speak and

understand, but for all the public places till *after fifteen* (except a play or oratorio) she should not know what they are, and then *very rarely*, and *only* with her mother or aunt. I believe you and I are perfectly well agreed on these points, and I am sure the general behaviour of the young people will not encourage us to alter our scheme. (Delville, 22 February 1752)

Dancing lessons would keep Mary safely occupied until she was ready to come on what Mrs. Delany called the stage. The minuet was an elegant social dance and was extremely popular with European aristocracy until the late eighteenth century. It was more an expression of social values than a dance. It functioned as the presentation and ritualisation of status through grace of body and display of fine clothing and jewels. To Mrs. Delany, torn between preserving Mary's modesty and showing her off, the minuet provided the ideal vehicle. It fell perfectly within the bounds of propriety. The minuet was performed in a moderate triple metre, and there were many variations, dozens of versions of setting or show-off steps and several ways to "cast off one couple". Dancers would dance differently depending on where they were, who they were and, most importantly, who was watching.

Minuets began and ended with a special sequence of honours, or elegant bows, to audience, to partners and to dancers, who faced each other in the centre of the floor. One couple danced alone while the rest of the company looked on. It had a fixed sequence of figures: lead-in, right-hand turn, left-hand turn and two-hand turn closing. These were punctuated by a Z figure. The basic minuet step-combination consisted of four steps in six beats, and Mary Dewes and her contemporaries spent hours being drilled by dancing masters to perform the dance to perfection. To be able to dance elegantly and well was a social imperative, and Mrs. Delany pressed the matter hard when she wrote again:

> Mary now is of an age to learn to dance ... It will help to strengthen her limbs, and make her grow, even though she may not be taught in the best manner. I hope you will give her every winter an opportunity of being taught either at the Bath or London, and of seeing a variety of good company, which is of more use in forming a gracious manner from the age of seven to fourteen than seven years afterwards! Every impression taken in our tender years is more lasting than when the mind is more filled with a crowd of ideas. (3 March 1753)

Her persistence was admirable. The following year she pressed again: "Shall I speak to Mr. Serise the dancing master, to secure him for Mary?" (Bulstrode, 14 January 1754). As the most fashionable dancing master to be had in London at the time, he was in much demand. Mrs. Delany nabbed him, and some months later she wrote: "Mr. Serise hopes to see Mary as straight as an arrow when she comes to town" (Whitehall, 5 November 1754).

Her crusade continued:

> The Dean and I shall be extremely mortified if you do not go to Spring Gardens; I think you ought to go on Mary's account; not only for confirming her dancing (*for which she has certainly a genius*), but to improve an acquaintance with her relations, who may hereafter be of use to her; so that when she is so unhappy as to want the protection she has at present, she may not

be a stranger to those with whom we may naturally wish she should keep up a good correspondence. As to a dancing I suppose Lady Cowper [godmother and cousin to Mary Dewes] will desire Dunoyer, and he is certainly the best now Serise is gone. Mr. Granville I suppose will lend you a clavichord; Mary has had *uncommon* advantages at home for the improvement of what is most material, and a foundation is laid, by her excellent and kind instructors, that will make her happy beyond this earthly tabernacle; but this is not all that is requisite, unless she is to turn hermit. There is a *grace* and a *manner* which cannot be attained without conversing with a variety of well-bred people, which when well chosen cannot efface what is certainly more necessary, but will give a polish, and by an agreeable recommendation render all the good part more useful and acceptable to those she converses with. These are my sentiments, and if I have said too much I hope you and Mr. Dewes will forgive my zeal for one that I look upon as my own child. (Delville, 27 January 1759)

Mrs. Delany's interference may seem excessive to our eyes but, as Lady Llanover explained, the role of godmother in the eighteenth century was not a sinecure with respect either to temporal or spiritual welfare. It conferred special duties of assisting in every possible manner with the proper settlement of the godchild in life. Mary Dewes' other godmother was drafted in to the cause as well:

Lady Cowper will like to be consulted about Mary's dress, and is a good judge. Dunoyer is now I believe the best dancing-master in London, his price is high ... I believe Lady Cowper has a good interest with him, and that may make him take more pains. (Delville, 16 February 1760)

The question of Mary's marrying arose when she was thirteen years old:

I am quite of your mind about marrying; I should be very sorry to have Mary married before she was twenty, and yet if a very desirable match offers sooner, I don't know how it can be refused, if *she must* marry *at all?* (Delville, 31 March 1759)

Mrs. Delany's ambivalence about marriage was ever present. "Why must women be *driven to the necessity* of marrying?" she wrote.

A state that should always be a matter of *choice!* And if a young woman has not fortune sufficient to maintain her in the station she has been bred to, what can she do, but marry? And to avoid living either very obscurely or running into debt, she accepts of a match with no other view than that of interest. Has not *this* made matrimony an irksome prison to many, and prevented its being that happy union of hearts where mutual choice and mutual obligation make it the most perfect state of friendship? (Delville, February 1751)

Despite these reservations, she participated with some skill in matchmaking, brokering several matches, including one for her goddaughter Sally Chapone. This was an area of the strictest propriety and ideally suited to her talents. The happy union of hearts she spoke about did not imply "love and a knapsack". Settlement terms were all important for both parties, and Mrs. Delany was a pragmatist. On marriage, the custody of the woman, her person and her possessions, were ceded to her husband. If her family had bargained well, she acquired status, a place in society, a house to command and a family. Netting a title was the goal for a relentlessly upwardly mobile society, and while a young lady's fortune might lure a title or forge a grand connection, the cost to dignity and purse could be high. The delicacy of these negotiations required the utmost tact, and while the men of the family took on the financial dealings, it was left to the women to accomplish the fancy footwork of the social manoeuvrings. Mrs. Boscawen confided to Mrs. Delany the difficulties of settling her eldest daughter, Frances, with the Honourable John Leveson Gower. His mother was the Dowager-Countess Gower, a cousin of Mrs. Delany's.

> *Our* great business goes on as well as it can do *without* any assistance, I had almost said *notice* from the *other side* ... *your* noble friend [Countess Gower] was so obliging to say she "had *no objection* to the lady." But yet one must see that they are *not pleas'd*, much less that they have any thoughts of giving us the pleasure to hear them say "You are welcome;" and yet, my dear madam, does not Admiral Boscawen's daughter with £10,000 now, and at least 5 more by-and-by, with many excellent and wife-like qualities, and no faults that ever they heard of, deserve some gentler welcome, especially as *nobody* asks *anything of them?* But this, my dear madam, *only* for the Duchess's ear and yours,

for I wou'd not go about *complaining*, – on the contrary, we mean to behave as if we had been received with the cordiality which (I think) we deserve! But I am partial, no doubt. *Our* poor little projects of settlement are now before my Lord Chief Baron [Smythe], when he returns them we shall submit them to Bill Hill [home of Lady Gower], tho' *perhaps* they may not deign to take any notice of them. I wish they could think as I do, that in this age it is a great blessing to marry one's child to a person of worth and principle. Such I am sure my daughter is, and as such I did expect she would have been kindly receiv'd in any family where there was not any *great* pretension to *fortune*, which Mr. Leveson certainly has not. (Audley Street, 7 June 1773)

Mrs. Delany advised Mrs. Boscawen how to gain interest with her formidable relation, and the marriage did come off.

Anne Dewes died in 1761 before she had the opportunity of seeing her daughter settled, and it fell to Mrs. Delany's lot as never before to guide Mary through the perilous waters of young womanhood. She went to her task with proselytising zeal. She wrote:

Pride is detestable, as it is productive of a train of ills. You may shine at a ball, be as well dressed as anybody, and by a *proper* and *prudent* behaviour give and receive pleasure, without the least imputation of pride; and you may visit your poor neighbours, and with your own hands bestow every comfort, without the imputation of meanness, but quite the contrary when it is done with true Christian benevolence,

> but if your charity is bestowed with ostentation
> and arrogance, you then are *proud*, – and if you
> are *affected* and *impertinent* in your behaviour at a
> ball, you *then are mean*. (Delville, 12 March
> 1765)

Avoiding the sin of pride was all very well, but Mary
faced far more corporeal dangers. Jean Jacques Rousseau, the
author of *Emile* and other radical works, had fled France and
come to England during the year 1766. He arrived at the
invitation of philosopher David Hume and fetched up in the
neighbourhood of Calwich, adjacent to Bernard Granville's
country estate. Bernard took him up and was deeply
impressed with him. He introduced Rousseau to his niece
Mary Dewes, who was visiting, and the author became very
fond of her. Alarm bells rang for Aunt Delany. Rousseau had
criticised religion in *Emile*, which had caused his books to be
burnt in France, and though she hadn't read Rousseau any
more than she had read Sterne, she determined her niece
would not fall for his heresy:

> Now for a word about Monsieur Rousseau,
> who has gained so much of your admiration.
> His writings are ingenious, no doubt, and were
> they weeded from the false and erroneous
> sentiments that are blended throughout his
> works (as I have been told), they would be as
> valuable as they are entertaining. I own I am
> not a fair disputant on this subject from my
> own knowledge of his works, as I avoid
> engaging in books from whose *subtlety* I might
> perhaps receive some prejudice, and I always
> take alarm when *virtue* in *general terms is the idol*,
> without the support of *religion*, the *only*
> foundation that can be our security to build

upon; that *great plausibility* and *pomp of expression* is deluding, and requires great accuracy of judgement not to be imposed upon by it. I therefore think it the wisest and safest way to avoid those snares that I may not have strength enough to break when once entangled in them. I remember a wise maxim of my Aunt Stanley's when I first came into the great world: — "*avoid putting yourself in danger, fly from temptation, for it is always odds on the tempter's side.*" (Autumn, 1766)

To her friend and contemporary Lady Andover, she wrote with more bite:

I am glad you have seen *the Rousseau*; he is a genius and a curiosity, and his works extremely ingenious, as I am told, but to young and unstable minds *I believe dangerous*, as under *the guise and pomp of virtue* he does advance very erroneous and unorthodox sentiments; it is *not* the "*bon tons*" who say this, but I am too near the *day of trial* to disturb my mind with fashionable whims. Lady Kildare said she would "offer R. an elegant retreat if *he would educate her children!*" I own I widely differ with her ladyship, and would rather commit that charge to a *downright honest parson*, I mean as far as to religious principles, but perhaps that was a part that did not fall into her scheme at all. (4 September 1766)

Emily, Lady Kildare, very soon to be Duchess of Leinster, came under Mrs. Delany's opprobrium again some years later:

I mentioned the Duchess of Leinster's marriage to her son's tutor, but I called him by the wrong name — his name is Ogleby. People wonder at her marriage, as she is reckoned one of the proudest and most expensive women in the world; but perhaps she thought it incumbent (as Lady Brown said of her Grace) to "marry and make an honest man of him." I pity her poor children. (Bulstrode, 1775)

Rousseau returned to France, to the great relief of Mrs. Delany, and the subject of Mary getting married began to re-enter the correspondence. She was twenty years of age, highly accomplished, elegant and well bred, ready for marriage. The first mention of her husband-to-be came from Bernard Granville when he wrote to his niece:

Mr. Port called here yesterday morning. I was sorry to hear Miss Sparrow has not been well lately, but I hope it not anything dangerous. I cannot add any more now, but my compliments to your brothers, and that you will believe me,
　　Dear madam,
　　Your most faithful, humble servant,
　　B.G. (Calwich, 18 May 1766)

Mr. John Port was a neighbour of Bernard Granville's. He had changed his family name of Sparrow to inherit the estate of his maternal Port relation, and Miss Sparrow was his niece. Mary confided her hopes of Mr. Port to Aunt Delany in Ireland. Mrs. Delany sent encouraging letters back and staked her claim in the decision making.

You know the worth of the friends you are already possessed of, and *when* you add one to the number that must be dearer to you than all the rest [Mary's prospective husband], one as will make you truly happy and do you honour, but on such occasions we must always *distrust* our *own* partiality, and call those in to our assistance whose affection for us must make them consider our real happiness, and whose judgements are unprejudiced. (Delville, 21 January 1765)

Mary Dewes and John Port married five years later. The delay was due to some perversity on the part of Bernard Granville. Lady Llanover, perplexed at his behaviour, wrote in her footnote:

> The marriage of Miss Dewes to Mr. Port of Ilam it was evident had long been opposed by her uncle, Mr. Granville, though on what grounds does not appear, as Mr. Port's family was very ancient, his estate very good, and himself very popular, and the contiguity of Ilam to Calwich might have been supposed a favourable circumstance, as Mr. Granville was so partial to his niece.

The Duchess of Portland was the catalyst. She intervened and Bernard Granville capitulated. The wedding took place at Bulstrode on 4 December 1770. The young couple spent their first few months as a married couple in London, close to Mrs. Delany. She was very pleased with the outcome and wrote to her friend Lady Andover;

> Mr. and Mrs. Port dine with me every day. They strive which shall show me most attention, and give me good reason to be satisfied with their union that I should be most unkind and unreasonable not to be contented. Mr. G. *has written* kind congratulations to them. He has been ill, and I believe at this time at the Bath. (The Thatched Cottage, 27 December 1770)

The following August, Mrs. Boscawen wrote to Mrs. Delany, who was with Mary at Ilam:

> Your dear niece being *pure well* is indeed an earnest of pure good news shortly. So experienced a person being with her is another satisfaction and a great one to me, for you must know I thought it very likely you would frighten each other where no fear was. The first time I experienced the pains of child-bearing, I concluded that no woman had ever endured the like upon the like occasion, and that I could not possibly recover it, whereas I danced a minuet about my room in ten days, to insult my nurse-keeper and set her a scolding for my diversion! ...
>
> Mrs. Mead will assure you, when you are terrified, that "all is well", and no more than what she has experienced *eight times!* And this will be a great comfort to you and my young friend in her *lit de misere*, so I enjoin and charge you to mind what Mrs. Mead *says*, more than what Mrs. Port *screams*, for scream she will and must. (Audley Street, 29 August 1771)

Those inevitable screams produced Georgina Mary Anne Port on 16 September 1771. She was variously called Georgina, Mary, Nancy, Paulinette, Georgi Anna, the little bird and the little dove, but mostly G.M.A.

❧

With a delightful new child's training to superintend, Mrs. Delany was revitalised. G.M.A. was only four months old when Mrs. Delany wrote concerning Mr. Port's niece Miss

Sparrow, who had proved a troublesome girl that might give bad example:

> I am obliged to you and your dear P. for taking my hint about "*speech*" so kindly. The strange behaviour of the young ladies of the present age makes one tremble for those that are *to come* on the stage; and I think much is owing to their want of that humble, respectful deference (to parents and elders) that we were taught in our childhood ... I think in some of my self-conceited moments I will write *a book of maxims* for G.M.A. (St. James's Place, 31 December 1771)

Miss Sparrow's efforts to correct her behaviour were commended:

> I am quite glad you find Fanny [Frances Mabel Sparrow] so much improved and so attentive; and hope her good sense will make her sensible of the happiness and advantage of having an uncle and aunt who are so sincerely her friends ... I am glad you wrap the Paulinette warm; those tender limbs require it, and I know you are of my mind; do *not* begin too soon to try and harden delicate plants; have every warmth but that of *always* hovering over a fire! You are wonderfully improved in your writing that I will not allow the word *scrawl* to appear in your letters; and I shall call it affectation. You will, I suppose, be careful in opening your box, as the mended bottle is stuffed into the ermine muff, wrapped round with gloves to keep it steady. (St. James's Place, 2 January 1772)

The tender watch continued: "I think G.M.A. is too young to sit long in her chair. Their little joints are weak, and want support. I approve extremely of your wrapping her up *warm*. It will be time enough to harden her" (St. James's Place, 27 January 1772).

On her first birthday, G.M.A. had the honour of receiving a letter from her grand-aunt.

> To Miss Port, of Ilam, aged 1 year, from her
> Aunt Delany, aged 72.
> Bulstrode, 16th Sept. 1772.
>
> My dearest little child, this is your birthday, and I wish you joy of its return; perhaps if you knew what a world your are enter'd into, *so abounding* with evil you would not say "*Ta*" to me for my congratulation, but the precepts and example of your excellent parents will teach you how to make so good a use of the tryals you will necessarily meet with, that they will not only be supportable, but lead to a state of happiness that will have no alloy. This is above your understanding at present, and a rattle or a little squeaking cuckoo will suit much you better; so for the present I leave you to your infantine amusements, which I shall be as ready to contribute to when I can, as I am to testifye how dearly you are beloved by,
>
> Your great
> A.D.

Aunt Delany was on duty again for the arrival of the first son John:

> You have named a longer day for my visit to Ilam than I had in *my mind's eye*. I suppose the

bantling will not be baptiz'd till your last week,
and would not that be a good time for me to
come to you?

As to the darling's stays, it may be time eno'
when you and I have had a *conference* about them;
but if a good air is not settled from the
beginning, it is as difficult to be attained
afterwards as good manners if neglected. Is not
the nurse in raptures with the dear child? (I
March 1773)

Toddlers, girls and boys, were dressed in floor-length gowns
under which they wore stiffened bodices or stays.

Reports went backwards and forwards, and history
repeated itself. "Does my little Mary (G.M.A.) bridle? And
does she scorn to be set down on the carpet, or Mrs. Prim in
the corner?" (Bulstrode, 3 July 1773); "I am delighted with
the dear little man's thriving state, and his dear sister's
schollarship. You may teach her the alphabet by rote, as she
has *so excellent* an *ear* and *memory*, and she will soon be
acquainted with it with her *eyes*" (Bulstrode, 13 August 1773).

❧

Good manners and propriety were always uppermost in Mrs.
Delany's mind. She wrote to her nephew the Rev. John Dewes,
doing duty as secretary to Bernard Granville at the time:

There are two little volumes come out on "the
improvement of the mind," addressed to a little
girl of fifteen [from Mrs. Hester Mulso
Chapone to her niece], that I will send my
brother the first opportunity; they appear to be
upon the best plan I have ever met on the
subject. It is plain truth in an easy elegant style,

and the sentiments natural and delicate. I have just finish'd it, which has insensibly lead me to give my opinion of it, which I did not intend doing, but as it has given me pleasure and edification I cannot forbear sending it the first opportunity. *It sells prodigiously.* Adieu. (St. James's Place, 25 May 1773)

Conduct manuals abounded, and Mrs. Delany had now found one that reflected her views perfectly. Hester Mulso Chapone, aunt of Sally Chapone and protegée of Samuel Richardson, published her *Letters on the Improvement of the Mind* to great acclaim in 1772. Mrs. Delany recommended them particularly for the wayward Miss Sparrow.

In her chapter "Politeness and Accomplishments", Mrs. Chapone outlined the proper conduct of a young person in company, an area where Miss Sparrow was deficient:

> You must appear to be interested in what is said, and endeavour to improve yourself by it … Then, when called upon, you must not draw back as unwilling to answer, nor confine yourself merely to yes or no, as is the custom of many young persons, who become intolerable burthens to the mistress of the house, whilst she strives in vain to draw them into notice, and to give them some share in the conversation.

More pointedly, Mrs. Chapone wrote:

> In your father's [or uncle's] house it is certainly proper for you to pay civility to the guests … Young ladies of near your own age, who visit there, fall of course to your share to entertain. But, whilst you exert yourself, to make their visit agreeable to them, you must not forget what is

due to the elder part of the company – nor by
whispering and laughing apart, give them cause
to suspect, what is too often true, that they
themselves are the subjects of your mirth.

Hester Mulso Chapone's arena was domestic, but the
essential guide to courtly conduct and political conniving was
also in circulation. Mrs. Delany was not enthusiastic, though
she wrote, "All the world are now reading Lord Chesterfield's
letters" (30 April 1774). Philip Dormer Stanhope, Fourth
Earl of Chesterfield, former Lord Lieutenant of Ireland
(1745–6), had had a glittering public career. A skilled courtier
and ambassador, his letters to his son Philip Stanhope,
advising him on his climb up the career ladder, had been
published.

Lord Chesterfield wrote:

My Dear Friend,
One observation, I hope you will make in
reading history; for it is an obvious and a true
one. It is that more people have made great
figures, and great fortunes in court, by their
exterior accomplishments, than by their interior
qualifications. Their engaging address, the
politeness of their manners, their air, their turn,
hath almost always paved the way for their
superior abilities, if they have such, to exert
themselves. They have been Favourites, before
they have been Ministers … The Prince himself,
who is rarely the shining genius of his court,
esteems you only by hearsay, but likes you by his
senses; that is, from your air, your politeness,
and your manner of addressing him; of which
alone he is a judge. There is a court garment, as
well as a wedding garment, without which you

not be received. That garment is an imposing air, an elegant politeness, easy and engaging manners, universal attention, an insinuating gentleness and all those *je ne sais quois* that compose the Graces. (London, 14 February 1752)

Bernard Granville commended the letters, but Mrs. Delany responded with her old tenacity:

I am not at all surprised you should be entertained with Lord Chesterfield's letters, and approve of many of them; as a politician and what is called a man of the world. The general opinion of these letters among the better sort of men is, that they are ingenious, usefull as to pollish of manners, but *very hurtful* in a *moral sense. Les graces* are the sum total of his religion. (Bulstrode, 4 September 1774)

With conduct manuals very much in vogue, Mrs. Delany herself was asked to draw one up for Miss Sparrow, who was still proving unsatisfactory. The tone is stern:

Rise at 7, sacrifice to cleanliness in the first place; neatness of person and purity of mind are suitable companions: then, with awfull attention, say your prayers, return thanks for the blessings you have received, and pray for their continuance and for grace to make the best use of them, etc. etc. If you have time, before breakfast read the Psalms for the morning in French, and some French lesson; most likely you may be called upon to read them afterwards in English. Write 3 or 4 lines, as well as you can, to offer to your friends at breakfast. Suppose you take in hand Mrs.

Chapone's letters to her niece; begin at page 3, "*Hitherto you* have," and *don't* exceed 6 *lines of her book at a time*, it will imprint it on your mind, and it would be an excellent exercise for your memory to get the historical and geographical parts of it by heart. I know no book for a young person (next to the Bible) more entertaining and edifying if read with due attention: I must again repeat, *not* to write more than *six* lines at a time, and that in perfection; for if you grow tired you will grow *careless*, and *that* is the bane of all improvement. I hope I need not recommend to you neatness and regularity in taking care of cloaths, etc. keeping them in nice order, and proper repair *not depending* on its being *done for you.*

Employ *two hours every day in plain work,* and *making up your own things*; it is an accomplishment necessary for every gentlewoman, and when you are in circumstances to make it less necessary or convenient you will be better able to know when it is well done for you. But this is not to exclude, at their proper seasons, works of ingenuity; if you have learned to draw, give *one* hour to that *every day*, but *not* to interfere, with what is more necessary. As the cleanly part of your dressing will mostly be done when you first get up, bestow as little time on *dress* as possible, but let it always be neat and suitable to your circumstances (or position), and never *extravagantly in the fashion,* which is very vulgar, and shows levity of mind. Be always punctually ready for your meals; it is very impertinent to make anybody wait for inattention or idleness, and the attention of young people should always be awake to do everything with propriety; after dinner retire to your room, and amuse yourself with anything that is *not study* for an hour, or walk if it is allow'd you, and the season proper for it, till you receive a summons to books or work for the evenings; the occupations of the day must of course vary with the season, and rules give way occasionally as engagements at home and abroad may sometimes interrupt them. Walking or playing with your little cousins may enliven part of your time; and your good sense and observance of the rules laid down in regard to them, will guard you against any wrong and mistaken kindness, and make you carefull and particular in all *your own* words and actions; as your good nature would be extremely hurt to *bring them under correction by your example.* You are now of an age to know how very improper it would be for you to interfere with their management, and that of the family; and be assured the only way to be beloved and happy (even in a parent's house) is to be humble, modest, attentive, and complying towards those who have taken you under their wing, adhering strictly to truth, and never *see* or say what is no busyness of yours, but be always civil and affable in your behaviour to the servants; you will then raise no jealousy or envy among them, and by not herding with them, you will gain and maintain their respect, and the confidence and friendship of the friends you are with, who have your happiness at heart, and are the only persons you should open your mind to without reserve. Avoid *intruding* on them when they may *like to be alone* — reserve on those occasions shows *observation* and *respect*; and the evening will close as the day began.

These are rude hints to be improved upon and filled up by *a better capacity!* (Bulstrode, 13 November 1774)

The rules had a remarkably good effect, in the short term anyway, because Mrs. Delany wrote a few days later: "I am glad that you think her improved" (Bulstrode, 18 November 1774).

Aunt Delany, always a great source of family news, sent this report with a cautionary note:

Sir Ed Winnington's son, of Worcestershire, is fallen desperately in love with Miss Anne Foley [a cousin], just 14 years old, and has proposed and is accepted, but not to be married these two years; but this must not be told to anybody. For Godsake, my dear Mary, don't let *my little Porty* think of anything but her lessons and her doll at 14 years of age! What behaviour and conduct can be expected for children's being so soon introduced into a state of life that requires the utmost prudence? But Mr. F. gives him a good character, and his estate joins Witley.

And as a postscript: "*Consider* before you determine about Fanny [Miss Sparrow] going to any water-drinking place with only so young a person as V. [Mrs. Vrankin]!" (St. James's Place, 27 April 1775).

G.M.A. was not likely to be married soon, but Aunt Delany nonetheless kept an eye on her potential competitors. She found fault with Lady Caroline Stuart, the granddaughter of Lady Mary Wortley Montagu. "She is extremely good-humoured and sensible," she wrote:

> but is one in whom many pleasing accomplish-ments are a little hurt by an awkward habit: she has *no affectation*, but a trick of a laugh at whatever is said or that she says herself. I should not mention this, but as it has proceeded from want of attention in her training up, which makes it so necessary to be watchful from infancy, and check in time any propensity to tricks.
>
> I think *my sweet bird* very free at present, if she has left off her little bashful way of lifting up her shoulders and elbows; but she has no odd tricks which she *can* learn *from you*, which is a matter of much consequence. (Bulstrode, 23 October 1775)

G.M.A., encased in her stays, was trained to curtsy and sink, keeping the upper part of her body straight as a ramrod. Hitching up shoulders and elbows would spoil the effect. There were varying degrees of bows or reverences to learn. To a parent or aunt a passing bow might be appropriate, but a more reverential sink would be required for someone like the Duchess of Portland. This would involve sliding one foot forward, transferring all weight to it, then taking a small sideways step and transferring the weight to that foot. The first foot then slides to join the other foot, heels touch, toes turn out, the knees bend outwards over the toes, a momentary eye contact is made and the reverence is concluded.

Mary Port had to ensure that G.M.A. received this early training in deportment. Meanwhile, reports from the Ilam nursery flew backwards and forwards, and Aunt Delany's guidance was sought. There were now three Port children,

G.M.A., John and George Rowe. Three more were to come, Bernard, Louisa and Harriet. Mrs. Delany replied:

> Alas, my dearest child, you call upon me for advice that I am little capable of giving ... your management must suit their *different* tempers. Your gentle, good-humoured dove must *not* be *roughly* opposed, but led with a soft *rein*, but a rein there *must* be, tho' a silken one; Whenever *our* little darling seems negligent or inattentive it should not pass by unheeded, and I am sure your tenderness will find means of gaining your point without severity, and avoid commands that may be difficult ... As to your son John I have less to say: a good school if he grows unruly will *tame him*; but even *a preparation* for *that* will be necessary, or the *discord* will never be resolved into a *concord* ... I suppose Miss Sparrow returns no more to school; and you will have an additional task to exercise your judgement upon: the subject a delicate one – for tho' she does not want for sense or good nature, they have hitherto met with many things to warp them. And I look upon schools as necessary *evils*, which under some *circumstances* are unavoidable; as the cabals, the party-spirit, the fear of the governess, the secret and foolish indulgences of the maids, sometimes teach dissimulation, jealousy, resentment, and revenge – a sad train, and as mischievous as the ichneumon fly that gets into the chrysalis of the poor innocent caterpillar, and devours its vitals.

Mrs. Delany helpfully concludes, "but do not be frightened, my dear Mary" (Bulstrode, 21 October 1774).

Two years later, John was still untamed, Aunt Delany wrote:

> I don't think severity will do if too often re-
> peated, and as he is a sensible child, perhaps
> treating him with some contempt when he is in
> his tantrums, or not seeing him at all that day, nor
> suffering him to keep company with sisters and
> brothers, but put to bed without seeing you or his
> papa, and not being worthy to ask your blessing
> till the next day, when you suppose he will be a
> good boy. (St James's Place, 9 April 1776)

❊

Miss Dolly Mode, of the chapter title, was sent to G.M.A. when she was five years old, and Lady Llanover in her footnote explained that her finery was a specimen of Mrs. Delany's skill and ingenuity in needlework. Aunt Delany sent wonderful presents to the children at Ilam, tempering her severity with unusual kindness. The doll was preserved in the family for many years. Mary had advance notice of the gift.

Aunt Delany had written:

> Sweet child, *how I love her!* I am dressing a doll
> for her; but oh, sad chance, the friseur who had
> her in hand let her fall and broke her nose, and
> as some of her clothes are made and her *tete* also
> fitted, it will be some time before I get another
> doll that will do. (St. James's Place, 29 April
> 1776)

The correspondence she started on G.M.A.'s first birthday was continued. "My Dear Child," Aunt Delany wrote, placing a heavy burden on six-and-a-half-year-old shoulders:

I look upon you as *my deputy* to take care of your dear and precious mama – to nurse her when she is sick, to read to her and lull her to sleep when she is not well eno' to *talk*, and she *is*, to cheer her with your innocent and lively prattle, and, by your own gentle manners, to set an example to your dear brothers not to disturb her with any noise. Nothing can make her so happy as to see you all improving every day, and attentive to all your lessons; and pray talk a great deal of French to her, – I am sure your good Mrs. A. Vrankin will enable and encourage you to do it: pray remember me very kindly to her. I hope you will like your cloak and apron; I did not edge it with fur, which is much the fashion, as I remembered you had one of that sort, and spring is coming on. I must now pack up the box that conveys this. Your uncles [Court and John] came to town last night, and I expect them every moment.

Say everything that's kind to your dear papa and mama, and believe me ever, my dearest child, your affectionate aunt and humble servt,

M. Delany. (St. James's Place, 22 January 1778)

Lady Llanover explained in a footnote that

Mrs. Delany had been under great anxiety in the course of the year 1778 in consequence of difficulties respecting the affairs of Mr. Port of Ilam. In that year, Mrs. Port visited her in London, bringing her eldest child, G.M.A., whose parents were persuaded by Mrs. Delany to leave their daughter in her care and she actually at the age of seventy eight by her own

earnest desire, took charge of her little grand-
niece of seven years old.

Flurries of letters were exchanged reporting on how
G.M.A. was getting on away from home for the first time:

Don't imagine I mean to scribble to you every
post; no such thing, for after this letter I shall
go on with my usual weekly journal; but I
thought a confirmation of my continuing well,
and that my dear little charge is *everything* we can
wish her, wou'd not be unwelcome.

Mary [G.M.A.] is now at my elbow looking
over a drawer of shells and insists on adding
"her duty," and that "when she hears *the organ* it
always puts her in mind of dear mama". (St.
James's Place, 27 February 1779)

G.M.A. was introduced into Mrs. Delany's elegant circle:

Sunday morning it being very fine I sent
G.M.A. to early chapel to St. James's with Mrs.
Silvestre [the person engaged by Mrs. Delany.
to attend upon her little grand niece] ... In the
evening came Lady Bute, Lady Beaulieu, Lady
Cecil Rice and her daughter, etc. and yesterday
(after some scruples) I yielded to an invitation,
made in a very kind manner, to your daughter
to dine and spend the day *en famille* with her, and
as she is a very tender motherly *discreet woman*, I
thought you would have no objection, and the
dear child was delighted to go; so after *we* had
performed *all our tasks, at two we* sallied out and I
took Lady Stamford in my way, who added not
a little to *her* happiness, by inviting her to come
and dine with her young people, and meet all

the young Thynnes and stay till seven or perhaps till eight o'clock next Saturday; but I have not yet told her the day as it is at a distance, and the hope of it is a spur (*en attendant*) to *our* industry. I carried her at three to Mrs. Pott's, and delivered her into her hands ... I then pick'd up *my little treasure*, had many thanks for the trust I had reposed in them, and came directly home, very impatient indeed for the happy tidings your dear letter brought me. I indulged Mary with reading it; which she did with no small sensibility ... Had I *less delight* in this dear child than I have the thoughts of its relieving you for some time of an additional care, and the satisfaction *your partiality* takes in her being some time longer *with me*, would be sufficient to make her a welcome guest. She has walk'd twice in the park; Mr. Bolton has come every day, is now with her, and I am in treaty with Monsieur French, Lady Stamford's dancing master, for one month to teach *us* to *walk* and *curtsey*. (St. James's Place, 27 February 1779)

G.M.A. sent her own report:

I am so happy with your letter that I longed to write to dear mamma, but Mr. Bolton was cruel, tho' A.D. is not; I am very happy here. I often think of you, and wish you could now and then step over here just to see how well A.D. and I agree, and that I might kiss my dear mamma and ask her blessing. I have seen a number of fine people, and Lady Cowper all in her jewels, with a rose in the middle of her bows. My A.D.

has had a frock made up and 3 caps, which Mrs. Silvestre has made. My A.D. insists on my wearing gloves, and she tells me that I am to take rhubarb – I don't like it, but I will do it because you desire it. Mr. French is very tall, and makes fine bows, takes a great deal of pains, and says "Bravo," when I do well; I have a great deal more to tell my dearest mamma, but can only add my duty and love to Ilam.

From your dutyfull and affectionate daughter,

G.M.A. Port. (St. James's Place, 20 March 1779

Mrs. Delany insisted on G.M.A.'s learning to dance as an essential part of her grooming:

Yesterday our dear child took her first dancing lesson of Mr. French, who can give us no other time than half-an-hour after four Mond., Wed., and Friday, so I dine at three to be ready for him. I *treated* myself with seeing her *first steps*, which promise to admiration; and her master was delighted to find her so well form'd to his hands, and so ready to take instruction. She curtsy'd, she hopp'd about and beat time, and after a few handings about, repeated the same by herself to the melody of the little Kit, which he says is uncommon, as he seldom finds them ready eno' for the fiddle till after a month or two's learning in hand: indeed he seems to have a particular good method, and she was much pleased ... Bolton commends his little schollar and will soon allow her to write to you; which *in her mind* she does hourly, as well as talk to you;

I hope notwithstanding her *great sensibility* of your tenderness which she truly returns, that she is well pleased, and she most cheerfully performs all her little exercises. (St. James's Place, 6 March 1779)

A pattern of visits was established, and tutors and masters were engaged annually to bring G.M.A.'s education up to a high polish.

As each visit ended, Mrs. Delany sorely missed her child. She wrote to G.M.A. en route for Ilam with her Uncle Court Dewes:

I can't go to bed till I have written a line or two to my dear G.M.A.; and tell her how I have passed *the melancholly day*. I tried to sleep after you left me, but instead of that followed your steps (in my imagination) till I thought you were near Salt Hill, I then got up that I might eat my breakfast much at the same time I thought you and your dear uncle might be employed the same way, and hope your breakfast was relished better than mine. When that was over I wrote a letter, and then went to my work and finished the flower I began yesterday; but my little handmaid was wanting, to pick up my papers, to read to me, to hum her tune, and to prattle to me ...

A propos, the little parokets told me as well as they could speak that they miss'd you sadly, so does everyone in the house, and Smith in particular, who is but very indifferent, and says she "can make me no more gooseberry-fool" since you are not here to eat it! Mrs. Silvester looks *very sad* but goes every day now to dress

> hair in perfection against she goes to "the
> *beautiful young lady*," that makes "such a *point of
> it!*" (St. James's Place, 22 May 1779)

G.M.A. was back in St. James's Place the following year, to
the delight of Aunt Delany. She entranced the household
anew and reports of her progress were dispatched post-haste
to her mother at Ilam:

> I began a letter yesterday, and wrote two pages,
> when alas! I pour'd the ink over it, instead of
> the sand, and must begin again, tho' your
> daughter has such an opinion of your cleverness
> and eyesight, that "she is sure you could read it"
> thro' its black cloud; however, I *will not set her* an
> *example* of laziness or of being satisfied to send
> you a letter in such a dishabille ...

> Mr. Bolton is not against her writing when
> anybody can look over her. *Indeed* she *has* a
> capacity *worth cultivating*; and when she is more
> advanced in the *most useful parts of education*, her
> lively parts will easily lead her to those
> accomplishments which are of *less consequence*,
> tho' they add an agreeable polish to the whole.
> She is now sitting by me casting up sums
> against Mr. Bolton comes, with as much
> importance, as a clerk in the Secretary's office. I
> find no difficulty with her about any of her
> studies, except what regards French, I can
> seldom prevail on her to speak it, tho' she is
> ready enough to answer me when I ask her a
> question; but it is only constant practise that
> can make that easy, but she reads it intelligibly
> and understands what she reads, and Mr.
> Marlheille says she is improved already by his

lessons; but hopes when she is at home that Mrs. Vrankin will keep her to speaking constantly. Mr. French says *"Bravo,"* it is pleasant to see her step and bound like a little fawn, as he leads her about the minuet step, as you desired. She is charming well and does her dear mama credit in every way. (St. James's Place, 14 March 1780)

Well now for our ball. Did I not write you word that Dr. Burrows had taken a fancy to our dear child's sweet countenance, and invited her to dance with his children, nephews and nieces? At six we set forward, and were some of the first. I saw the ball begun, and G.M.A. dance down one dance like *any fairy*, and worthy of a more practised partner than came to her share. However she looked *so well* and *so happy* that I left her, quite satisfied. The Mistress Burrows' are very good sort of people, and tho' ranked among the female *geniuses*, *not* unmindful of *necessary attentions!* And they were delighted and *much obliged* by my trusting such a charge with them. She had nothing but simple cake and warm milk and water. I beg'd she might have no negus or lemonade, as one is *too strong* and the other *too cold* for children. I sent Rea for her in the Dss's coach *at 9 o'clock.* She came home before my circle was broke up, and entertained them all with the entertainment she had enjoyed, and assured me she could have danced 2 hours longer. She slept near 10 hours, and is vastly well, and at this time with Mr. Marlheille; and another engagement is ready for her this evening. (St. James's Place, 28 March 1780)

I think her spirits much greater than they were last year; I believe Rea being young, and cheerful, and very fond of her, is an agreable circumstance to her as well as to me, and they have *everyday* a good *game of romps*, which I wink at, as *youthful spirits must have a vent*. Her quickness of observation is often surprizing, and a very little encouragement would make her an excellent mimic – a quality which encouraged might give a turn of acrimony to her natural sweetness of disposition; I therefore check it, and tell her (which she understands very well) that those painters who deal in *Caracatura*, never produce anything that is *beautiful*. (St. James's Place, 11 April 1780)

I had a visit this morning from Mrs. Chapone and her friend Mrs. Smith and they have run away with *my child* to dinner, promising to return her between 7 and 8. The house is a *desert* without her, a stillness and void that is quite uncomfortable ...

The dear child is full of glee with the expectation of seeing the King and Queen and all the royal family on the 4 or 5th of June, the King's birthday. Mrs. Stainforth has desired me to send her to her at one o'clock on that day, and she will place her where she will see and be seen very plainly. At present her little head is full of an invitation *she* has given to the Dss of Portland, and to the Bishop of Litchfield and Mr. Montague to dine here on my birthday. I am to have *nothing* to do with it! She and Rea are to settle the dinner; and she has written to her uncle Court to be sure to be in town by that day, to assist her to entertain the company. Don't imagine I am spoyling your child, and making her conceited; far be that from me; and it is a point I have been very watchful about. (St. James's Place, 17 May 1780)

G.M.A.'s thank you letters on her return home, however, did not meet with unqualified approval:

I am always happy my dear child to receive any mark of your attention and kindness and thank you for your letter which I receiv'd this morning with one enclosed to the Duchess Dowager of Portland. Remember when you write to persons for whom you have a particular respect, that *abbreviations* are *not* respectful; and I must beg you to be *more attentive* when you write, for my credit is concerned as well as your own, and your dear mama is not well eno' and has too many fatigues to go thro' to be able to direct you in an exercise which indeed is in your own power to do well, and in which you have been so fully instructed. You know, my dear little pupil, that it was the condition of our correspondence that I should criticize your letters and I am sure you will take it as kindly as I mean it. (Bulstrode, 9 July 1780)

G.M.A. was back with Aunt Delany again the following year but returned home to assist her mama, who had another baby, a sister named Harriet. As the visit drew to a close, Aunt Delany squeezed every last drop from the tutors:

> I hope you and her papa will excuse G's not writing, as she wishes much to do, but every spare moment I wheedle her to her harpsichord as it is a pitty she should not profit as much as she can by Mr. Snow's directions. (St. James's Place, 3 May 1781)

> I am to make G.M.A.'s apology for the shortness of her letter; very willingly would she have filled a folio, but a Mr. Bolton, a Mr. French, *a Mrs. Delany*, and a Mr. Snow, make such demands on her that she must bottle up all she has to write till she can present it by word of mouth. She is pure well. (19 May 1781)

G.M.A. was almost ten when Harriet was born and Mrs. Delany encouraged her attendance at her mother's confinement:

> I am so impatient to wish my dear child joy of her mama's being brought to bed safe and well, and of your having another sister ... at present I imagine you all attention to your dear mama, delighted to be of use to her, and a comfort during her confinement; great quietness is so necessary to restore strength that there cannot be too much caution, especially this very hot, oppressive weather; but you have two such excellent assistants in your papa and A.V. [Mrs. Vrankin] that I think no lady in the straw will be better nursed, and so I leave the rest of my letter till tomorrow. (Bow Window, Whitehall, 20 June 1781)

Confinement involved complete bed rest for the mother for up to six weeks, even after a normal delivery. The great quietness alluded to by Mrs. Delany could include covering the floors and stairs with carpets and cloths, oiling the hinges of the doors, silencing the bells, tying up the knockers and, in noisy streets, strewing the pavements with straw.

Had G.M.A. learned her lessons well? A young lady of fourteen wrote to her papa from London:

> As my A.D. writes to mama, and as it is my turn to write to you, it is with great pleasure I sit down to give you an account of what I have seen and done since you last heard. First, then, I commence by saying I had the happiness of seeing Lady Tweeddale last week; she enquired after you and yours. Secondly, I have begun dancing with Slingsby, and I like him much; he has made very good scholars, and is of course a very good master. Thirdly, I have begun music with Richards, and I like him. Fourthly, I have been to see Lunard's [sic] beautiful balloon; the gallery is white and pink satin, with gold fringe. He has a table and four stools in it. I should like to go up with him, provided he does not cross the sea, as there is no danger in the world; for if it should burst it descends so gradually it is impossible to be hurt. He goes up the end of this month. Fifthly, and lastly, I go this evening to Lady Julianna Penn's; my chaperones are Lady Dartrey and Miss Hamilton. (St. James's Place, 12 February 1785)

Did Papa allow her to go up in Lunardi's hot air balloon? It was the rage of London. "All the world give their shilling to see it," Betsy Sheridan wrote to her sister in Dublin. Is it likely Aunt Delany would have ventured her precious child? The height of her aspiration for G.M.A. at that time was enclosed in the lines she wrote for her. G.M.A. was fourteen and Aunt Delany was in her eighty-fifth year:

Allons, Ma'amselle, votre reverence,
Hold yourself straight – mind time when you dance,
Sink gracefully – and *bound* with *ease;*
(*No affectation, if you please;*)
The polish of the person, and the mind
In gentleness, with spirit join'd,
Your task perform'd – then curts'y low,
And Mr. French will say – Bravo!
Your busyness done, and you at ease
To take your game at spilakees;
May conquest crown your dextrous touch!
I never can express how much
I wish you *every grace* and *Prize*
That can endear you to the good and wise.

pink
lutestring:
mrs. delany's
wardrobe

I have made her up a pink lutestring for the
King's b. day; as perhaps some of the Royal
Family may spy her out when she is peeping at
them. I *have* tried her hair up, but her forehead is
now too bald, tho' it will not appear so another
year with a little management of shaving the
young hair. She has a very easy, good air, and a
fine chest. The coat maker advises girts to be
fastened on the top of her stays, and crossed
over her shoulder blades and fastened before,
which will not appear being under her slip, to
keep her back flat for a year or so, but I *would not*
have it *done* without your approbation. Tho' *I
don't turn up her hair* I don't *suffer it* to make a
dowdy of her by *covering her forehead*, but only a
little thin shade about *an inch* over it, which looks
becoming and natural. (St. James's Place, 24
May 1780)

Lutestring was a thin, finely corded silk with a glossy surface.
It comes up frequently in Mrs. Delany's fashion correspondence as a fabric of choice for special gowns – on this occasion,
for the King's birthday. The colour pink was regarded as
highly appropriate for young girls and perfect for G.M.A.'s
first appearance at court. Eighteenth-century women were
alert to a sense of what was suited to their age, thirty being
the onset of middle age and a time to abandon frivolities like
pastel colours, feathers and flowers. Mrs. Delany had worn
pink lutestring herself as a young girl and had a particular
fondness for it.

Hairdressing was another major concern. Mrs. Delany
always made a point of it. Miss Mary Hamilton, who

recorded her stay at Bulstrode in the 1780s, said that Mrs. Delany insisted on sending her waiting woman Astley to Miss Hamilton's room to dress her hair better than her own maid could do it, and she was forced to submit. G.M.A.'s forehead and hair were very important to her general appearance. The ideal forehead was white, smooth and open, the hair not allowed to grow too deep upon it. The nine-year-old's hairline had been shaved to strengthen the young hair and clear her forehead. A letter written to G.M.A. herself drove home the point: "I forgot to tell you Miss Beckingham's hair is turned up, which has improved her looks extreamly, and they think her forehead like yours" (Glanvilla, 23 July 1781). Putting the hair up meant turning it up and back, but this would have made G.M.A. look like an owl, so Aunt Delany, ingenious as always, devised another way – a light draping of locks an inch forward – to take the bald look from her.

Contemporary advice on the care of boys' hair was on offer:

> First, every morning thoroughly wash the child's neck with cold water, especially behind the ears: and let it be well dried with a coarse cloth. Rub the head well till it smokes; this promotes circulation and dissolves all secretions and stagnations in the head. Afterwards, comb the hair with a large comb; then take about the bigness of a large nut of sweet pomatum, put it in the palm of your left hand, and with the points of your right fingers rub it well into the pores of the head all over; after which, let it be pretty well combed with a small comb, but not too much. This will sweeten the head, take all scurf from the roots of the hair, and nourish it exceedingly, always remembering that the hair be cut regularly every new moon,

and that by an experienced hand. (Richard Corson, *Fashions in Hair: The First Five Thousand Years*)

With the proper management of the hair well in hand, Aunt Delany turned her attention to G.M.A.'s stays. She was a great believer in stays for children – boys and girls – having earlier supplied the Dewes children: "I must send my little Jacky a pair of stays, and his sister, let me know what size I must bespeak" (Pall Mall, 15 January 1747). Fashions changed and, towards the latter end of the century, there was a shift in attitude towards children's freedom of movement, inspired in large by the teachings of Rousseau. However, Mrs. Delany, decidedly not a devotee, continued to promote stays for G.M.A. that she might cultivate a good air. She went further and suggested girts to brace and straighten her. This practice was quite common. She had earlier reported: "Lady Sophia Carteret is grown and improved in her person, but not in her face and she has a steel back fastened with strings round her shoulders, which she constantly wears" (Bulstrode, 29 December 1757).

Juliana-Susannah Seymour wrote with some feeling on the subject in her book *On the Management and Education of Children, 1714–1775*:

> To me there is nothing so terrible as the Sight of a Child of Quality armed and surrounded with Steel; the Back held flat by one Piece, the Shoulders kept back by another; a Bow over the Breast, and a Rib at each of the Legs ... You have seen Stays made of Packthread, let your Daughters wear these: Every body has indeed heard of and seen them, but I would have you use them. If it is difficult to find a person to make these, let them have no Stays at all; which,

perhaps, if I might speak my Mind altogether freely, is much better. I would have a Girl, till she is fourteen, wear no Stays; a tight Waistcoat may serve the Purpose.

William Buchan, too, railed against stays in his *Domestic Medicine* (1760), saying they were the bane of infants and that a volume would not suffice to point out all the bad effects of this ridiculous piece of dress. He also said he was very sorry to understand that there were still mothers mad enough to lace their daughters very tight in order to improve their shape. Aunts were equally condemned, of course, but Aunt Delany was unrepentant.

❉

From the very beginning of her correspondence, the then Mrs. Pendarves was avidly interested in fashion and clothes. Though somewhat restricted by her gouty, bad-tempered husband Mr. Pendarves, she managed to escape him sufficiently often to attend weddings, balls, operas and royal gala occasions, where the great aristocratic families dressed to kill. The correct dress was a prerequisite for participating in these events. Richness of dress indicated rank, wealth and belonging. The art of dressing well was not just a point of good manners but also a necessary prop to established society. It marked the territory of the ruling élite until the insolent middle classes began to ape them when cheaper imports of silks, satins, damasks, laces and finery flooded the English market from the middle of the century. Then it was more difficult to tell the difference.

Making the grand figure was the prerogative and duty of the aristocratic families. Anne Granville would not lag in the fashion stakes, and Mrs. Pendarves (later Delany) spared no pains in sending lavish descriptions of the London styles to

Gloucester. "Now for the modes: – There is a great liberty taken in dress; everybody pleases themselves. A great many people curl the hair round the face, the young and handsome become it. Ribbon is not very much worn" (Somerset House, 11 November 1727). Anne was kept supplied with patterns and fabrics and instructions. The letters at this stage of the correspondence are young and lively. Mrs. Pendarves revelled as much in describing the fashions as her alter ego Mrs. Delany did in describing her menus. Meanwhile, wedding settlements and society entertainments formed part of the girlish gossip.

A newlywed's trousseau always aroused great interest:

> Yesterday I was to see the bride my lady Walpole who was married the day before. She was excessively fine, in the handsomest and richest gold and white stuff that ever I saw, a fine point head, and very fine brilliant earings and cross. Mrs. Rolle [mother of the bride] was in a pink and silver lutestring, and Mrs. Walpole [mother-in-law] in a white and gold and silver ... Everybody had favours that went, men and women: they are silver gauze bows, and eight of gold narrow ribbon in the middle: they cost a guinea a piece; eight hundred has already been disposed of. (28 March 1724)

The marriage of Margaret Rolle to Lord Robert Walpole, son of the former prime minister and brother of Horace Walpole, proclaimed by its opulence the arrival of this couple onto the world stage. There was no doubting their wealth or rank. Mrs. Pendarves described Lady Walpole's white and gold silk damask as "stuff", a term that originally applied to plain woollen cloth but one she frequently used to describe fine fabrics. Lady Walpole's point head was a needlepoint headdress or cap, made for this occasion of the finest Brussels, Mechlin or Valenciennes lace.

> Lady Frances Hamilton is soon to be married to Mr. Sanderson, a brother of Lord Scarborough; she is to have ten thousand pound down, and ten thousand pound after Lord Orkney's death ...
>
> I must tell you of a new entertainment I have had, which was the Masquerade last Tuesday. We dispatched Moll and Bess before us, and said not one word of our design of going, but as soon as they were gone we dressed ourselves in black dominos ... I was much pleased with it, and like it so well as to hope one day to have the pleasure of going with you to one ... I will dress up your head, and am proud you should prefer my fingers before any other. (London, 16 May 1723)

> Next Wednesday the Duke of Norfolk gives a masquerade; everybody is to be extravagantly fine, and to pull off their masques before they leave the house. (Somerset House, 11 May 1728)

Masked balls or masquerades were entertainments where the participants dressed in coy or outrageous costumes and parried witty epithets to conceal, or possibly reveal, their identities. There was a verbal code of introductory set phrases, such as "I know you" or "Do you know me", providing fertile ground for flirtation and ribaldry. When the writer Mary Wollstonecraft was employed as a governess in Ireland, her long-suffering mistress, Lady Kingsborough, cajoled her into attending a masquerade in Dublin in 1787 and lent her a black domino. This was a dark, loose cloak of Venetian origin, which disguised the whole person. It represented intrigue, adventure, conspiracy and mystery and was worn by both sexes for that extra *frisson*. The mask, concealing the gender, was kept on by means of a glass bead fixed inside, which was held between the teeth.

The Kingsborough party first visited the houses of several people of fashion whose task it was to discover the identities behind the masks, and Mary Wollstonecraft seized on the opportunity to show off.

> We ... were a tolerable, nay, a much admired group. Lady K. went in a domino, with a smart cockade. Miss Moore dressed in the habit of one of the females, of the new discovered islands, Betty D. as a forsaken shepherdess – and your sister Mary in a black domino. As it was taken for granted the stranger who was just arrived, could not speak the language, I was to be her interpreter, which afforded me an ample field for satire.

The youthful Mrs. Pendarves attended masquerades with glee, though the middle-aged, censorious Mrs. Delany strongly disapproved of them. They became quite notorious, not least because the intermingling of classes blurred the caste lines but also because "the whole Design of the libidinous Assembly seems to terminate in Assignations and intrigues" (Roy Porter, *English Society in the Eighteenth Century*). The most famous masquerades in the latter part of the century were hosted by Mrs. Teresa Cornelys, a famous impresario who converted her house in Soho Square in London to host subscription balls. Mrs. Delany mentions them with disapproval in the correspondence. For one such ball at Mrs. Cornelys's establishment in 1770, ordinary dominoes were forbidden; elaborate disguises had to be hired or made, and one swain turned up as Adam in flesh-coloured silk with an apron of fig leaves embroidered on it "fitting the body with the utmost niceness", which led to "unavoidable indelicacy" (Liza Picard, *Dr. Johnson's London: Everyday Life in London 1740–1770*).

❧

Fashions changed slowly through the eighteenth century but, allowing for fluctuations, the typical outfit of a gentlewoman like Mrs. Pendarves, later Mrs. Delany, was a multi-layered construction. Next to her skin she wore a chemise, a short, straight underskirt like a half-slip, sometimes called a "coat". Over this she wore a knee-length chemise or slip with a low neckline gathered on a ribbon drawstring and usually lace-edged. These undergarments were usually made of fine linen or lawn. Stockings came next, knitted or machine-made, of wool or silk. The finest silk stockings were decorated at the ankles and up the leg with embroidered trimmings called clocks. Garters held the stockings up, either above or below the knee. Knickers or drawers were not known until early in the nineteenth century, when an open-leg variety appeared. Eighteenth-century women found the chemise and "coat" perfectly adequate. During menstruation women resorted to sedentary occupations or retired to the sofa altogether, hence one of the many tags used to describe having a period: "being the French lady". Menstrual rags were made from torn strips of cotton or linen.

Over the chemise came the ubiquitous stays, a stiffened corset or bustier-like garment made usually from two layers of heavy linen or buckram stiffened with paste or glue. Further stiffening of cane, straw or whalebone was sewn in vertical rows of backstitching, and for a particularly formal gown, the ribs were sewn in a horizontal direction as well, forcing an erect posture. Ribbons or laces were threaded through eyelet holes along the edges to lace the stays tightly. It was believed that stays were necessary to give support to the bust and to push the shoulders back. Lighter versions were even worn at night. While approving of stays, Mrs. Delany did not hold with any kind of excessive lacing and poor Miss Sparrow was in the firing line again. Mrs. Delany wrote:

> I hope Miss Sparrow will not fall into the absurd fashion of the *wasp-waisted* ladies. Dr. Pringle declares he has had four of his patients martyrs to that folly (indeed *wickedness*), and when they were open'd it was evident that their *deaths* were occasioned by *strait lacing*. (Bulstrode, I October 1775)

As the century progressed, the desired shape of the bosom changed from a wide expanse in the early part to a flattened effect in the middle years, achieved by high lacing of the stays. By the 1780s, a pouter-pigeon, stuffed crop look was fashionable, the natural bosom augmented by layers of starched muslin or even "bosom friends" of wool or flannel. Miss Sparrow was probably trying to achieve this effect.

The next item of dress was the hoop. Structurally, hoops were like the scaffolding of a dome, but the parabola changed through the century as the fashions changed to give bell-, oval-, tulip-, kidney- or fan-shaped curves as each came into vogue. The hoops, usually made of whalebone or cane, were tied with tapes around the waist. Side-hoops or "false hips" replaced full hoops, except for court-wear, by the 1750s; these were hinged to the waist. False rumps, bosoms and patent bolsters made of horsehair and wadding were worn by the latter part of the century – the weight must have been quite considerable.

The correct manipulation of the hoop, particularly when it was very wide, in the 1730s and 1740s (and throughout the century for court), was a sign of good breeding. This was where the dancing master came in. His pupil had to learn how to move backwards from the royal presence. For presentation at court, she had to curtsy in a huge stiff-bodied gown with hoop and kiss the hem of the queen's gown, having first taken off her glove. She then had to command sufficient composure to hold a brief conversation. Next came the retreat, where she had to move backwards making three more curtsies along the way, manipulating the enormous train of her dress as she went. This feat had to be carried off in a seemingly effortless glide under the beady eyes of the entire court.

The petticoat was an underskirt that went over the hoops and distended towards the hem. The stomacher, which was usually covered in a matching fabric, was a separate piece. It was a stiffened pasteboard panel or shield, which narrowed from the neckline to a point over the stomach. It met the petticoat at or below the waist. The stomacher, along with the stays, reinforced a rigid upper body. A busk was a strong piece of wood or whalebone

> thrust down the middle of the stomacher to keep it streight and in compass, that the Breast nor Belly shall not swell too much out. These Busks are usually made in length according to the necessity of the Persons wearing it: if to keep in the fullness of the Breasts, then it extends to the Navel; if to keep the Belly down, then it reacheth to the Honour. (Randle Holme, *The Academy of Armory*, 1688)

The most formal open-robed gown was called a mantua. Typically, this was a skirt and bodice ensemble, open in front to show off the decorated stays or stomacher and petticoat. It was somewhat like an open coat that did not meet in the middle. The bodice was anchored with pins, hooks and eyes or buttons or laced across the front of the stays with bows called echelles. The skirt opened in front to show the petticoat. To this ensemble a handkerchief was added around the neckline for modesty, a lace cap and heeled shoes donned and the outfit, though devoid of laces or ruffles, trimmings or jewellery, was suitable for a gentlewoman of quality to make or receive her visits.

The original mantua was a kimono-like construction, which evolved into the open robe. It is thought to have acquired its name either from the French *manteau* or because early examples were made from Italian silk from Mantua. The style became so widespread that dressmakers were commonly called mantua-makers. Other types of gowns included the "closed robe", which was a joined bodice and skirt dress with no front opening; and the sack dress, which was a particularly elegant gown with distinctive box pleats falling down from the neckline at the back, making a pleated, floor-length train. For household tasks a separate skirt and bodice combination was sometimes worn, the bodice unboned for ease and comfort.

For ladies of leisure or those not involved in the supervision of servants, a fashionable dishabille or undress called a "wrapping gown" or nightgown was sometimes worn. This gown had fullness in the back, was crossed-over or wrapped in the front and secured with a clasp, brooch, sash or girdle at the waist. It was worn for morning strolls in the park but was not considered full dress. While this gown gave an appearance of freedom, stays were worn underneath.

Most gowns appeared to be very substantial garments but were actually precariously fastened with pins to hold everything in place. The *manteau de lit* was a wrap-over worn in the evening before retiring or in the morning before dressing.

Getting dressed and undressed required the services of a lady's maid. Her job was to lace the stays, fix and tie the tapes and panniers, pin the bodice to the stays or stomacher, curl and powder the hair and pat, tweak and pull the whole ensemble into perfection. This job required nimbleness. In her later years, Mrs. Delany used her influence with Queen Charlotte to obtain a position as dresser for the novelist Miss Fanny Burney. Lady Llanover, editor of Mrs. Delany's letters, who was deeply unimpressed with Miss Burney's presumption, wrote:

> Mrs. Delany ... had not seen enough of her to be aware how utterly unfit she was for any place requiring punctuality, neatness, and *manual dexterity*; [Queen Charlotte used to complain to Mrs. Delany that Miss Burney could not learn to tie the bow of her necklace on Court days without giving her pain by getting the hair at the back of the neck tied in with it] and that she had not sufficient sound sense, judgement, or discrimination to preserve *her own equilibrium*, if placed in a sphere so different to that in which she had been brought up.

❧

There was a great many fine clothes on the birthday. Lady Sunderland was very fine and very genteel. Her clothes were in the finest pale blue and pink, very richly flowered in a running pattern of silver frosted and tissue with a little white, a new Brussels head, and

Lady Oxford's jewels. Bess [Elizabeth Tichborne, Lady Sunderland's sister] had on a pale lemon-coloured lutestring and look'd like a witch, at least her sister's good looks were no advantage to her. I was at Lady Carteret's toilette, whose clothes were pretty, pale straw lutestring and flowered with silver, and new Brussels head ... Lady Carteret has just sent to me to go to the opera with her. (Beaufort Buildings, 30 May 1724)

Lady Carteret's toilette was a sort of audience of admirers at her dressing-table, a warm-up before going out for the day. Male and female hangers-on commonly gossiped and twittered while the hair was dressed and the final touches were added. The looking-glass on the dressing-table was usually as adorned as the lady. Mrs. Delany sent fulsome instructions to Anne and later to Mary on the fitting out of their dressing tables. Queen Caroline, the reigning monarch, had a looking-glass that was a veritable altar to beauty. It was draped in crimson damask with "head" made in Brussels bobbin lace and tied with a silver tassel, her silver gilt toilet set arrayed before it. The young Mrs. Pendarves of this period was not exempt from the vanity of the toilette either. "I am to be curled and friz'd," she wrote, "and am not yet a bit dressed; I can no longer rob my toilette of my person, but must take my leave of you for this post" (Somerset House, 14 March 1728). "Yesterday (as my tail was pinning up) he came [a suitor]: he was not very gay, but enquired very much after you, and entertained me with his journey to town" (19 November 1728). On another occasion she wrote, "Tomorrow is the Birthday. I shall be fine, but like the jay in borrowed feathers ... My head is drest, and Mr. Wise who is at my toilette says, 'prodigious well'" (28 February 1729).

She cut a dash.

On Saturday the first day of March, it being Queen Caroline's birth-day, I dressed myself in all my best array, borrowed my Lady Sunderland's jewels, and made a tearing show. I went with my Lady Carteret and her two daughters. There was a vast Court, and my Lady Carteret got with some difficulty to the circle, and after she had made her curtsey made me stand before her. The Queen came up to her, and thanked her for bringing me forward, and she told me she was obliged to me for my pretty clothes, and admired my Lady Carteret's extremely; she told the Queen that they were my fancy, and that I drew the pattern. Her Majesty said she had heard that I could draw very well (I can't think who could tell her such a story); she took notice of my jewels; I told her they were my Lady Sunderland's (I think it is a great condescention, after all this, to correspond with a country girl!) ...

The King was in blue velvet, with diamond buttons; the hat was buttoned up with pro-digious fine diamonds. The Queen was in black velvet, the Court being out of mourning only for that day. Princess Royal had white poudesoy, embroidered with gold, and a few colours intermixed; the petticoat was very handsome, but the gown looked poor, it being only faced and robed with embroidery. Princess Amely had a yellow and silver stuff, the pattern marked out with a thread of purple, and purple ribbons with pearl in her head, which became her.

Princess Caroline had pink colour damask, trimmed with silver. The Prince of Wales was in mouse-colour velvet, turned up with scarlet, and very richly embroidered with silver; he dances very well, especially country-dances, for he has a great deal of spirit. Lady Carteret's clothes were the finest there – green and gold, embroidered and trimmed; Miss Carteret yellow and silver. Lady Hartford had a blue manteau, embroidered with gold, and a white satin petticoat; it looked very whimsical, and not pretty. (Somerset House, 4 March 1729)

Tailor's paper patterns existed from the seventeenth century and patterns were also often taken from unpicked gowns. These were exchanged between sisters, cousins and friends and improvised along the way. Mrs. Pendarves was highly skilled in drawing and cut-work and drew up her own patterns. Pattern-making continued to be a necessary and useful skill into the next century. Mrs. Rundell gives directions on how to make black paper for drawing patterns in her *Domestic Cookery*, 1806. Many ladies designed their own dresses and, as silk and fine materials were very expensive, they refurbished and remade their old ones. The mantua-maker generally made the basic dress and the milliner made the trimmings, though these distinctions were not absolute. A lady's maid who could sew well and adjust the trimmings to her mistress's liking would prove an invaluable asset. A prodigious amount of hand-sewing was done. Gentlewomen commonly brought sewing in their workbags from house to house and worked away on their ruffles, fringing or knotting during their visits. Grander decorative schemes might require reinforcements, and there are many instances in the correspondence of sewing-bees. Women of Mrs. Pendarves' class were usually proficient if not superlative needlewomen. As her own talents extended to design, she created sumptuous decorative schemes for her own court dresses.

Gowns from the 1720s to the 1740s were usually worn untrimmed except for court. The silks were very heavy but crisp and fell into such lovely sculptural folds that no other decorations were required. Figured damasks in white, pale blue, pink and bright, clear yellow were very popular. There were also brocades and figured silks with large floral designs, and also with wide stripes. Silks from the looms of the Huguenot weavers in Spitalfields in London were especially beautiful at this period, though the weavers were constantly embattled against a tide of smuggled imports from France and Italy. Mrs. Pendarves wrote:

> My clothes were a French silk, I happened to meet with a great pennyworth – they cost me seventeen pounds ... the ground dark grass green, brocaded with a running pattern like a lace of white intermixed with festoons of flowers in faint colours. My ribbons were pink and silver, my head well drest, French and a cockard that looked smart. (14 March 1729)

Her clothes were indeed a great pennyworth. Seventeen pounds sterling translates roughly in contemporary values to eighteen hundred pounds sterling, which gives a good idea of the money Mrs. Pendarves had at her disposal for personal adornment and of the amount she was willing to pay for French silk, which may or may not have come from the Spitalfields looms. French manners and fashions, while derided on the one hand, were carefully noted on the other. Mrs. Pendarves sent this account to Anne following her reading of *Female Falsehood or the Life and Adventures of a late French Nobleman*:

> They wear their stays extravagantly low, their sleeves very short and wide, petticoats short, English dormeuses, and the girdle not in the least peaked down; you have not had so much of

fashions from me since my being in town, and may not have so much again till next year, so make much of this. (Lower Brook Street, 28 March 1734).

More French fashion was to come:

> I was not at the *Cour* [Court], therefore cannot be very particular in my account of the Birthday ... The only particular lady was the Duchess of Richmond, who is just returned from Paris. She was quite in the French mode, her clothes very fine and handsome – silver tissue ground and velvet flowers; her head was yellow gauze, and her lappets tied with puffs of scarlet ribbon about two inches distance. A long train was worn over the petticoat. (Extract undated)

Lappets were pendants, usually of lace or cambric, hanging from the headdress at either side of the head.

After the royal wedding of the Princess of Orange in 1733, Anne was informed: "the Princess of Orange's dress was the prettiest thing that ever was seen – a *corps de robe*, that is, in plain English, a stiff-bodied gown". However, the long hours circulating and curtsying in boned gowns, stays and stomachers were exhausting, even for the most enthusiastic courtier:

> Last night I returned from Court, cold and weary ... into bed I tumbled about half an hour after one. I slept tolerably well, dreamt of nothing at all, waked at eight, roused Mrs. Bell, huddled on my clothes, bought eighteen yards of very pretty white silk for Trott, something in the nature of shagreen, but a better colour than they ever are; it cost sixpence a yard more; the

piece came to three pounds and twelve shilling.
(19 November 1728)

Throughout the 1720s, long lists were sent from Gloucester for fabrics, laces and fripperies, and Mrs. Pendarves supplied, not just Anne, but also the neighbourhood. Trott's white silk shagreen was a kind of silk velvet taffeta that imitated the pimpled texture of shark- or fish-skin. "I want to know how you like your things," Mrs. Pendarves asked.

> Your laces look very grey, but they are Mrs. C.'s doing; the English head is not well dressed up but I had not time to alter, for they came home but just before they were packed up. I am afraid Miss Matt will not like her fan, but tell her quadrille is all the mode, and the sticks were mended in so many places that they told me they did not deserve a better mount; the price was three and sixpence. I am very happy in the good account I have of my dear mama. (12 December 1724)

In the same letter, she advised on mourning garb:

> I think her (Mrs. Carter) in the right in buying a white satin to top her black, for the reasons she gives me; but she can only wear as a nightgown, and if she was in town she should wear only mourning when she is dressed, but in the country that will not be minded, white gloves, coloured fan and coloured shoes, and edgings if she pleases, and black or white short apron and girdle which she likes best. My mama must not wear black handkerchiefs with her second year's mourning. Mr. Pendarves is

confined with the gout in his foot: he has had a
very violent cold, but it is now pretty well again!
(12 December 1724)

Mourning etiquette was rigidly complied with, and Mrs.
Pendarves was something of an expert. Strict rules governed
the degree of mourning, its duration and the colours to be
worn. Mourning was donned not just for members of the
immediate family but also for distant relatives. It was *de rigueur*
for royal deaths. White was also worn for deep mourning,
sometimes on the death of a child. When Mrs. Pendarves
referred to Mrs. Carter's "nightgown", she meant a loose
wrap-over or wrapping gown worn informally, mornings or
evenings, not a nightshift for wearing in bed. A nightgown was
an intermediary dress worn before being fully formally
dressed. It was worn with stays or sometimes even a hoop, so
any suggestion of comfort was an illusion.

On another occasion she wrote:

> In the box with the linnen there is mama's black
> poudesoy gown and petty coat, your white
> pettycoat, and mama's two hoods; (but I will
> never again employ these people), also three
> japan bords, six forks and spoons, and French
> silver saltsellers, and a pair of China ones, which
> you may think old fashion, but it is the new
> mode, and all the saltsellers are now made in
> that manner. There is a little Tunbridge jewel box
> which Mrs. Tillier [sic] desires you to accept as
> her fairing; in the first partition there is three
> cakes of lip salve in the next a solitary ring ... in
> the next is the overplus money of the five
> guineas, and in the last is my mother's six pound
> ten shillings, and Mrs. Badge's account how she
> has laid out the money. (5 October 1727)

This wonderful box held Mama's black gown and petticoat of poudesoy, which was a strong, corded grosgrain silk. The Tunbridge box, a gift from Mrs. Tellier, was well stocked. Mademoiselle Tellier had been Mary Granville's French governess at her Aunt Stanley's. In one of the small compartments there were three cakes of lip salve. This type of cosmetic was often made up at home, so Anne probably relished hers from a London apothecary. Sarah Neale's manuscript book has a receipt for lip salve. It directs:

> 4 ozs of fresh beef suet or marrow, unsalted butter or hogs lard (whichever you like best) – 3 ozs beeswax – half an ounce of Alcany [Alkanet] Roots, half an ounce of Storax [a balsam of Liquidambar orienatalis], half an ounce of Gumbenjamine [a resin], one slice Peppin – 2 ounces of Loaf Sugar – 6 spoonfuls of Clarret and 4 of Sack. Let all these ingredients boil together till it is of a good colour then strain it off and drop it into 6 penny worth of Balsam of Peru [a balsam or resin from Myroxylon Pereirae, an excellent application for sore nipples or cracked lips].

The alkanet root provided the red colour, the sack and claret the preservative, and the suet, balsams and beeswax the unguent lubrication and pleasant perfume, a delight for any beaux.

> We dine tomorrow with Sir John at Somerset House: at four o'clock in the afternoon comes my lawyer and my taylor, two necessary animals. Next morning I send for Mrs. Woodfelds to alter my white tabby [a glossy watered silk] and my new clothes, and to take my black velvet to

make; then comes Mrs. Boreau to clip my locks, then I dress to visit Lady Carteret, then I come home to dinner, then I drink coffee after dinner, then I go to see my niece Basset and Mrs. Livingstone ... I will give you a full and true account of all the fops and fopperies I meet with. (Northend, 8 November 1726)

News of the fops, fopperies and fripperies went directly to Anne, who was staying in Bath at this time, convalescing from a bout of illness:

> Your white satin came home last week, and is prodigiously pretty. I have sent it to be made and shall send it to the Bath this week. I shall send at the same time my Brussels night-clothes, which I desire you will wear, and tear if you please, as long as you flaunt it at the Bath. (16 September 1729)

There was more frippery news.

> I have this morning bought me a scarlet damask manteau and petticoat, and a gold-colour tabby night-gown. (Somerset House, 9 October 1729).

> I hope I shall be able to send the box by Saturday's carrier with Mrs. Greville's gown which I sent to the man as soon as I received it, and shall today get the screen and the buckles ... Gauze heads are now the top mode: I will send you one exactly in the fashion and charge you to wear it without any alterations. You will think it strange coarse stuff, but it is as good as the Queen's and sure that's good enough for you. (20 November 1729)

I am going to get ribbons, gloves, and some more frippery things for my journey. (Upper Brook Street, 15 October 1730)

The journey was to Ireland where the young widow, Mrs. Pendarves, was warmly welcomed on her first visit. She reported on a state ball at Dublin Castle, which was a little less sophisticated than she was used to:

> on the first of March we went to Court in the morning ... and listened to music and songs ... then bad dinner and went again at seven. The ball was in the old beefeaters hall, a room that holds seven hundred people seated, it was well it did, for never did I behold a greater crowd. We were all placed in rows one above another, so much raised that the last row almost touched the ceiling! The gentlemen say we look very handsome, and compared us to Cupid's Paradise in the puppet-show. At eleven o'clock minuets were finished, and the Duchess went to the basset table.
>
> After an hours playing [basset was a popular card game] the Duke, Duchess [of Dorset] and nobility marched into the supper table ... When the doors were first opened, the hurly burly is not to be described; squawling, shrieking, all sorts of noises, some ladies lost their lappets, others were trod upon. Poor Lady Santry almost lost her breath in the scuffle, and fanned herself two hours before she could recover herself enough to know if she was dead or alive. (I March 1731)

Mrs. Pendarves took up the cause of Irish textile man-ufacture on arrival. She praised the Irish glovers and sent gifts of several pairs to Anne. William Shubridge of Watling Street and Edward Sweehenham of Dame Street are among the glovers listed for the year 1732 in *Watson's Almanack*. Their handiwork may have graced Anne's small white hands. Mrs. Pendarves planned to smuggle her some Irish "stuff", probably poplin, at the first opportunity. Poplin was a mixed fabric of silk warp and worsted (wool) weft. The beauty of its soft sheen and its durability made poplin very popular. In the previous century Irish wool exports had threatened the English wool trade, and a protectionist policy was instituted to inhibit the free export of Irish cloths. A bill of 1699 ordered:

> Laying four shillings duty on every twenty shillings value of broad cloth (woollen cloth) exported out of Ireland and 2 shillings duty on every twenty shillings value of serges, baizes, kerseys, stuffs, or any other sort of new drapery made of wool or mixed with wool.

Poplin was just such a new drapery mixed with wool.

Jonathan Swift had published a pamphlet in 1720, *A Proposal for the Universal Use of Irish Manufacture, in Cloaths, and Furniture of Houses, etc. Utterly Rejecting and Renouncing Every Thing Wearable that Comes from England.* This was the spur for a certain coterie, Mrs. Pendarves among them, who determined to promote local manufacture. They set an example by sporting Irish cloths to the gala occasions at the Castle, Dublin's answer to the royal court:

> Mrs. Donellan and I have each of us made a brown stuff manteau and petticoat, and have worn them twice at the assemblies; pretty things they have produced … We gave sixteen pence a yard! I wish I could convey a suit to you, but they are prohibited; however I will, when I return try if I can cheat for you. (Dublin, 17 January 1732)

This was an object lesson to the upwardly mobile run of Castle society, who were generally more anxious to show off expensive foreign imports than support local enterprise. Some Dublin mercers fought back:

> Hoggart and Vincent, Woolen-Manufacturers, at the Hibernian Industry in Cork-Hill opposite Dame St. Dublin make and sell all sorts of Irish Broad Cloaths, Beaver Druggets, Ratteens, Lutherines, Proneloes, Shags, Shagreen and Variety of Linings, with Velvets as good as any Imported from Genoa or Holland; and sundry other Draperies at the most Reasonable Rates. NB Livery cloths d'yed in the Wooll. (*Dublin Daily Advertiser*, 1 November 1736)

Meanwhile, there was news from England that Mrs. Pendarves' fine bachelor brother, Bernard Granville, was setting trends of his own:

> You said not one word to me about Bunny's wearing his own hair. I had a letter yesterday from Lady Carteret; she writes me word that he "looks *very well* with his new-adorned pate." Tell me what you think? I *fancy* a wig became him better; what provoked him to cut *so bold a stroke?* (Killalla, 4 February 1733)

Men wore wigs as part of everyday dress, the most popular being the "bob wig" with a central parting and curls like sausage rolls on either side. The maintenance of the wigs was a constant fuss and expense. They required a battery of equipment, including wig-bags and ribbons, wig boxes, stands, ivory or wide-toothed combs, wig powder and bellows. The powder was usually some form of starch, which could be scented with orange flower, lavender or orris root or tinted a pink, blue or mauve hue for that extra *élan*.

A gentleman's head was close shaven to fit the wig snugly, and at home in retirement he would remove his wig and put on his nightcap, a turban-like affair to keep his head warm. He would also don his banyan or loose wrap-over gown, worn over his shirt and breeches, and thus attired would retreat to his library to study or read or chat with his friends. By "wearing his own" hair, Bernard Granville would avoid all the fuss, and his new requirements could be supplied from Dublin if necessary:

> John Grace. Ivory Comb-Maker from London, next Door to the White-Lyon, opposite to Mountrath Street in Pill Lane, makes and sells all sorts of Ivory-combs by Whole sale and Retail, at reasonable Rates. As Toirtoise-Shell and Silver Combs. NB The Silver-Combs turns the Hairs of the Head or Eyebrows from Grey or Red to a fine Mouse Colour. (*Dublin Daily Advertiser*, 21 October 1736)

Hairstyling for men became almost as demanding as for women towards the latter quarter of the century. Court Dewes described his experience of *haute coiffeur* while on a visit to Paris in 1776:

> For the first ten days I was in lodgings at 2 guineas a week, had my coach and my laquais, besides Edmund, my own valet de chambre. The day after my arrival (which you will think more incredible) I sat *two hours* to have my hair dressed, and I had 36 papillotes in it, which I had the curiosity to count; but do not imagine from that I am going to turn out a fine gentleman at an age

when it would be time (as to externals at least) to lay that character aside. I intend all the flutter shall pass away as I pass from Paris, and fancy you will see me return as *plain* and as *frugal* as ever. (Paris, 6 November 1776)

❧

On her return to Dublin after her marriage in 1743 to Dr. Patrick Delany, the new Mrs. Delany settled happily in Delville outside Dublin. She took up her support for Irish textile manufacture again. Floods of imports from England swamped the market. By 1753, the *Dublin Directory* lists such imports as:

Beaver Skins and Beaver Wool, French Indigo, Old and New Drapery; Silks, raw, thrown, and manufactured; Cambricks, Hollands, Lawns, Muslins; Cotton, Silk and Thread Stockings; Worsted and Silk ditto and Breeches; Calicoes; Silk and Hair Shags; Silk Ribbon, Cottons, Mohair-Buttons, Fustians, Chequers, Tapes, Kentings, Gold and Silver Thread and Lace, Bone-Lace, Linsey-wool-seys, Camblets, Millinery Wares, Hoops ... Looking-Glass Plates etc.

Lord Philip Dormer Stanhope, Fourth Earl of Chesterfield, and his wife, Melusina de Schulenberg, were due to arrive in Dublin for their first tour of duty when Mrs. Delany wrote:

The yachts are to go this day for my Lord Lieut., so in a few days I suppose we shall have them. I design to make my first visit in an *Irish stuff manteau and petticoat*, and a *head* the Dean has given me of Irish work, the prettiest I ever saw of the kind; he has made me also a present of a repeating-watch and a diamond ring; the diamond is a brilliant, but such gems are only valuable when they are testimonials of a kind and affectionate heart; as such to me they are inestimable. (Delville, 24 August 1745)

Lady Chesterfield took up a campaign of promoting Irish industry, though Mrs. Delany gave herself the credit.

On the Princess of Wales's birthday there appeared at court a great number of Irish stuffs. Lady Chesterfield was dressed in one, and I had the secret satisfaction of knowing myself to have been the cause, but dare not say so here; but I say, "I am glad to find my Lady Chesterfield's example has had so good an influence." The poor weavers are starving, all trade had met with a great check this year. (Delville, 23 November 1745)

The crusade was kept up: "Next Monday we are all prepared to appear at the Castle in Irish stuffs; I have bought a *sprigged* one"(18 January 1746). "Yesterday I went to the Castle to pay my compliments to Lady Chesterfield, who has had a very long confinement with St. Anthony's fire; she looked very ill. I was dressed in my Birthday poplin and looked very fine" (Delville, 18 January 1746).

The Delanys went even further and presented Irish stuffs to family and friends in England:

I am very glad you like the poplin, and the Dean is very proud my mother approves of hers. I have got one for Mrs. Viney and for each of her daughters, which I will send to England by the first opportunity. I desire their directions, who they shall be consigned to. I can't undertake to bring them as they are prohibited, but a person skilled in those affairs has undertaken care of them. (Delville, 5 April 1746)

A visit to England every third year was part of the agreement reached between Dr. and Mrs. Delany on their marriage, though in twenty-odd years of marriage they actually spent only fourteen in Ireland. On home soil, her fashion reporting took on a glamour she could not match in Dublin. On a visit in 1746, her social life had picked up extraordinary pace. In the space of a few days after her arrival, she had been at St. James's, the Duchess of Queensbury's, Whitehall, Carlton House, Mrs. Montagu's at Hanover Square and at Leicester House for the queen's birthday. She sent this report:

> The Duchess of Portland was in white satin, the petticoat ruffled, and robings and facings. She had all her fine jewels on, and looked handsomer than ever I saw her look in my life ... There was not much new finery, new clothes not being required on this Birthday ... They curl and wear a great many tawdry things, but there is such a variety in the manner of dress, that I don't know what to tell you is the fashion; the only thing that seems general are hoops of an enormous size, and most people wear vast winkers to their heads. They are now come to such an extravagance in those two particulars, that I expect soon to see the other extreme of thread-paper heads and no hoops, and from appearing like so many *blown bladders* we shall look like so many *bodkins stalking about*. (Pall Mall, 21 January 1746)

The Duchess of Portland's rig-out was trimmed with ruffles, robings and facings. Robings, often noted in letters by Mrs. Delany, were bands of lace or embroidery brought around from the back of the neck, over the shoulders and fastened to the edges of the stomacher or stays, like an ornate collar. They were worn on state occasions. The size and shape of hoops had changed with the century to the enormous flattened oval of this period. Gowns worn in this fashion were often too wide to go through doorways, so the wearer had to pivot in sideways. Headdresses had changed, too, from petite lace caps fitting snugly to the back or top of the head. Caps now were circular, edged with ruffles of linen or lace, or the round-eared cap, which curved like a bonnet to the level of the ears. From the mid 1740s there was a fashion for wiring the side frills of these caps, hence Mrs. Delany's winkers.

From the centre of the fashionable world, once the trip was over, it was back home to Delville, where life was very happy but humdrum:

> Yesterday morning I for the first day since I came worked four hours at *my Quilt*, and Mr. Greene read to us. Bushe painted, and Mrs. Greene made a night-gown for the little boy. One day next week we are to go a house-warming to her. Mantua-makers and housekeeper etc. call me away. (Delville, 13 June 1747)

This quiet life notwithstanding, she was able to fill Anne in on the gossip: "All you have heard of the Miss Gunnings *is true*, except their having a fortune, which I am afraid they have a *greater* want than that, which is *discretion!*" (Delville, 8 June 1750).

The Gunnings, Elizabeth and Maria, were the two lovely daughters of John and Bridget Gunning of Castlecoote, Co. Roscommon. Their mother was the former Bridget Bourke, sixth daughter of Viscount Bourke of Mayo. They were launched on the London scene, allegedly in clothes borrowed from the Irish actress Peg Woffington. They were so beautiful they literally brought the city to a halt, with hundreds of onlookers coming out to gape at them wherever they appeared. They may have lacked discretion – there is an anecdotal report that Maria on meeting George II told him the only grand spectacle she longed to see was a coronation. He, apparently, was very amused. They certainly lacked fortune – that much was true – but they were abundantly supplied with other attributes. Many an ambitious mama was thwarted when the Gunnings netted a title each. Elizabeth married the Sixth Duke of Hamilton and Maria married George, Sixth Earl of Coventry, and became the Countess Coventry.

When the newly married Lady Louisa (Lennox) Connolly, bride of Mr. Thomas Connolly of Castletown House, Co. Kildare, made her debut in London she met the Gunning sisters at a ball in Richmond House. She reported, "The Duchess of Hamilton is lovely!" and went on to describe Lady Coventry as fashionably dressed in a "cap perched up three miles high, and puffed lappets set hollow from the head in order, I believe, to look like wings". Lady Louisa had come over from Ireland with a great reputation for beauty, and Lady Coventry is reported to have declared when she saw her, "Well, thank God! She is not near so handsome as Lady Kildare [Louisa's sister, Emily]. Now I have seen her I am easy."

❧

On the Dublin scene, Mrs. Delany had rivals of her own:

> Wednesday, the Birthday. I went with Mrs. Clayton *at her request, but will not again* for reasons too long and impertinent to insert in a letter ... I went to *Madam* in my coach at one o'clock; she was in her sedan, with her three footmen in

Saxon green, with orange-coloured cockades, marched in state, I humbly followed. A stop kept me about half an hour on the way; she got to the Castle without interruptions, and went on into the drawing room directly. Can you tell *why* she desired me to go with her? I can. She was superb in brown and gold, and diamonds; I was clad in the purple and white silk I bought when last year in England; my littleness set off her greatness! These *odd fancies* make me laugh, and not a bit angry: only rather self-satisfied, that I feel myself above doing the things which make the actor so despicable. (Delville, 2 November 1751)

Domestic life took precedence over fashion as Mrs. Delany made plans for the trip to Mount Panther:

Thursday, settled affairs for the North, have taken a workwoman into my house, who is to have charge of all my *household* linen, and to wash my laces, as Smith is not now able to do all. (Dangan, 3 June 1752)

I have sent my niece Mary, by Mrs. D., a strong piece of cloth for *frocks*, and have got coats for the boys, but no opportunity yet of sending them, as they must go privately; you must forgive my *homespun tokens* to the dear children. I had hopes of fitting their coats on this year, but since that hope is blasted, you must not chide me for this little indulgence. On Tuesday, please God, we set out for Mount Panther. I shall not be able to write, I fear, till I get there, and my letters will take an unmeasurable round. (Delville, 13 June 1752)

> Pray send me cut in paper the pattern of a bib
> that exactly fits Mary's coat, and the length of
> her petticoat from the hips and from the peak
> of her stays; it is to *try an experiment* in a coarse
> sort of work which, if it succeeds, you shall see;
> if not, forget I mentioned it. (Delville, 17
> March 1753).

Mrs. Delany kept up her interest in Irish manufacture:

> Just here Bushe made me go with her to
> Drumcondra, half a mile off, to see a new man-
> ufactory that is set up there of printed linens
> done by copper-plates; they are excessive pretty,
> but I will not describe them as I hope to bring
> you a small sample next summer. (Delville,
> 9 December 1752)

Some time earlier she had taken a jaunt to Co. Kildare:

> Yesterday we spent a very pleasant day in the
> country with Mr. and Mrs. Lawe at their bleach
> yard, 9 miles off, near the famous salmon leap
> of Leixlip. They have a pretty cabin there, and
> gave us some fine trout caught out of their own
> brook just at their door, that were excellent, and
> many other good things. I wished you there, it
> was so new a scene; and the men at work laying
> out the cloth etc. on the grass full in our view
> was very pretty; the machine for rinsing the
> clothes is very curious. (Delville, 20 June 1747)

While English trade restrictions inhibited the export of
wool and printed cottons, the linen industry in Ireland was
encouraged and promoted. The Linen Board, set up in 1711,
offered premiums and prizes to manufacturers to improve their
product, and with such encouragement and ideal growing

conditions, Irish linen became a superlative product at home and abroad. Flax-growing thrived where growing conditions were suitable, notably the northern half of the country. It grew better on shallow, sharp land that remained damp even in dry spells. Very rich land was not suitable, as the crop grew too tall and broke before it was ready for harvesting.

The sight of hanks of linen spread out to finish in bleach yards along riverbanks was a common sight in the country, though new to Mrs. Delany at the time. Bleaching the linen was a difficult and disgusting process. The brown raw linen from the looms of the weavers was given at least twelve boilings in concoctions of cow's urine, cow dung, buttermilk, potash, bran, salt and other ingredients. Between each boiling, the bleaching solution was rinsed out in the nearest river or stream. The cloth was then spread out on grass to dry, after which it was again watered and dried. The boiling process was then repeated. At the end of all the boilings, the cloth was beetled by hammering it on a flat stone with a wooden mallet or beetle. Only a minority of weavers, who were usually peasant farmers and their families, bleached their own linen. The cloth was generally sold unbleached at linen markets to enterprises like Mr. Lawe's at Leixlip to finish. The industry was very progressive and embraced new technology. Mrs. Delany had noted machinery, probably Dutch bleachers, which were brought in to mechanise the washing and rinsing of the raw linen.

However dutiful an Irish industry correspondent Mrs. Delany was, she was irrepressible as a fashion reporter. On another visit to England she wrote:

> All I can learn of fashions is that people's heads are dressed much as they were last year: hoops *only worn* when full dressed, and those large. (Bulstrode, 15 January 1755)

> I don't know what you mean by a *pompadour*,
> unless it is what we call in this part of the world
> a *pelisse*; which in plain English is a long cloak
> made of satin or velvet, black or nay colour,
> lined or trimmed with silk, satin, or fur
> according to fancy, with slits for the arms to
> come out and a head like a *capuchin*. They are
> worn by everybody, they come down half way
> the petticoat. (Bulstrode, 20 January 1755)

Whatever confusion arose about a pompadour and a pelisse, there was a hairstyle named after Louis XV's mistress the Marquise de Pompadour (1721–64). The hair was swept up straight from the forehead into a high roll and turned back on a pad. Sticky dressings called pomades were combed through to keep the pompadour upright. Mrs. Rundell's receipt, aptly named "Pomade Divine" gives a good idea of the type of ingredients used. She directs to:

> Clear a pound and a half of beef-marrow from
> the strings and bone, put it into an earthen pan
> or vessel of water fresh from the spring, and
> change the water night and morning for ten
> days; then steep it in rose-water twenty four
> hours, and drain it in a cloth till quite dry. Take
> an ounce of each of the following articles,
> namely, storax, gum-benjamin, odoriferous
> cypress powder, or of Florence, half an ounce
> of cinnamon, two drachms of cloves, and two
> drachms of nutmeg, all finely powdered; mix
> them with the marrow above prepared …
> Strain the ointment through a linen cloth into
> small pots, and, when cold, cover them. Do not
> touch it with anything but silver. It will keep
> many years.

Margaret Trouncer, in her biography of Madame de Pompadour (1936), described her at her dressing table in Versailles. It was laden with philtres and fineries, paints, pastes, patches, scents, vermilion rouge, vegetable rouge, mineral rouge, chemical white, blue for veins and Maille vinegar against wrinkles. She went on to describe the Pompadour seated before her mirror being laced into her stays when a scratching at the door would announce her first caller, a "conceited looking hairdresser, comb in hand", who "began undoing the edifice he had erected two weeks before, while Pompadour relieved the itching of her head by means of an ivory hand on the end of a stick".

Mrs. Delany witnessed such outrageous fashion at first hand when she saw the trousseau and jewellery of a new society bride, Miss Margaret Poyntz. The very fortunate Miss Poyntz married John Spencer, a son of Countess Georgina Cowper, and she was immediately annexed as a new Granville relation. Mrs. Delany wrote:

> If I had sooner known all the particulars relating to our new cousin Mrs. Spencer, you should not have been so long ignorant of them. She had four negligees, four nightgowns, four mantuas and petticoats. She was married in a white and silver trimmed. I cannot remember the rest, only a pink satin with embroidered facings, and robings in silver done by Mrs. Glegg. Her first suit she went to Court in was white and silver, as fine as brocade and trimming could make it; the second, blue and silver; the third, white and gold and colours, six pounds a yard; the fourth, plain pink-coloured satin. The diamonds worth twelve thousand pounds: her earrings three drops all diamonds, *no paltry scrolls of silver*. Her

necklace most perfect brilliants, the middle stone worth a thousand pounds, set at the edge with small brilliants, the large diamonds meet in this manner [Mrs. Delany included a drawing of the clasp]. Her cap, all brilliants (made in the fashion of a small butterfly-skeleton), had a very good effect with a pompon; and behind, where you may suppose the bottom of the caul, a knot of diamonds, with two little puffs of diamonds where the lappets are fastened, and two shaking sprigs of brilliants for her hair; six roses all brilliants for her stays, set in this form [another drawing]. Her watch and etuy suited to the rest … Her jointure, I hear, is four thousand a-year, I don't know what her pin-money is, I suppose in proportion to everything Mr. Spencer has done, which has shewn his nature to be good and generous. Lady Cowper says he may spend near thirty thousand pound a-year without hurting himself. (14–17 January 1756)

This golden couple became parents the following year to Georgiana, the future Duchess of Devonshire. With such a trousseau, the new Mrs. Spencer was kitted out for life. The idea of a gown reserved for just the wedding ceremony was a nineteenth-century notion, as clothes were then comparatively cheaper. In the eighteenth century, even the most singularly elaborate dress had to serve for more than one occasion, and the new Mrs. Spencer was presented at court the following day in her wedding dress. Far more emphasis was laid on the pre-marriage settlement than on the actual wedding ceremony.

Mrs. Spencer's negligees were not to be confused with her nightgowns. The negligee was an earlier import from the French court. It was a looser and floatier dress, sometimes called a *robe volante*. The style smacked of indecency to many commentators when it made its first appearance. A French periodical, *La Bagatelle* (1718), found that the new *robes volantes* gave women "an air of coming pleasures" and their bodies "freedom to expand and thicken". The negligee fitted over the bust on a coarse cloth bodice lining that laced behind and, again, even under this loose-fitting gown women wore their stays.

In her inventory of the sumptuous jewellery, Mrs. Delany mentioned an etui. This was a small, decorative needle case of a type often carried by gentlewomen, suitably bejewelled no doubt. Many years later, Mrs. Delany was given such an etui by Queen Charlotte. Rea, her waiting woman, sent an account of it to G.M.A.:

> the Queen came up to Mrs. Delany and put a packet into her hand, and said, in a most gracious manner, she hoped Mrs. Delany would look at that sometimes and remember her. When your aunt opened it it was a *most beautiful* pocket case, the outside white sattin worked with gold, and ornamented with gold spangles; the inside – but it is impossible for me to describe it, it is so elegant; it is lined with pink sattin, and contains a knife, sizsars, pencle, rule, compas, bodkin, and more than I can say; but it is all gold and mother of pearl (Bulstrode, December 1779)

Anne followed up the astonishing account of Mrs. Spencer's trousseau with some queries of her own, and Mrs. Delany lost no time in replying:

> Many thanks to my dearest sister for her letter of the 21st. I will endeavour to answer all your questions. Mrs. Spencer's negligee sleeves are *treble*; the ruffles are much the same as at Bath, long at the elbow and pretty narrow at top; I

think they *pin* their gowns *rather closer before*; hoops are as flat as if made of pasteboard, and as stiff, the shape sloping from the hip and spreading at the bottom, enormous but *not* so ugly as the *square* hoops … Heads are variously adorned, pompons with some accompaniment of feathers, ribbons or flowers; lappets in all sorts of *curli murlis*; little plain cypress gauze *trolly* or fine muslin; long hoods are worn close under the chin tied behind, the earrings go round the neck, and tye with bows and ends behind. Nightgowns, worn without hoops; I have seen no *trollopees* since I came from the Bath. If you mean to communicate this intelligence to your neighbours, I desire you will *translate* it, as the language is known but to few! (Spring Gardens, 24 January 1756)

The height of fashion in headwear was achieved by another style introduced by Madame de Pompadour called the pompon. Mrs. Delany remarked it as part of Mrs. Spencer's headgear. A pompon was usually a small spray of flowers, feathers or jewels placed either centrally or to one side of the head. The piece was sometimes *tremblant* on wires, worn on its own or with a small cap. When Mrs. Delany mentioned not having seen any trollopees since coming from Bath, she was harking back to her beloved *Clarissa*, where the prostitutes wore "a shocking dishabille, and without stays their gowns hanging trollopy". This was a general sideswipe at the laxity of dress.

From this zenith of wealth and ostentation, Anne was now plunged into mourning: "At last Princess Caroline has left this painful life … It will be a general mourning – dark crape negligees or nightgowns and bombazeens; it is not yet known whether for three or six months" (Bulstrode, 29 December

1757). "About mourning," Mrs. Delany continued in a follow-up letter:

> bombazeens quite plain, broad-hemmed muslin, or *white crape*, that looks like old flannell, seven shillings a yard, and won't wash; Turkey gauze is also worn, which is thick and white, but is extravagant, as it does not wash, dirties in two days and costs 5s. a yard; the mourning will be worn *six months*, three in crape and bombazeen.
> (17 January 1758)

Bombazeens and crapes were the fabrics usually reserved for mourning. Crape was a puckered and crinkled semi-transparent fabric, usually dyed black, and bombazeen was black open twill weave, with a silk warp and a worsted weft, though cotton and linen wefts were also used. Gossip of the Gunnings filtered through the mourning gloom – they were not forgiven: "The Duke of Hamilton's death has made a very fair widow, and *at present* a very disconsolate one" (Spring Gardens, 21 January 1758). Elizabeth confounded them all again by marrying Colonel Campbell the following year; he later became the Duke of Argyle.

❈

Mundane matters were also reported from Mrs. Delany's well-run household. A good housekeeper saw to it that adequate stores of personal linen, domestic linen, sheets and napery were properly made, laundered, starched, dried, stored and mended. Household linen was valuable, and articles were itemised in household inventories. Servants with particular skills with textiles who could wash and refresh laces, sew, mend and do fine needlework were cherished. The cleaning of stockings, particularly gentlemen's stockings, was a business in itself. A well-turned leg was considered very attractive. Bundles of stockings were delivered to the stocking cleaner where they were washed, often dyed pale blue, green or pink, treated for stains and hung out to dry. Outer garments were cleaned only rarely, usually by specialists outside the household; the rest went to the washerwoman.

> We had like to have lost all our week's linen and three suits of the finest Irish damask; the washer-woman's goods were seized by her merciless landlord, and the steward threatened that if we did not lay down six guineas our linen should be sold! I sent for Mr. Chapone [Sally's brother], who has got us our linen, only paying for the washing. (Spring Gardens, 11 February 1758)

Aunt Delany's mind, as we know, constantly turned on the Dewes family. Mary Dewes, and the figure she would make in the world, was a high priority; "I must take the liberty of begging you will lay that [money] out for my Mary in the way you like best. Is she not tall enough for *a robe*? And would not a full pink colour satin become her?" (Delville, 23 December 1758). Mary Dewes was twelve years of age at this time, and though children's clothes did not differ sub-stantially from adults', Mrs. Delany appears to suggest this robe as an advance for Mary and again favoured the colour pink. She followed up her theme the next month, but another royal death upset her plans:

> I think Mary will become a robe very much; but if the mourning is to be the same as for Princess Caroline, she must lay her *costly robes aside* for some time, and dress like other girls of her age. For second mourning, if she is in town, a white satin may do as well as pink; but I

believe the deep mourning will last till April.
(Delville, 27 January 1759)

Her gowns were discussed again the next year, and from this extract it seems that Mary had ventured to hope for a closed robe with front-fastening bodice. Mrs. Delany did not approve and wrote to her mother:

> I can't but think the Pauline would become a *negligee* very well; for constant wear young people (as you say) are better in a dress where their carriage may be more observed; but I don't by any means approve of gowns that button before. Anything that drags the shoulders forward at the growing-time is a great disadvantage.

She made a concession, however:

> but if she likes the appearance of it, a stomacher may be made to *pin on*, and that will look as well as if it really buttoned. The *vanity* and *impertinence* of dress is always to be avoided, but a *decent* compliance with the fashion is less affected than any remarkable negligence of it.
> (Delville, 2 February 1760)

The Gunnings entered the correspondence again:

> And what a wretched end Lady Coventry makes after her short-lived reign of beauty! Not contented with the *extraordinary share* Providence had bestowed on her, she presumptuously and vainly thought to mend it, and by that means they say has destroyed her life; for Dr. Taylor says the white she made use of for her face and neck was rank poison; I wish it may be a warning to her imitators. (Delville, 2 February 1760)

A white complexion was the desired look, and society beauties went to great lengths to achieve it. Maria Gunning already had the startling complexion of the consumptive, but lead used as a whitening pigment in her pastes and powders probably sealed her fate. Painters ran the risk of lead poisoning as a matter of course and were often afflicted with what was called painter's colic. Lord Chesterfield had remarked in a letter, several years before Lady Coventry's death, that he had been "near enough to see manifestly that she had laid on a great deal of white which she did not want and which will soon destroy both her natural complexion and her teeth" (17 March 1752).

Other cosmetic camouflages were achieved by wearing patches. These were usually made of taffeta or leather, cut in odd little shapes, such as stars or half-moons, and stuck on with glue. The original idea was to cover pockmarks, but the patches were considered so alluring they were often applied where there was no underlying blemish. The veins in neck and chest were sometimes accentuated in blue to highlight the fairness of the breast. Eyebrows were plucked thin and pencilled high and curved. Rouge was applied in round or triangular shapes. Lips were painted into a bee-sting, a shape that softened out as the century progressed to a rosebud. Carmine, a derivative of cochineal, alkanet root and beetroot were used to colour rouges and lipsticks.

A fair complexion was still the goal for G.M.A., as it had been for the Gunnings, though moderation was the keynote. Mrs. Delany wrote to her when she was visiting Matlock, a spa town on the river Derwent: "You must be pleased with Matlock's beauties, and going upon the water. I shall expect to see you a little gipsy, but never mind if you are well, for *health* is better than a *fair* face!" (Bulstrode, 14 September 1781). On a more modest scale, but in as earnest a pursuit of white skin as the society beauties, Dorothea Herbert recounted the attempts she and her sister made under the influence of a young visitor, Miss Hare from Cashel, Co. Tipperary. The fourteen-year-old Miss Hare was more sophisticated than the Carrick-on-Suir girls. Dorothea wrote in her *Retrospections*:

> She led us into a new Species of Culinary Preparations – Namely making up washes and beautifying Lotions – We had two or three of the Tenants every day hunting the Country for different sorts of Herbs, and such Plaisters and Milk Washes as We made up would be enough to ruin all the fair Skins in the Circassian Marts – Every night we were Wraped up like Pomatum Sticks in greasy brown Paper, and I'm sure if any Stranger had seen us at Night they would have taken She, Fanny and I for three Egyptian Mummies ready Embalmed – Our Hands, Faces, and Chests were completely cover'd with Tallow and Brown Paper, made into various sorts of Ointments.

A visit to some wealthy Herbert relations, the Blundens in Castle Blunden, Co. Kilkenny, followed the heroic effort. Dorothea described how they spent the week before the visit redoubling their cosmetic labours and dyeing, clearstarching and gaufreying their old fripperies. She wrote:

> The first Mortification we experienced was to find that the Blundens had what we so earnestly sought and Miss'd, viz the Whitest Hands, Noses, and Teeth in the World – The More we scrubb'd the more desperately Red did our Skins grow – Every Day after Dinner we retired to our

Room with Shame and Dismay at the redness of
our Hands and Noses – which was encreased by
the Blundens mischievously laughing at it.

Visiting wealthy relations could be a severe trial. The
business of an unmarried young lady was to make herself as
amiable and marriageable as possible. She was on probation
and, as Mrs. Delany pointed out, family credit was at stake.
Mary Dewes, staying at Richmond with her other
godmother, the fashionable Lady Cowper, needed her very
best finery to carry off the visit, but Aunt Delany had it in
safe keeping. She wrote:

Alas! My dear M. so very careful was I of your
painted silk negligee, as to *lock it up* in my japan
chest, and cannot well give that key to anybody;
but the instant I go to town I will send it away
to Richmond, that it may make its appearance,
though the wearer wants no tinsel ornaments to
set her off to advantage, and if her merit cannot
be read in her eyes, those faithful intelligencers
of her heart, a rich robe will only allure those
who are not worthy of more valuable allure-
ments! All this is to reconcile you to my over
carefulness about your *negligee*. As to the patterns
you are to have from Mr. Ashburner, I fear you
cannot judge very well of a pattern silk. I
should have no objection to a rich pink, plain
satin, if they are fashionable; but a flimsy satin
is very ugly: perhaps you may see something you
like of mixed colours, (some pink by all means,)
and what you like I shall most certainly like. It
might be made, and sent to meet you at
Richmond, and then, perhaps, you will not
want the other. I should be afraid, as it is

delicate, that packing backwards and forwards might hurt it; but I will send it carefully to all who remember me, and tell Mrs. Venor I *fear* cards usurp the *needle's* dominion at Welsbourne, or your ruffles would be done long ago. (Bulstrode, 19 October 1769)

As Mrs. Delany grew older, the fashionable world became an object of ridicule. She wrote to her nephew the Reverend John Dewes, who also liked to be well informed, "I don't hear a word of news. Diversions, *rouge*, and every fantastick fashion in male and female daily multiply" (St. James's Place, 21 May 1771). Our rural fashion correspondent, Dorothea Herbert, actually confirmed Mrs. Delany's worst opinion. She wrote in her *Retrospections* about her cousin Ned Eyre, an object of fascination to his relatives:

> He was heir to an immense property ... He had a Glass Coach and a glass Vis a vis where he sat dressed out from Top to Toe in a suit of the Gayest Colour Silk or Sattin lined with Persian of a different Colour – He wore Sattin Shoes and Set Buckles had two or three sets of paste Buttons that cost an immensity – His Hair was dress'd like a Womans over a Rouleau or Tete, which was then the fashion among the Ladies – He sometimes carried a Muff, sometimes a Fan, and was always painted up to the Eyes with the deepest Carmine – His Manners and Actions were as Outre as his Dress ... we all doated on him.

Mrs. Delany maintained her dislike of dandies and fops and so-called macaronis. In a letter to Mary, now Mrs. Port of Ilam, she wrote:

The chief topick of conversation yesterday was Lord Villiers' appearance in the morning at Court in a pale purple velvet coat, turned up with lemon-colour, and embroidered all over with S.S.'s of pearl as big as pease, and in all the spaces little medallions in beaten gold, *real solid*, in various figures of *Cupids* "and the *like*" (as *Smith* would say). At best it was only a fool's coat. (St. James's Place, 2 January 1773)

She was now in her seventies but had lost none of her bite. She sent Mary this account of her grandee friends setting off for a ball:

This morning I made a visit to Lady Dartmouth; found her and her excellent lord at home ... Lady Dartmouth was just going to submit to the friseur's tyranny, in order to make her appearance at the French ambassadour's ball tonight, where all the fine world are going to shine away. It is to be the most brilliant thing that has yet been exhibited, and even our dear Dss goes, with whom I dined, and am just return'd from Whitehall, where I left *a groupe* all ready to set off ... Lady Bute and her two daughters, Lady Weymouth *most splendid* in jewells, but in came Mrs. Montagu [Elizabeth Montagu, the famous bluestocking], who *rivall'd her* in sparkling gems. I could not help calling to mind (on seeing her so beset with jewells) Lady Clarendon's answer to Lady Granville, when she ask'd her "what was become of her jewells?" (as she had not seen them in a great while). "They are in my cabinet. When my eyes outshone my *diamonds* I wore them; now *they* outshine my eyes

I lock them up," and I thought if Mrs. M.'s *coronet of brilliants* which crown'd her *toopee* had been in her cabinet it would have been their proper place. It is wonderful that a mind so well stored shou'd find a corner for so frippery a thing as vanity. (I March 1773)

On 7 June 1774 the wedding took place between Georgiana Spencer, eldest daughter of the lavish Spencers, and William Cavendish, Duke of Devonshire. It was the most splendid match of the season but a miserable marriage. The whole of society looked on as the cold duke froze the blood in the veins of his delightful, spoilt, good-natured bride. She turned instead to the crowd for approbation and affection, just as her descendant Princess Diana did many generations later. The crowd supplied it. She was an unconventional beauty with a strong individual sense of style, and she soon became the rage of the day. Everything she wore, everything she said and did was copied. She was queen of her own very fashionable set and in time lost her constitution to dissipation, her fortune to gaming, the vice of the age, and her reputation to adultery. Mrs. Delany, related to her through her Granville blood, was horrified. She wrote;

This bitter reflection arises from what I hear *every*body say of a *great* and *handsome* relation of ours just *beginning* her part; but I do hope she will be like the young actors and actresses, who begin with *over* acting when they first come upon the stage ... but I tremble for her. (St James's Place, 10 March 1775)

Long before her downfall, Georgiana had enjoyed a honeymoon of enormous popularity. Amanda Foreman relates, in her biography *Georgiana, Duchess of Devonshire*, that hairstyles were already top heavy but Georgiana took things a stage higher by creating three-foot hair towers. She used false hairpieces and pads and glued the whole lot together with scented pomades. The constructions were then decorated with ornaments. Once she carried a ship in full sail on her head, another time an arrangement of stuffed birds, another time waxed fruit. On one occasion, she even had a pastoral tableau nestling in her coiffure with little wooden trees and little wooden sheep. Mrs. Delany had remarked the frisseur's tyranny in a very modest context, but Georgiana's towers required the help of at least two hairdressers and took several hours to assemble. Mrs Delany now wrote: "The ladies head-dresses *grow daily*, and seem like the Tower of Babel to mean to reach the skies!" (St. James's Place, 22 February 1776).

The edifices made any quick turn of the head impossible, and the only way to ride in a carriage was to sit on the floor. Mrs. Delany wrote:

> I hear of nothing but balls and high heads – *so enormous* that nobody can sit upright in their coaches, but *stoop forward* as if they had got the children's *chollick*. Surely there is an influenza of the *brain*, which must account for the present vagaries, and be some excuse. (St. James's Place, 21 December 1775)

The coiffeurs could last several weeks before needing to be rebuilt, but meanwhile the ladies had to sleep in semi-recumbent positions. Fashionable society went mad as women competed with one another to see who could construct the tallest head, despite the fact that they became the butt of the popular caricaturists of the day.

Bluestocking Hannah More wrote to her sister on the same subject:

Nothing can be conceived so absurd, extravagant, and fantastical, as the present mode of dressing the head ... have just escaped from one of the most fashionable disfigurers; and though I charged him to dress me with the greatest simplicity, and to have only a very distant eye upon the fashion, just enough to avoid the pride of singularity, without running into ridiculous excess; yet in spite of all these sage didactics, I absolutely blush at myself, and turn to the glass with as much caution as a vain beauty, just risen from the small-pox; which cannot be a more disfiguring disease than the present mode of dressing. (*The Life and Correspondence of Hannah More*, Volume I)

The dress, the manners and the morals of the so-called bon ton greatly offended Mrs. Delany:

Nothing is talked of now so much as the ladies *enormous* dresses, more suited to the *stage* or a *masquerade* than for either *civil* or sober societies. The 3 *most* elevated plumes of feathers are the Dss of Devonshire, Lady Mary Somerset, and Lady Harriet Stanhope, but some say Mrs. *Hubert's* exceeds them all.

The plumes referred to were excessively expensive ostrich feathers. Georgiana had started this fashion by attaching one, four feet in length, in a wide arc across her head.

Mrs. Delany continued:

It would be some consolation if their manners did *not* too much correspond with the lightness of their dress! But the Lady H. Stanhope is *much*

commended for the propriety of her behaviour.
(St. James's Place, 10 March 1775)

Lady Harriet Stanhope came in for favourable mention because the following year she married Mrs. Delany's cousin, the Hon. Thomas Foley, and she paid her a formal visit:

> She came next day between two and three, very polite, a very fine figure, and *I think* very pretty; her address is remarkably pleasing, but there is a *particular affectation* in speaking now practised by the present "*bon ton*" in twisting their mouth, and *spreading* it out to shew their white teeth, that appears to me *a great blemish*, but it is in vain when people can perswade themselves that a *fault* is a *perfection* to hope to see it amended. (St. James's Place, 9 April 1776)

Lady Harriet had adopted a mannerism of speech called the "Devonshire House Drawl". It was part baby-talk, part affectation. Amanda Foreman explained that the word "hope" was written and pronounced "whop"; you became "oo". Vowels were compressed and extended so that cucumber became "cowcumber" and yellow "yaller". Lady Harriet's new husband, Thomas Foley, was already one of the set. He was an *habitué* of Newmarket and as profligate a gambler as any of the Devonshires could wish for, until his credit ran out. Mrs. Delany later reported in dismay the shabby ending to the whole saga when Lady Harriet Foley was handed out of her own house by the bailiffs about a year after her marriage.

On a more edifying note, to celebrate Mary's birthday she wrote:

> I have put on *all* my *birthday geer, new white sattin,* best covers on my chairs, and the knotting furniture of my bedchamber, with window-

curtain of the same. Tender recollections and warm wishes will supply the place of bonfires and illuminations, an offering more worthy of the occasion than what is prostituted to every (factious) *patriot* unworthily *so-called*. Can any thing in the world more strongly prove the strong political tincture that infects every human mind at present, that even on the most foreign occasions a dash will appear; or why *should I* bring in a patriot by head and shoulders? Indeed, my dearest Mary, *I am sick* of the mischiefs of politicks. They tear asunder the very vitals of friendship; set familys and friends at variance; and, to compleat our ruin, *vice and extravagance knows no bounds* (St. James's Place, 22 February 1776)

Whig politics was the new toy of the Duchess of Devonshire, and her active participation was another new disturbance to Mrs. Delany's sense of propriety. She had the comfort of her old cronies, though, who found the new fashions and behaviour of the ton as appalling as she did:

Last night I had Lady Weymouth, Lady Stamford, and a short visit from Lady Frances Bulkeley, who came on purpose to enquire after you, which she did most kindly. I had also her Grace of Queensbury, *very droll* about the fashionable heads. She says "they are too bad to look at," and so she "only looks at the ladies buckles;" and "to mortify them for their folly she advises everybody to do the same." What do you think? (St. James's Place, 15 February 1776)

Last night I was at Mrs. Walsingham's concert ... the concert was splendid; rows above rows of fine ladies with *towering tops*. Not having been much used to see so many together I must own I could not help considering them with some astonishment, and lamenting that so absurd, inconvenient, and unbecoming a fashion should last so long, for though every year has produced some alteration, the *enormity* continues, and one of the most beautiful ornaments of nature, fine hair, is entirely disguised...

The Dss Dowager of Portland carried me to Mrs Walsingham's at a little before 8; I had a comfortable seat on the sofa by her Grace and Lady Bute, and *we* were the only *flat caps* in the room! The music was charming." (St. James's Place, 24 May 1780)

Reports of fashion excesses were all very well, but the ever-practical Mrs. Delany, at seventy-eight, continued to provision Mary Port's family, just as she had Anne's and the Gloucester neighbours all those years before. History repeated itself.

I have been at as great a loss to get you a few yards of *true* Indian dimity. Your neighbour, Manchester, has brought that manufacture to so great a perfection, that it is difficult to know *which* is the *right!* However, I cut that matter short by sending you four yards, ell-wide, that I had by me, of finer than I can meet with, and I *am sure* it is Indian, tho' *not now* as white as Manchester, but will wash of a very good colour. I have got a piece of Nankeen, and propose sending the box next week. (St. James's Place, 10 January 1778)

She had known court life from her earliest years and now, towards the latter end of her life, the royal family took her up and she was regularly invited into their company at Windsor. Her descriptive powers were as sharp as ever. She sent this account to G.M.A.:

> The Queen was dressed in an embroidered lutestring; Princess Royal in deep orange or scarlet, I could not by candlelight distinguish which; Princess Augusta in pink; Princess Elizabeth in blue. These were all in robes without aprons. Princess Mary (a most sweet child) was in cherry-coloured tabby, with silver leading strings; she is about four years old; she could not remember my name, but, making me a very low curtsey, she said, *"How do you do, Duchess of Portland's friend; and how does and how does your little niece do. I wish you had brought her."*
> (Bulstrode, 10 October 1779)

Though her life spanned the best part of a century, and changes in fashions accelerated to her horror in the last quarter, Mrs. Delany's attachment to pink lutestring was fast from beginning to end. She entertained the king and queen with this story of her girlhood and told it to Miss Mary Hamilton, who recorded it in the journal of her stay at Bulstrode:

> When she was very young, and lived with her parents in Gloucestershire (Buckland), she had an invitation to dine at a gentleman's house in the neighbourhood, which her mother allowed her to accept. As there was to be company she was very smartly dressed, and as the road was too bad for a carriage, she was mounted on a

pillion behind a steady old domestic. On their way they met a pack of hounds; Miss Granville was enchanted, the mettle of the horse was roused, and old John was easily prevailed on to join the chase. The consequence was the (pink) lutestring slip was rent in many places, the smart shoes lost, and the hat and streamers blown over the hills and far away … But alas! After joy came sorrow, she kept the dinner waiting, and dreaded returning home in her tattered garments; Mrs. Granville reproached her severely, and this unfortunate chase cost many penitential tears.

This story may have been some consolation for the oft-disapproved-of Miss Sparrow – if only she had known.

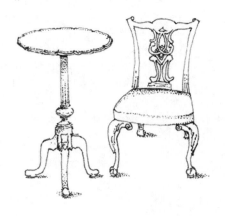

crimson
damask:
mrs. delany's
decor

Mrs. Mary Pendarves and Dr. Patrick Delany married in June 1743. The following year they remained in England, making their wedding visits and waiting for preferment for Dr. Delany. When the Deanery of Down was secured, they set sail on the *Pretty Betty* for home. Their residence was called Delville, which was on the outskirts of the much smaller eighteenth-century city of Dublin. Nothing of the house remains. It was demolished in 1951, and the Bon Secours Hospital, to the north of Glasnevin, now stands in its place. Delville itself was a solid three-bay house rebuilt on the site of an earlier one.

In 1719 the lease of a house called the Glen was signed over to Dr. Richard Helsham and the Rev. Patrick Delany, both fellows of Trinity College Dublin. Jonathan Swift is said to have named the house Heldeville in honour of its new tenants, but Helsham relinquished his interest shortly afterwards, and the name became Delville after its sole encumbant. Francis Elrington Bell in *A History of the County Dublin* asserts that Dr. Delany displayed an ambition of making a figure in the world throughout his life and so lived in a style that his means did not justify. "At Delville, he sought to gain the reputation of an improver, and for many years he indulged there in reckless outlay. He levelled the original house, the Glen, and another was designed without any regard to the dimensions or his purse." This was the house Mrs. Delany was welcomed into. The house, gardens and lands were on rising ground overlooking the Tolka river. The small but very pleasant estate of about eleven acres was adjacent to what are now the Botanic Gardens and, on a bright day, the new chatelaine Mrs. Delany wrote, she could see the masts of the ships in Dublin harbour from the windows.

This was not her first sight of her new home. On her earlier visit to Dublin in the 1730s she had been a guest at Delville. She wrote on that occasion about Jonathan Swift and the fascinating company she met at the Thursday Club, which was held in Dr. Delany's townhouse in Stafford Street in Dublin. She included encomiums on Dr. Delany, a prominent figure in Swift's circle, but she did not remark on either of his houses. Marriage was far from her mind. She had no notion of Dr. Delany, nor he of her. During that first Irish visit, while the young widow Mrs. Mary Pendarves was enjoying the hospitality of her Irish hosts at Killala, he had married the rich widow Mrs. Margaret Tenison.

The new Mrs. Delany, a bride in her middle years, now returned to Dublin with great energy. The miniature estate of Delville was her husband's pride and joy, and it became hers as well. She was at last mistress of her own house, and she went to the task with an enthusiasm that did credit to her fifteenth-century ancestor Sir Roger Granville. He was dubbed the Great Housekeeper for his improving works. Letters to Anne at this period were extremely detailed – such was Mrs. Delany's eagerness to share the delights of her new home.

Though Delville was a modest house compared to the great houses such as Castletown, the Connolly mansion in Kildare, or Bulstrode, the home of the Duchess of Portland, it nonetheless reflected the Delanys' position in society. A grander version of Delville, thankfully still standing today, is Newbridge House in Donabate, Co. Dublin. This house was designed and built for the Reverend Charles Cobbe, Archbishop of Dublin, by George Semple in 1749. It was enlarged again by Lady Elizabeth Cobbe in the 1760s. Archbishop Cobbe was a senior prelate and the Cobbes were wealthy landowners; their house reflected their position in society. Dr. Delany was always ambitious and Delville, though smaller, was part of what would be termed today his image. Through the eighteenth century, expensive decoration was usually reserved for the rooms for public entertaining, the hall, staircase and a suite of possibly four to six rooms. Houses such as Delville or Newbridge were more cohesive, being smaller, but their public rooms would send all the right messages. They proclaimed status, cultivated taste and, in the case of the wealthy Cobbes, power. These establishments were intended to impress.

> Yesterday morning (for Tuesday I spent the whole day in settling shells and papers) my upholsterer came, and my new apartment will be very handsome. The drawing-room hung with tapestry, on each side of the door a japan chest, the curtains and chairs crimson mohair, between the windows large glasses with gilt frames, and marble tables under them with gilt frames; the bedchamber within hung with crimson damask, bed chairs and curtains the same; *the closet* within it is most delightful, I have a most extensive and beautiful prospect of the harbour and town of Dublin and a range of mountains of various shapes. This bedchamber and closet are on the left hand of the drawing room; on the right is a very pretty square room, with a large dressing room within it, which I hope will be my dearest sister's apartment, when she makes me happy with her company. (Delville, 28 June 1744)

D.D., as she fondly called Dr. Delany, had given her *carte blanche* and she lost no time in setting to: the upholsterers were on the doorstep within days of her arrival at Delville. Mrs. Delany sent Anne a veritable inventory of the house and furnishings to enable her to imagine it all. The drawing-room was the grandest reception room of the house, situated upstairs on the first floor. It probably spanned the front of the house. This room was hung with tapestries, a décor that gave colour and interest but was a little old fashioned by 1744. Lighter painted panelling, stucco [plaster] work and fabrics, especially rich furniture damasks, had become popular for use as hangings by this time. The Granville family were interested in tapestries, fashionable or not, possibly because of their own superb needlework talents.

No less a judge than Bernard Granville had written to Mary Dewes about the appointments in the house of their Foley relations:

> I am glad you have seen the Foleys, and agree with you in thinking the tapestry the finest of their kind that I have seen. Did not you admire the looking-glasses between the windows? The fringe to the window curtains seemed to me to be the best I ever saw, but the tapestry is a constant entertainment, and the *story* a very proper one to admit of variety of expressions.
> (Calwich, 10 May 1767)

We do not know what the "proper" story of the Foley tapestry was, but epic tales from Greek or Roman mythology, heroic battles and chivalrous deeds of knightly valour were common subjects. Magnificent tapestries of earlier periods came from Antwerp and Brussels but a lighter style of tapestry, from this later period, was being produced by the Gobelins factory in France.

Mrs. Delany wrote there was a japan chest at either side of the door. These are likely to have been a pair of highly decorated painted lacquer chests on stands of a style that had been popular from the late seventeenth century. The English of the East India trading company, stationed originally in Guangzhou province, sent wondrous Chinese lacquered screens, fan frames, tables, boxes, *objets d'arts* and cabinets back to Europe. The arrival of these exotic trinkets, along with Chinese tea and Chinese porcelain to drink it from, began the first chinoiserie craze. Exquisitely painted and inlaid lacquer panels were also exported. The panels and other components were sometimes assembled onshore to make finished cabinets and chests, like the japan chests at Delville. These pieces were designated Japanese or Chinese or Indian quite indiscriminately – the differentiation of country or even continent was not necessarily reckoned.

Years earlier, every bit as *au fait* with interior décor as with fashion, the then Mrs. Pendarves had written to Anne to say, "I was yesterday at Lady Sunderland's, and supped there. Lady Sun. is very busy about japanning: I will perfect myself in the art against I make you a visit, and bring materials with me" (23 August 1729). Two weeks after that she wrote, "Everybody is mad about japan work; I hope to be a dab at it by the time I see you" (Somerset House, 9 September 1729). A year later she wrote, "The soot is incomparable; a thousand thanks for your care about it, pray let it be sent by the first opportunity, and many thanks for the lamperns" (Upper Brook Street, 15 October 1730).

Mrs. Pendarves became a dab hand at everything she did, so we can be confident japanning was yet another accomplishment. Japanning was the painting on of layer upon layer of lacquer to a very high finish. It became a huge fad, with ladies lacquering small objects from snuff-boxes to tea tables. Lacquer was made from the sap of the lac tree, native to China. The process of distilling the resins, seed lac and shell lac, was messy, painstaking and even dangerous, so it was not usually undertaken by amateur artists, even stalwarts such as Mrs. Pendarves. She thanked Anne, however, for the "incomparable soot"; this was the blackening pigment of her lacquer. An over-the-counter preparation of black japan was available from the varnish-maker Williamson of Ripon, and others no doubt, at this period, but that would be too easy. Mrs. Pendarves chose to colour her own. Soot, lampblack or candleblack were used as the pigments for black paints too. The soot was crushed wood-charcoal residue, rendered down from pine trees and other vegetation. Particularly fine qualities were prepared for artists from peach stones and other vegetable matter. The soot Anne took so much trouble over may well have been of this superior artist's sort.

Returning to Delville, Mrs. Delany's drawing-room was a lavish room by any standards. It would have glowed with the deep-crimson mohair curtains and chair covers. Crimson was a very popular colour at the time and had a more purplish hue than crimsons of today. Mohair was an expensive fabric made from the hair of the Angora goat, often used in grand furnishing in the early eighteenth century. The large glasses or mirrors hanging between the windows were placed to reflect the light, especially candlelight. Pier glasses, as they were called, were often fitted with pendant candle branches or sconces to capture as much light as possible. Mrs. Delany had described "marble tables between the windows, and looking glasses with gilt frames" (21 October 1731) on her first visit to the home of the Claytons at 85 St. Stephen's Green. This décor may have inspired the scheme for Delville. Console tables topped with marble, possibly Italian, Carrara or Siena, were positioned beneath the looking-glasses. No expense was spared; this grand room proclaimed wealth, status and style.

Adjoining the drawing-room was Mrs. Delany's bedchamber. A bedchamber of this formal sort was in a semi-public progression of rooms – the visitors trooped from one to the other and admired everything *en route*. The bed hangings and chairs were covered in crimson damask, which was a silk fabric (originally from Damascus) woven with a rich, raised pattern, usually floral. The closet was not, as we might think, a wardrobe. It was a small inner room, often situated at the corner of a larger room. Mrs. Delany was very fond of her closets, and they feature frequently in her correspondence from Delville. Author Samuel Richardson made much of the closet, too: in his novel *Pamela* it served as a place of concealment for Pamela's master and seducer, Mr. B. In one of her candid letters to her parents she wrote of his treachery:

> I pulled off my Stays, and my Stockens, and my Gown, all to an Under-petticoat; and then hearing a rustling again in the Closet, I said, God protect us! But before I say my Prayers, I must look into this Closet. And so was going to it slip shod, when, O dreadful! Out rush'd my Master, in a rich silk and silver Morning Gown. I scream'd and run to the Bed.

If there was any excitement of that sort in Delville, we were unfortunately not informed of it. The truth was generally more prosaic. Pamela had earlier described the closet as belonging to the housekeeper Mrs. Jarvis, where she kept a few books, a chest of drawers and "such-like". Closets were commonly used for sewing or handiwork, to write letters in or just to have a quiet chat. They were small rooms, sometimes equipped with a little fireplace, and so easier to heat and much cosier than formal reception rooms. When the family was not required for entertaining, the closet was a welcome bolthole. Mrs. Delany wrote some time later that she too had placed a little chest of drawers in her closet within her bedchamber, "from whence I send you this letter. How blest should I be could we have a tete-a-tete in it with you! It is calculated for that purpose, being retired from all interruption and eaves-droppers" (11 July 1747).

Mrs. Delany also mentioned another square room, the opposite number to her bedchamber. This room, she said, had a large dressing-room within it. This apartment was intended as Anne's guestroom for the visits she never made.

❦

I have described my house very awkwardly to you, but to be regular: it stands on a rising ground, and the court is large enough for a coach-and-six to drive round commodiously. The front of the house is simple but pretty – five windows in front, two stories high, with a portico at the hall door, to which you ascend by six steps, but so well sheltered by the roof of the portico that it is secured from rain. The hall is 26 f. by 22 and 12 f. and a half high, the ceiling finished in compartments, with a Doric entablature in stucco round the room. On the right hand is the eating parlour, 26 f. long and 16 f. and a half wide, with a projection in the middle, which opens thirteen foot and is eight foot deep, with three windows, and large enough for two side-boards, one window between the tables and one at each side, which lights the room very agreeably; it is a very charming room, cool in Summer and warm in winter; the chimney is at one end and a window over against it; on the left hand of the hall is another large room, which at present is unfinished, but is designed for a chapel when we are rich enough to finish it as we ought to do.

At the end of the hall is a very neat stone stair-case, well finished with stucco, which leads to the apartment I have described above. Beyond the stair-case, below, is a little hall; on the right hand is a small parlour, where we breakfast and sup, out of it our present bedchamber and a large light closet within it; it is but a small apartment but very pretty, and lies pleasantly to the gardens, and as we sit by the fire-side we can see the ships ride in the harbour. From the door of the little parlour are about ten steps that carry you to my English room, and another flight of the same stairs lead to the rooms over the little parlour, and bedchamber and the maids rooms, and serve for back stairs to the great apartment ... I forgot to add, that out of my English room you go into the library, which is *most plentifully filled*, and D.D. has filled up the vacancies of my shelves with the modern poets nicely bound. (Dublin, 12 July 1744)

The hall Mrs. Delany described at Delville was high and airy. The ceiling was blocked out in small stucco coffers or sunken squares. Anne, or any educated person, could readily picture a Doric entablature. The classical orders of architecture were Doric, Tuscan, Ionic, Corinthian and Composite. In origin, the orders described ancient door shaft and lintel construction. This basic structural motif was developed through antiquity into a highly stylised classification system, which codified the architectural laws of proportion and decoration. The Doric entablature in the hall at Delville was a system of stucco mouldings on the upper part of the wall following these rules. The first layer was an architrave, which represented a crossbeam. The frieze above that was a band of plain stucco. The cornice topped that – this was a slightly projected moulding, intended in its ancient Greek origins to throw rainwater off the door. The Doric order, which had simple columns (pillars or shafts), capitals (heads or caps on top of the columns) and entablature, was considered an appropriate order for a hall or vestibule. The orders ascended in importance to the Corinthian or Composite: these had the most elaborate capitals and were used in the grandest rooms.

By the beginning of the eighteenth century, it had become fashionable to have a separate room in which to eat. This eating parlour or dining-room may not have been the grandest room of the house, but it was very dear, as we know, to Mrs. Delany's heart. The dimensions she gave were generous, and the rectangular projection she wrote of appears on the right-hand side in drawings and photographs of Delville. From about 1700, it was fashionable to create a niche within the dining-room to contain the sideboard, and Mrs. Delany intended to put two sideboards into the niche. At this time, a sideboard or buffet was essentially a serving table. On formal occasions, the best pieces of plate or family silver were set up on the buffet or sideboard. When guests crossed the threshold of the eating parlour, they were arrested by the showy display across the room. The new "terrene" with its "chasing mighty well done" (Delville, 25 January 1746) that they had made was just the sort of item that would have taken pride of place. Wealth and status were demonstrated at every opportunity. Though dinner was eaten mid-afternoon, the silver would sparkle and catch the light as winter evenings drew in and the candles were lit.

Until the middle of the eighteenth century, the average dining-room contained virtually no cupboard space; the napery was brought in by the servants, the cutlery was contained in knife boxes or cases and the plate was on show on the sideboards. Other items such as plate carriers or plate buckets, plate warmers, dumb-waiters, wine coolers, cheese coasters, bottle sliders and cellarets were introduced at a later stage. Another piece of furniture called a gentleman's comforter or a gentleman's necessary was part of the dining-room appointments. This contained a chamber pot or potty. When the ladies withdrew after dinner, the gentlemen relieved themselves into this article to the satisfaction of all parties.

Life was always more difficult for ladies, and some were less delicate than others. Lady Louisa Connolly recorded that their visitor Lady Barrymore, a great old friend of the Connolly and Kildare families, on one occasion jumped up and said:

> Well, I vow to God, I can stay no longer here. I am dying with the gripes – want to shit most dreadfully and stay letting it bake out of civility to you Lady Anne. Jane, Jane, this instant, child, show me to the little house or I'll break your head, Run, I say!

When Lady Barrymore rejoined her company, she gave a description of her expedition to the "house of office", how charming and comfortable it was and how happy it made her.

Dining tables from this period were functional and not very big. Furniture was moved around a lot, and a second table was often drafted in if the numbers were too great. Mrs. Delany often refers to her second table. The most common shape was oval with two folding or drop leaves supported by extra legs, which swung out from knuckle joints underneath. These tables were intended to be versatile; they could be folded down and put back against the wall when not in use. Another wave of dining tables became popular around the 1760s. These were designed to accommodate more people. The drop leaves of the new tables were now rectangular in shape, and an extra free-standing table was added at each end. These accessory tables were usually D-shaped or semicircular, now regularly referred to as D-ends. They were clipped on to the main table. When unclipped, they could be used separately as side or pier tables.

Small, neat drop-leaved tables were used for breakfast and supper, but as time went on, more elbowroom was required. Jane Austen, the great observer of society, reflected this trend. *Emma* was published in 1816 and in it Miss Woodhouse, the heroine of the novel, prevailed on her company to take their seats around the large, modern circular table that she had introduced at Hartfield:

> and which none but Emma could have had power to place there and persuade her father to use, instead of the small-sized Pembroke, on which two of his daily meals had, for forty years, been crowded. Tea passed pleasantly, and nobody seemed in a hurry to move.

In Mrs. Delany's day, crowding around the table, sitting like ramrods on straight-backed chairs was the norm. "To tell the plain truth," wrote Madame Marie Anne Fiquet du Boccage in her *Letters Concerning England, Holland and Italy* in 1750:

> There are scarce any armchairs in their apartments; they are satisfied with common chairs. The women who use no paint and are always laced, (as was formerly the custom in *France*), are fond of these seats; in their court dresses they resemble the pictures of our great grandmothers; but they are extremely affable and obliging in their behaviour.

❧

Closing the door on the eating parlour and crossing the hall brought the visitor to another fine room, destined to be the chapel. Mrs. Delany brought her artistic talents to bear on the chapel some years later. Her initial reports on Delville went on to describe the stone staircase, which was the formal staircase giving access to the drawing-room on the first floor. She described a secondary hall towards the back or return of the house. The parlour they used for breakfast and supper and their current bedchamber with ubiquitous closet was situated on this hall. A short back staircase took visitors up to Mrs. Delany's English room. She was fitting this apartment out to her own taste, which was why the upholsterers were summoned with such alacrity. She wrote:

> I expected a great deal of business, but not so much as I find; I have workmen of all sorts in the house – upholsterers, joiners, glaziers, and carpenters – and am obliged to watch them all, or their work would be but ill-finished: and I have not been one day without company since I came. (Delville, 26 July 1744)

Plans to visit the Deanery of Down for the first time threatened to halt proceedings, and a slightly discommoded Mrs. Delany wrote:

> If I could be reconciled to leaving Delville I should be very well pleased with this little pilgrimage, but I own I leave it for a day with regret. We shall take this opportunity of having our house whitewashed, and some part painted, and many other finishings which we are now very busy in giving directions about. (Delville, 28 August 1744)

"My English room is quite unfurnished again," she wrote a few weeks later:

> and under the painter's hands. I have had it painted a sort of olive, somewhat lighter than my brother's, for the sake of my pictures, and because the room is very light. I have had the frieze painted with festoons of flowers and shells alternate, and you can't imagine what a pretty effect it has; as soon as the room is dry, which will be about a fortnight hence, I shall be very busy in replacing my goods. We now live in our great parlour, which is a most comfortable room. Oh that I could bring you and our dearest mama to this dwelling with a wish!
> (Delville, 23 September 1744)

Olive was one of the staple colours of the house-painter's trade. It occurs in the price lists of the famous London paintmaker and supplier Emmerton from 1730 as "ready-mixed and ground in oil at 8 pence to 1 schilling, per pound". Mrs. Delany clearly chose this colour because it provided a good backdrop to pictures – gilt frames looked very well against olive green – but it was also in emulation of a room belonging to that arbiter of taste Bernard Granville. The frieze was her own design, one of many executed at Delville, of painted garlands alternating with pendant shell collages. Some of Mrs. Delany's exquisite shell-work survived in Delville up to the 1950s.

Mrs. Delany kept her eye in on her regular visits back to England. She wrote to Anne about their accommodation at Pall Mall in London:

> My lodging consists of one parlour (staircase is light and easy) and a drawing-room, a size larger than what I had in Clarges Street: tapestry

hangings, crimson stuff damask curtains and chairs, and tolerable glasses between the windows. The bed-chamber backwards, new and clean; crimson and yellow flaring hangings of paper, and a bed of the same materials as the curtains in the dining-room; but it looks into a pretty garden, and over the Prince of Wales's into the park, which is cheerful and pleasant. The two pair of stair rooms and the garrets all very tolerable. The rent four guineas a week; the situation is next door to the Cocoa Tree, which is the direction for me. Foley and Gran come to town tomorrow. (Pall Mall, 15 January 1747)

On another occasion they stayed at Cornbury, the home of Lord Douglas, son of the Duke and Duchess of Queensbury, from where she sent a detailed description of their apartments:

I never saw anything equal to it. It consists of two large rooms and a bedchamber: the first room is hung with flowered paper of a grotesque pattern, the colours lively and the pattern bold and handsome, (that is the Dean's dressing- room); the next room is hung with the finest Indian paper of flowers and *all sorts of birds*, (that is my dressing-room); the ceilings are all ornamented in the Indian taste, the frames of the glass and all the finishing of the room are well-suited; the bedchamber is also hung with Indian paper on a gold ground and the bed is Indian work of silks and gold on white satin; the windows look into the park, which is kept like the finest garden and is a Paradise. (Cornbury, 30 October 1746)

The term "India" paper was the name given to exotic, expensive hand-painted Chinese wallpaper. Before the 1740s, these wallpapers were only available from the east, and the confusion over naming arose because importation was through the East India Company. The earliest and finest examples of India paper were separate self-contained pictures, each on individual panels of paper. The most expensive kind depicted the human figure in Chinese life. The next price range depicted birds and flowers, which was the type Mrs. Delany admired at Cornbury. She also reported that the ceiling and mirror frames were "well suited" — they were probably an eclectic feast of Chinese fretwork with rococo scrolls and chinoiserie motifs, miniature pagodas and the like. This was high fashion of the period. Some of these ideas might have been stored away for future reference, though Mrs. Delany applied decorum to her decorating as to every other facet of life. India paper might be all very well in a grand house such as Cornbury but perhaps not in Delville.

There were shops or Chinese paper warehouses selling India papers in at least three locations in London. In Dublin, John Russell "at the Indian Woman in Bride Street, Paper-Stainer" is recorded as early as 1737, advertising papers both "flocked and plain", but it is unlikely that he actually stocked India paper because, as late as 1758, when young Lady Louisa Connolly was making her wedding visits in England, she wrote home to her sister Lady Kildare at Carton: "I shall not bring over India paper for the bedchamber and dressing-room, as they will not be done this year, and then perhaps there may be something new." Lady Kildare herself created what she called her Chinese room at Carton the following year, but when the panels of Chinese or India wallpaper arrived there were not enough to cover the walls. Accordingly, she had borders made in whimsical Chinese shapes, fans and such like, and fitted her wallpaper panels into the shapes. She had the intervening empty wall space painted in peacock blue to set off her Chinese scenes. The effect she achieved was not unlike that of a print room, another great fad among eighteenth-century leisured ladies.

The most outstanding print room still surviving in Ireland is Lady Louisa Connolly's at Castletown, dating from around 1765. This is, as the name suggests, a room or gallery hung entirely with prints or engravings. The theme of Louisa's gallery is family life and domesticity, and a key to the various engravings hangs in the room.

Mrs. Delany, always at the cutting edge, literally and metaphorically, was well ahead of Castletown. A letter written to her brother in 1751 suggests she was creating something of a print room herself:

> I have received the six dozen borders all safely, and return you, my dear brother, many thanks for them. They are for framing prints. I think them much prettier than any other sort of frame for that purpose, and where I have *not* pictures, I *must* have prints; otherwise, I think prints best in books. The manner of doing them is to have straining-frames made as much larger than your print as will allow of the border; the straining-frame covered with coarse cloth, the print pasted on it, and then the borders, leaving half an inch or rather less of margin round the print. Mr. Vesey has a room filled with prints made up in that way, and they look very well. (Delville, 11 April 1751)

Improvements continued to be made and new furnishings were introduced, including a bespoke cabinet to display Mrs. Delany's shell collection:

> We are very busy in settling all my drawers of
> shells, sorting and cleaning them. I have a new
> cabinet with whole glass doors and glass on the
> side and shelves within, of whimsical shapes, to
> hold *all my beauties*. One large drawer underneath
> for the register drawer ... (Believed to be 11
> July 1747)

Mrs. Delany had a lifelong interest in the natural world. She
used huge quantities of shells in her shell grottoes and
decorative festoons, but she also collected and classified
specimen shells. Collecting was a very fashionable pursuit of
her class and shared amongst her friends; the Duchess of
Portland was a formidable exponent. Mrs. Delany traded shells
all her life with the avidity of the most zealous collector, and
she paid significant sums for unique examples. The register
drawer housed her lists of shells, possibly her accounts and the
code or plan of the cabinet. Similar glass cases to the cabinet
she described are still to be seen at Newbridge House in
Donabate. A dedicated room there, the famous museum of
curiosities, though of later date, displays the Cobbe family
collections of shells, fossils, minerals and all sorts of
curiosities from exotic parts. Anne, too, collected shells; she
passed the interest on to Mary Dewes who in turn passed it on
to G.M.A., and later Mrs. Delany urged the providing of a
little cabinet or bureau for G.M.A. to order her shells.

❧

> We are going to be very busy in settling the
> library. The Dean has made an addition at the
> end of it of a sort of closet, to which you
> ascend by one step; it opens with an arch, five
> foot and a-half wide; there is to be a window at
> the end which is east, and on the south side,
> opposite to the south window, there is to be

looking-glass representing a sash window, which will reflect the prospect, and prevent the cold of the north: it is to be all stucco, and adorned with pilasters, a table in the middle for writing and holding papers, and only convenient room left for going round it and for seats. The old part of the library is 32 ft long, and about 11 feet wide; it holds a great many books and when finished will be very pleasant; the prospect from the new window charming. How often shall I wish for you to help me to settle the books – an employment you always were fond of; here you would meet some that would amuse you very well. The addition is 12ft. sq. (Delville, 6 October 1747)

The library was an important room in the house: a gentleman's library reflected his taste and cultivation. It was the domain of the dean. The young widow Mrs. Pendarves had been impressed by Dr. Delany's scholarship when she first met him. It was a quality she found most attractive. When he made his proposal years later, she hoped his learning and the respect he was held in by his peers would offset his lack of birth or fortune. However his library, no matter how well stocked, did nothing to assuage Bernard Granville's dislike of the match.

Building works did not daunt the Delanys. They added niches, windows and extensions and generally made it up as they went along – something that makes for interesting reflections on today's planning regulations. A photograph of Delville taken in 1946 shows eight sash windows to the front of the house, four on the ground floor and four on the first. A drawing by Letty Bushe done in 1754 shows five windows on the first floor. Mrs. Delany, in her first despatch (12 July 1744), cited five windows in total to the front of her house, two on the ground floor and three on the first. Expediency and their own taste were the only authorities the Delanys applied to, and Delville was altered at will.

❧

"Wednesday, I travelled all over Dublin shopping; bespeaking paper for hangings, linen for beds, and a thousand things too tedious to be here inserted" (Delville, 8 June 1750). The thousand things Mrs. Delany calls tedious are precisely what interest us today, and we know she bought locally because in another letter she proudly declares:

> I have done up a little apartment, hung it with
> blue-and-white paper, and intend a bed of blue-
> and white linen – *all Irish manufacture*; and hope
> some day to be so happy as to show it to you,
> but your apartment is allotted in another part of
> the house. (Delville, 15 July 1750)

The street directories show that wallpaper manufacturers, or paper-stainers as they were called, generally had two premises, a retail outlet in a fashionable street and a "factory". Wallpaper making thrived in Dublin at this period. Mrs. Ada Leask (Mrs. H. Longfield) in *History of the Dublin Wallpaper Industry in the Eighteenth Century* (1947) lists around one hundred paper-stainers working in Dublin between 1700 and 1800. Bernard and James Messink of Blind Quay advertised wallpapers made "in imitation of Tapestry or Needlework, fit for hanging of Rooms" in 1746. In 1777 Michael Boylan of Grafton St advertised "Plain Papers now so much used in London and Dublin" and listed some of the colours available: "Pea Green, verditer, Blue, Peach ... Queen's Brown, Hair Stone, Lemon". The principal source of design patterns for Dublin paper-stainers at the time was London. Without regard for copyright, at the start of each season the wallpaper makers of Dublin would travel to London, returning with examples of the latest patterns. These would be copied post haste and advertised for sale. This also happened with clothing, where style changes were pirated wholesale.

Until the late 1830s, wallpaper was printed on lengths formed from individual sheets of handmade rag pulp paper measuring approximately twenty-one by eighteen inches. They were glued together by overlapping the edges. Hand-blocked paper was printed with thick distemper paint and stuck on with a flour and water paste or animal glue size. The paper-stainer was responsible for arranging to have the paper hung, and many paper-stainers also describe themselves as house-painters in the trade directories. Paper-staining, though a highly specialised art, seems to have been carried on in conjunction with other allied skills, such as cotton and linen printing. Mrs. Delany's scheme involved a blue and white paper with matching blue and white linen for the bed. Her paper and linen were probably bespoke from the same manufacturer. In the majority of cases, other aspects of interior decoration, such as house painting, gilding or floor-cloth making, also went with the paper-straining trade.

Mrs. Delany now had some practical design advice for Anne:

> I suppose when you turn your kitchen into a parlour, you will fit the wainscot of the best bedchamber there, and hang the bedchamber with paper. Whenever you put up paper, the best way is to have it pasted on the bare wall; when lined with canvass it always shrinks from the edges. I have stripped down old stuff beds and sent them to Mount Panther, and in their stead am putting up blue and white linen and blue and white paper hangings, this has taken up a good

deal of attention, as I am new sashing the room, new setting the grate, enlarging the room, and several alterations that require my overseeing and must be done before we leave Delville that the rooms may be fit for use by the time we return. My work-room I am going to new model, the wainscot wants new painting, is cracked and has started in some places; the paper I have chosen is pearl coloured caffoy paper; the pattern like damask: the pictures look extremely well on that colour, and the crimson damask window-curtain and chairs will suit very well with it. (Delville, 30 June 1750)

Anne's house was topsy-turvy, the kitchen was being converted into a parlour. The wainscot from her best bed-chamber was to be pulled out and re-fitted in the new parlour. A wainscot was a boarded panelling, made in the previous centuries of oak. By the middle of the eighteenth century, oak wainscot was deemed hopelessly old fashioned. Reception rooms and stairwells in fashionable houses were covered in fielded panels usually made in Baltic pine. The advantage of this type of panelling, which had raised, flat central areas, was that it made for much lighter interiors, and unlike the old oak panelling, it could be painted and repainted from time to time to ring the changes. Stuccoed walls eventually replaced fielded panelling. This was not only a whim of fashion but also because wood panelling was a serious fire hazard. This upheaval in Anne's house was to the considerable dismay of the generations of mice thriving behind the wainscot.

Anne's bedchamber was to be new hung with wallpaper. Early wallpapers were pasted to stretched hessian or canvas linings, which provided a smooth flat finish, an idea very similar to Mrs. Delany's method of framing prints. Wooden laths or battens were fastened to the walls, hessian was tacked on to the battens and the wallpaper was pasted on top. A gap between the battens and the wall also gave the mice a free run, and they were safe to return until Mrs. Delany upset their plan by suggesting Anne paste her paper directly on to the surface of the wall itself.

Then she wrote quite imperiously:

> I beg your pardon, Madam, I am not for your shutting up any window in the new parlour but that which you propose doing. A workroom must have light *near the chimney*, or it is very inconvenient and uncomfortable, so go on with your scheme, which is a very good one. A room cannot be handsome which does not well answer the purpose it was designed for. (7 November 1751)

Anne was undecided about her parlour and must have also reconsidered the wainscot idea because Mrs. Delany advised her anew: "If your parlour is stuccoed (though I think I should rather hang it with stucco paper), you must have plugs of wood where you think to hang pictures to fix nails in, as they cannot be driven into stucco" (Delville, 11 January 1752).

Delville itself was a hive of activity. Mrs. Delany was enlarging rooms and new-sashing windows and setting new grates. The work-room she referred to was about to be redecorated. This was the closet adjoining the crimson-damask bedchamber. The wainscot, reaching from floor to chair rail, needed re-painting. The new wallpaper to go above that was to be a pearl-coloured caffoy. Caffoy was a stamped woollen velvet used in the first half of the eighteenth century, a type of flocked wallpaper. The designs for flocks were drawn or stencilled on sized or sticky paper, which was then thickly covered with clippings of wool, creating the raised damask effect. The all-important pictures would look well against the pearly tones, which in turn would contrast beautifully with the crimson scheme next door. The texture of the caffoy paper would echo the texture of the damask curtains and chair covers. Mrs. Delany thought of everything.

> I am going to make a very comfortable closet;– to have a dresser, and all manner of working tools, to keep all my stores for *painting, carving, gilding,* etc; for my own room is now so clean and pretty that I cannot suffer it to be strewed with litter, only books and work, and the closet belonging to it to be given up to prints, drawings, and my collection of fossils, petrifactions, and minerals. I have not set them in order yet; a great work it will be, but when done very comfortable. There is to my working closet a pleasant window that overlooks all the garden, it faces east, is always dry and warm. In the middle of the closet a deep nitch with shelves, where I shall put whatever china I think too good for common use, but trifling and insignificant is my *store-room* to what yours is! Mine fits only an idle mind that wants amusement; yours serves either to supply your hospitable table, or gives cordial and healing medicines to the poor and the sick. Your mind is ever turned to help, relieve, and bless your neighbours and acquaintance; whilst mine, I fear (however I may sometimes flatter myself that I have a contrary disposition), *is too much filled* with amusements of no real estimation; and when people commend any of my performances I feel a consciousness that my time might have been better employed. (Delville, 6 October 1750)

The eighteenth-century notion of a closet is difficult to grasp, and in this extract Mrs. Delany is writing about two separate closets, creating even more confusion. When she spoke of "her own room", she referred to her olive-green English apartment, the private domain where she allowed the dean temporary refuge while his library was in disarray. The closet adjoining this room was an important one because it housed her prints, drawings and her special mineral collections. It was like her cabinet of curiosities and print room combined.

This room exemplified the eighteenth-century hunger for knowledge of the natural world and other worlds, a curiosity that later characterised the period known as the Enlightenment. In that spirit, she approved mightily of a drum or gathering to view noted scholar Dr. Pocock's collection:

> Next Tuesday we are to go in the afternoon to an Egyptian drum at Dr. Pocock's. Instead of spreading his table with cards, I hope he designs to cover them with drawers of curiosities, and instead of the tittle-tattle of the town to give us some philosophical lectures! It would be pleasant enough to see the surprise of the smart beaux and belles when they observe such an entertainment prepared for them; and instead of the rooms being decorated with china, japan, indian paper, and looking glasses, to observe nothing but Egyptian deities on pedestals, tables covered with precious fragments such as toes and fingers, lumps of stone that have neither shape nor beauty of colour, Turkish robes hanging on pegs, travelling kitchen utensils, etc. and a medley that would make

much too large a catalogue for my paper to contain. (Delville, 22 April 1752)

She wrote of a new "very comfortable closet" to store her tools for painting, gilding and carving. This closet was to have a small suite of cupboards or a dresser fitted. It also had a "deep nitch with shelves". These niches were built for display purposes and often had shell- or scallop-shaped canopies overhead. Mrs. Delany's fine china would look very well on open shelves in a niche of that sort. The working tools would remain hidden behind the dresser doors only to appear when Mrs. Delany's *meitheal* or group of co-workers came around.

She was always happy to contribute to Anne's decorative schemes, and a sewing bee could be called on if there was pressure to finish a project:

> I am glad your works go on so well, and am sorry I have no knotting of the sort you want done. I cannot promise too much for you till I have finished a plain fringe I am knotting to trim a new blue and white linen bed I have just put up; as soon as that is finished I will do some sugar-plum [a knotting stitch] for you; but I fear you will want it before I can do any quantity: let me know, and mine may lie by till yours is done, and send me the sized knotting you want; I have a good friend also that I can employ I believe for you. (Delville, 27 October 1750)

Working co-operation was not confined to Anne. In the same letter she wrote:

> I wish your house finished, as this is a bad time of year to be incumbered with workmen. Monday, I went to Dublin, was two hours and a half

choosing worsteds for a friend in the North,
who is working *a fright* of a carpet! (Delville, 2
November 1751)

❧

Mrs. Delany wrote to her brother, a noted horticulturist:

> I am now considering about a greenhouse, and
> believe I shall build one this spring; my orange-
> trees thrive *so well* they deserve one. I propose
> having it 26 ft by 13, and 13 high, and a room
> under it (with chimney for my poultry-woman)
> that will open into a little back garden, which I
> intend to make my menagerie. Will you tell me
> if the chimney will be any disadvantage to my
> orange-trees? I am called upon to dress. Adieu!
> (Delville, 19 January 1751)

Mrs. Delany's gardening is a subject for another book, but the
garden cannot entirely be ignored because, though small, it
was quite famous in its day and was central to the Delanys'
charmed existence at Delville for the years they spent there.

Around the house was a small parterre on which they
successfully grew orange trees. The neighbourhood was, and
still is, in a mild climate belt, a sort of microclimate, which
allowed the cultivation of orange trees. This microclimate is
very much enjoyed by the Botanic Gardens today. To the north
of Delville, a walkway led to an Ionic temple, adjoining the
church, and above the portico was the inscription *"fastigia
despicit urbis"*, a pun on multiple levels attributed to Swift,
proclaiming that the inhabitants vomit from a great height
upon the despised city of Rome – in this case, Dublin. Swift
had been unhappy with Dr. Delany's defection to what he
considered inaccessible country. Nearer the house there were

walks lined by fruit trees, a bowling-green, flowers and sweet briars. At the end of one of these walks was a grotto-cave with a seat in the opening to take in the view. There were paddocks for the cattle and deer sloping down to a stream, which flowed into the Tolka River. Temples, rustic bridges, trees and shrubs, among them arbutus, ilex, elms, oaks and yew, ennobled the scene.

Edward Malins, writing about the landscape at Delville in the *Quarterly Bulletin of the Irish Georgian Society* in 1968, said that the garden at Delville had been the first of its kind in Ireland and was a model for many on a larger scale. Parts of the garden, he suggests, must have been

> very similar to parts of the nearby Botanic Gardens today, especially in the treatment of water in the glen.
>
> It was what was called a *ferme ornée*, though in miniature. The fields were used as pasture for cows, and the grass paths and walks meandered round them. The garden led out into fields and woodland, and by judicious planting in these paddocks, a series of vistas and key points could be made which did not interfere with agricultural practice. And this is exactly how the Delanys laid out Delville. The Delanys had eighteen head of deer in the fields, and the orange trees thrived, and in the summer they used to breakfast out of doors, amid the roses, jasmines and pinks, or sometimes under the shade of the nut trees with an Irish harper playing old tunes to them.

Amongst other improvements, Mrs. Delany planned a nine-pin bowling alley and a house for cultivating auriculas at the end of the garden. Her shell-work extended to a chandelier for the grotto. By eighteenth-century standards, its eleven acres were very small, yet at his death Dr. Delany was said to be virtually bankrupt. Swift had intimated as much in his "An Epistle upon an Epistle":

> But you, forsooth, your all must squander
> On that poor spot, call'd Dell-ville, yonder;
> And when you've been at vast expenses
> In whims, parterres, canals and fences,
> Your assets fail, and cash is wanting;
> Nor farther buildings, farther planting;
> No wonder when you raise and level,
> Think this wall low, and that wall bevel.
> Here a convenient box you found,
> Which you demonish'd to the ground;
> Then built, then took up with your arbour,
> And set the house to Rupert Barber.

❧

Back in England, on one of her many visits to Bulstrode, the home of the Duchess of Portland, Mrs. Delany enquired of Anne:

> Have you begun the shade for your toilette? If not, I believe you must do it to wash, for the catgut in time grows very limp, and the silk fuses. I should think a border the same as that of our great-grandmother's netting, and the middle part worked plain in the common way on the very coarse catgut would be best.
> (Bulstrode, 21 December 1753)

Lady Llanover said in her footnote to this piece that she believed Mrs. Delany invented this type of netting. The groundwork was like catgut in squares, upon which were worked "by the eye" beautiful and intricate designs in white thread, like lacework, in all sorts of stitches. When finished, it was put on coloured silk for toilet tables. Ladies' dressing-tables and the mirrors above them were often draped, and this mode lasted for a number of years.

History repeated itself frequently with Mrs. Delany, and fourteen years later she directed Mary Dewes in the very same employment:

> I think your fancy about taking a gimp round the flowers on the toilet would be pretty, but too much work, nor would it I believe quite answer; I should think your best way would be to put the flowers between two fine catguts, and tack them slightly round the edges, to keep them in their place, with very fine thread or silk, and if with a brush pencil you put a little starch (which is better than gum) on the back of the flowers and leaves when you place them on the catgut that is to be the ground, it would give a stiffness that would be an advantage to the whole: it must be done in a frame, and were you to do it in flounces as mine was done, you would I think be better able to manage it; three flounces would be enough, and they should hang a little full; your largest flowers must be at the bottom. I am sure you will do better than I can direct you, this is only in complaisance with your request, and so with love and best wishes from all here, I end my long recipe for a toilet! (Delville, 23 April 1767)

As Dr. Delany advanced in years and the Tenison case pressed harder, he determined Mrs. Delany should have the security of a house of her own, and he bought a house in

Spring Gardens in London for her security. This house was a source of great work and satisfaction, as Mrs. Delany wrote from Bulstrode:

> We came to town on Monday as we had designed. Much disappointed at finding the house no forwarder; but we have set all hands to work. The house is small, but very pretty, convenient, and in a delightful situation ... On Monday, after some fretting, a great deal of scolding and expostulation with Mr. Lambert, our builder, came to Whitehall. Lord Titchfield [second son of the Duchess of Portland] made us a visit, he is a charming youth: we engaged him to dinner, and eat our beef-steak and roast fowl at 3, considered our house over and over and read between the whiles. Yesterday morning, after an hundred interruptions and settling where the dressers, boiler, stoves, etc. etc. were to be placed, we went to see Mrs. Donnellan at Fulham. (Bulstrode, 25 October 1754)

While waiting for the house to dry, she wrote:

> Mrs. Vesey's house in Bolton Row is empty, and if they are not in England when I come to town after Xtmas we go there till our own house is perfectly aired and safe. The stucco men have not yet done the dining-room. (Whitehall, 5 November 1754)

Fielded panelling in deal had been dispensed with in favour of stucco walls, and some comfortable chairs were also thankfully introduced by this time:

> I have bespoke four armed chairs and six other stuffed rushed for the drawing-room, and seats

low and easy such as we love; but Mr. Dewes shall have a chair of *his own* when he does me the favour to come in *every room*, or at least a cushion to raise him. I have bought a charming old-fashioned cabinet for eight guineas that I dare say was not made for twenty. (Bulstrode, 24 November 1754)

London was expanding at a great rate in the 1750s. The houses at Spring Gardens were part of the new speculative building boom of the time. Graceful new terraces were being bought up by the upwardly mobile middle classes, but the Spring Gardens scheme was aimed at a higher end of the market. The following extract gives a very good account of a "day in the life" of Mrs. Delany at that period:

On Thursday morning at ten, D.D. went into the City, and I to the terrace in Spring Garden, where I scolded at some things that were and some things that were not done. Lady Dorothy Hotham, who is next door to us, (on whom I called,) had been in her house these six weeks, and says they have got no cold. We shall not go to town till this day fortnight, and that depends on Lady Harriet and Lady Margaret gathering strength [they were recovering from smallpox], and an alteration of weather. When I had done in Spring Garden, I went to Mr. Pitt's auction of shells, and met two *fine men* there by appointment – *Mr. Granville* and Capt. Kirke, but had not time to examine half the treasure of shells there displayed. Called at a print shop to see a specimen of some exotic coloured plants that Mr. Miller [Philip Miller, Superintendent of the Society of Apothecaries Physic Garden, Chelsea] is going to publish: they are pretty well done: I shall subscribe, they come out monthly, 6 for a crown. Then went to Craven Street, to Mrs. Granville, who is very much out of order with a slow fever; went from her home to dress at two. Called on Mrs Montagu, [bluestocking hostess and author], Hanover Square ... By half-an-hour after three I got to Mrs. Donnellan's – nobody dined there but her nephew; my brother came by the time we had dined, then Mrs. Foley, then Mrs. Montagu, then Mr. Campbell, Mr. Bernard, and Miss Cooley, – so that I left her in company again without the opportunity of saying one private word. In my way home I called on Lady Tweeddale, Lady Wallingford, and Dash – nobody at home. On Friday morning I settled accounts and gave orders. (Bolton Row – Mrs. Vesey's house, lent to the Delanys till their own was ready – 22 February 1755)

When the house was finally finished, Anne was given directions to it:

I had a letter today from Mr. Shuttleworth, who assures us our house is dry and safe, and I hope nothing will prevent your being in town on Saturday se'night the 22nd. The street we live in is called New Street in Spring Garden, and our house is the last in the row. I wish you to come from your coach in a chair, as you will have a good way to walk. (Bulstrode, 12 March 1755)

The snag list was not a new phenomenon. Mrs. Delany wrote, "I like my house *mightily*, but some of my chimneys smoke, and we are trying to cure them" (Spring Gardens, 18 March 1755). She got into her decorating stride again:

My "*dining room*," vulgarly so called is hung with mohair cafoy paper, (*a good blue*) curtains not up, chairs not covered, mahogany cabinet very pretty fills up the recess between the window and chimney, and new glasses are put up between the windows ... Instead of the red and white Irish linen I shall put up a stuff and silk damask bed. At present we have brought down your blue bed and placed it in our alcove. (16 December 1755)

The following year, the Delanys were at Bath, both unwell:

The Dean is rather better this evening; if well enough to preach a charity sermon on Sunday at St. James's, but I think he will hardly be able. I had a letter last post from my brother, who is much pleased with his *new bath*. (4 November 1756)

Washing with water had become popular in the wake of Rousseau's eulogising of nature. Baths of the period were portable, usually made of wood, copper or lead. The servants, of course, had the job of hauling the pitchers of hot water to fill them. A quick rubdown with a spirit of wine would have sufficed before this, but bathing with soap (called washballs) and water now came into vogue. Louis XV of France had a dedicated bathroom installed at Versailles around 1770. This bathroom was plumbed and had two tubs, one for washing and one for rinsing. He also had a vermeil-lined (silver gilt) exotic veined-wood bidet. It seems that Bernard Granville, a great man of fashion himself, may actually have been ahead of the French court.

Cleanliness was next to godliness, and once back in Delville, the chapel finally had to be tackled:

I am going to make a wreath to go round the circular window in the chapel, of oak branches, vines and corn; the benches for the servants are fixed, the chairs for the upper part of the chapel are a whim of mine, but I am not sure till I see a pattern chair that I shall like it; it is to be in the shape and ornamented like a gothic arch. If it pleases me in the execution I'll send you a sketch. (1758, part of a letter).

By this time there was a move away from the type of ordered Palladian classicism exemplified by the library extension the Delanys had instituted. The French (Rococo), Chinese and Gothic tastes and a new style that blended all three were being adopted in England by makers of furniture as well as by architects and builders. Mrs. Delany, always moving with the times, bespoke her chairs with back splats in the shape of the gothic lancet window.

The Gothic taste was finding expression in sham castles and picturesque ruins. On a visit to England some time later, she visited another private chapel, one she highly disapproved of:

Last Thursday we went to Old Windsor to see Mr. Bateman's [a noted collector], which I had not seen since his converting it from the Indian to the Gothic. Its outward appearance is venerable – arched porticos and windows, Gothic towers and battlements ... I was a little provoked at his chapel ... it is an exact representation of a popish chapel expensively decorated – not a circumstance omitted, and more than I can enumerate; but all I can say of it, it is like peeping through a show-glass in a box. There are many crucifixes in it, ivory figures of saints, crowns, and crosses set with sapphire, a little case called the treasury filled with rosaries, crosses, and a thousand things relating to ceremonies that I don't understand; and it is so adorned, so crowded, that is it almost impossible to distinguish one thing from another, but what must offend every serious observer must be the intent of this chapel, for if he does *not* make use of it in *good earnest*, his making a joke of it is *shocking*; and at least he should have omitted the *sacred figure*, which ought to strike with awe and reverence, besides nobody can justify turning any religion into ridicule, though some ceremonies may be trifling and absurd, but I don't suppose he desires to be thought of a papist, and perhaps he would rather be thought a heathen! (Bulstrode, 10 October 1768)

New projects continued apace in Delville:

I have had my new gardener (who I like mightily) with me to consult about the order of my flower-garden, which is under my dressing-room window, and between us I believe we shall make it very gay and pretty; it is a great amusement to me to see the people at work in it, digging and planting. I can't say my four days confinement upstairs was dull. My bed-chamber is very large, comfortable, with pleasant views and the bow closet! I have now completed it by two looking-glasses that fill the side panels of the bow window, and reflect all the prospects. You would say indeed I am greedy of prospect were you to see it, *not to be contented* without those reflectors; the glasses reach within a foot of the cornice of the ceiling, and are fastened up with double knots of gilded rope. They were put up whilst I was above stairs, and a great amusement. Working and reading, and a little cribbage go on. (Delville, 30 December 1758).

Mrs. Delany had been ill and confined to bed for four days when this extract was written. It must indeed have been very pleasant to watch the workmen dig, a pastoral scene of honest toil afforded only to the idle rich, though Mrs. Delany, in justice, was never actually idle.

❧

When the dean died in 1768, Mrs. Delany was thrown into confusion. The energy, love and vast amount of money they had poured into Delville was a thing of the past. Dr. Daniel Sandford acted as her attorney in Dublin, and Delville was sold with dispatch. In her grief, she considered retiring altogether to Bath, but the Duchess of Portland prevailed on her to stay in London where she would be among friends. Moving house, considered today one of the major traumas in life, did not phase Mrs. Delany. She changed house with ease, even in old age, and between times picked up her traps and visited the homes of her friends for long stays. From the time of the dean's death onwards, she spent the summer months of every year at Bulstrode.

She sent many accounts of the royal visits to Bulstrode. They give a good idea of how Bulstrode was appointed:

> A gracious visit from her R. H. Princess Amelia, has made some little disturbance even in this palace. All the comfortable sophas and great chairs, all the piramids of books (*adorning*

almost every chair), all the tables and *even the spinning-wheel* were banish'd for that day, and the blew damask chairs set in prim form around the room, only one arm'd chair placed in the middle for her Royal Highness ... She was delighted with the place and her entertainment, which was magnificent and pollish'd to the last degree, yet everything conducted with the utmost ease. The Princess went all over the house and garden ... We dined at three, and she had a polite attention to every ingenious ornament on the table, and you may be sure Mr. Levier's [the butler's] ingenuity, etc. was *not idle* on this occasion. (Bulstrode, 14 September 1772)

When even more honoured visitors, the king, George III, and Queen Charlotte, visited some years later, The Honourable Mrs Hamilton sent this description:

Two chairs were placed in the middle of the great drawing-room for the King and Queen. The King placed the Duchess of Portland in his own chair, and walked about himself. Breakfast was prepared in the long gallery that ran the length of the great apartments (suite of eight rooms and three closets). The King and the royal family did not choose to have breakfast brought to the drawing-room, but went to the gallery, where tables were spread with tea, coffee, chocolate, and cakes, fruits and ices, to which succeeded (as if by magic) a cold repast. The Queen remained in the drawing-room, with Mrs. Delany standing at the back of her chair, which was worked in chenilles by Mrs. Delany from nature, of which the Queen expressed great admiration. (Bill Hill, 21 August 1778)

In the three years following the death of her dear D.D., Mrs. Delany sold the house in Spring Gardens and leased another house, which she variously called The Thatched Cottage or The Little Thatch. She bought her last house in St. James's Place. She wrote to her friend Lady Andover about her new home:

> I suppose your ladyship cannot be ignorant of so important a transaction as the present possessor of the "*little Thatch*" having purchased some old walls in St. James's Place, in order to remove thither by the end of July, and she has put *on all her spurs!* But such gentry as carpenters, bricklayers, etc. etc., are invulnerable, and I fear my spurs will not avail; but in order to be ready (should they perform articles), before I came out of town I took down all my books, all my china, packed them in order for removing, that I might come to this paradise with my friend, and have no unneccessary calls to London. (Bulstrode, 3 June 1771)

She made progress and wrote to Lady Andover again at the end of the month:

> Next week I must take a trip to London to look after my workmen, in hopes of being able to remove my furniture and maids into my new house, where I hope to have the honour and happiness of seeing my dear Lady Andover next winter, and placing her in as snug a corner as at the little Thatch. (Bulstrode, 28 June 1771)

St. James's Place was her last home, excepting the cottage in Windsor offered for her use by the king and queen after the death of the Duchess of Portland. True to her extraordinary energy and optimism, she was as enthusiastic about setting up the house in St. James's Place as she had been about Delville. She wrote to Mary Dewes:

> I shall miss them very much [Mary's brothers]; they have worked for me like little horses, and all my books are in pretty good order, and everything else, indeed; but as to comfort or quiet I might for the three last days past as well have lived in a paper-mill, a pewterer's-shop, etc. such sawing, hammering, and all sort of noises, but all pretty well over – and by way of exercise to my lungs I have scolded as smartly (as Dicky's mother could do) at absurd blunders and negligences – but with all faults 'tis *mine own*, and it will appear faultless to me when my dear Ilam friends pay it a visit! I have been more tormented about a carpet than anything else, the old one would not do, and Captain Lechmere gave ten pound for it, which was its full worth; however, he had other conveniences given up to him in THC [The Thatched Cottage] that made matters even, and Mr. Shuttleworth (born to be my torment, and I infatuated to employ him), has disappointed me day after day, and at last in a fit of despair I have submitted to take a very vulgar one, (carpet I mean). (St. James's Place, 7 December 1771)

The continuation of this letter shows the volume of traffic and social life the elderly Mrs. Delany enjoyed in London:

> When I came home I found my table covered with visiting tickets, Lady Bute and her two

daughters, Lady Mansfield and her two nieces, Mrs. Drummond, Miss Auriole – I was sorry they came when I was abroad, which will very seldom happen, for I find the love of my chimney-corner increase, and any hurry a little more than ordinary too much for me; though I assure you I am very well, only lazy, or (as a fine lady not long ago said) "*indigent*," meaning "*indolent*". Apropos to *indigent*, what do you think my bricklayer's bill alone comes to? – £146. I have called in the rest, and if they are all in proportion high, I *may* write "*indigent*" for "*indolent!*" (St. James's Place, 7 December 1771)

Though pressed for funds and battening down the hatches against the cold, Mrs. Delany was planning more improvements:

Mr. Pit called on me yesterday morning; a solitary evening; and this morning I have had list nailed round my doors, and stopping every crack and crevice that let in cold air, which, with good fires, makes my house very comfortable, and I have much reason to be satisfied, though it has been more expensive than is convenient, as I shall not this year be able to make some alterations that I proposed; however, I will hope that Easter Term will finish my Irish affairs, and then I can indulge myself. (St. James's Place, 2 January 1772)

Still concerned about her bills, she wrote to her nephew John Dewes:

I am very comfortably settled in my new house, which is warm, airy, and convenient. At present my head is confused with calling in my bills and making up my accounts, for I think nothing my own till all is paid for, and the people tease me by *not* bringing in their bills; however it is almost accomplished, and I hope then to sit down in peace for the time Providence allots me, thankful for the blessings I have received and humbly hoping that those afflictions and trials I have gone through may be a means of future happiness. (St. James's Place, 7 January 1772)

To her brother she wrote:

I have no news; I am quiet in my chimney corner, and amuse myself with settling my shells that have been all jumbled together, and feel great comfort in having a place I can call *my own*, though it has cost me more than I intended, but not more than with prudent care I can answer; and at the latter end of life, when living abroad is irksome and impracticable, a convenient home is a consolation for the infirmities of age. (St. James's Place, 16 January 1772)

Mrs. Delany, in her seventies, was far from housebound. She got out and about and was as keen-eyed as she had been in her twenties. Along with the rest of London, she visited the newly re-furbished home of Mrs. Elizabeth Montagu, a leading bluestocking, who had built a sensational new town-house at 23 Hill Street. Everybody wanted to see it. Mrs. Delany had already remarked on Mrs. Montagu's penchant for youthful attire, and it seemed she dressed mutton as lamb across several disciplines:

If I had paper and time I could entertain you with the account of Mrs. M.'s (Hill Street) *room of Cupidons;* which was opened with an assembly for all the foreigners, the literati, and the macaronis of the present age. Many and sly are the observations how such a *genius* at her *age*, and so *circumstanced*, could think of painting the walls of her dressing-room with bowers of roses and jessamins entirely inhabited by little Cupids in all their little wanton ways, is astonishing! Unless she looks upon herself as the wife of old Vulcan, and mother, to all these little loves!

I hear the prancing of horses, so must say adieu to my dearest M. (St. James's Place, 28 May 1773)

Mrs. Delany wrote matter-of-factly to Mary:

I will endeavour to get the materials for your work-bag before I go to Bulstrode. Before I go I shall have a troublesome affair to settle, which is taking down my pictures in my drawing-room in order to have the ceiling cleaned and whitewashed; at present it looks fitter for Morpheus's cave, the god of sleep, than for the sprightly circle that so often honour it. (St. James's Place, 10 May 1774)

In the next letter, the following month, she turned her attention from smoky ceilings to imperial dinner plates:

I am just returned from viewing the Wedge-wood-ware that is to be sent to the Empress of Russia. It consists I believe of as many pieces as there are days in the year, if not hours. They are displayed at a house in Greek-street, Soho, called "Portland House"; there are three rooms below and two above filled with it, laid out on tables, everything that can be wanted to serve a dinner; the ground the common ware pale brimstone, the drawings in purple, the borders a wreath of leaves, the middle of each piece a particular view of all the remarkable places in the King's dominions neatly executed. I suppose it will come to a princely price; it is well for the manufacturer, which I am glad of, as his ingenuity and industry deserve encouragement. (St. James's Place, 7 June 1774)

All of London flocked to see this commission for the Imperial Russian court.

Mrs. Delany was always interested in new gardening trends, and Capability Brown, who was commissioned to work on the park of her friends Lord and Lady Bute at Luton, was the fashionable landscaper of the day. Lancelot Capability Brown, along with others such as William Kent and Humphrey Repton, redesigned nature for his wealthy patrons, on occasion razing entire villages that spoilt the view from their houses. The rich at this time wanted their houses and parklands set in sentimental rusticity, but not necessarily the real thing. This taste for what was called more "natural" landscaping, fostered by Capability Brown and others, bent nature herself to the "improving" taste of the rich.

Mary Dewes received a detailed account of the refurbished house and lands at Luton. Mrs. Delany was not impressed:

> The situation you know. They have opened a view to the river, and the ground and plantation are fine. It would be better if there was a greater command of the river, and if Mr. BROWN had not turn'd all the deer *out of the park*; they are

beautiful enliveners of every scene where there is range sufficient for them.

She went on to describe the house:

The only objection to the house is the 42 stone steps, which you must ascend whenever you go up to the lodging appartments. When you are there there is no fault to find, as they are fine rooms, and very commodious; five compleat appartments – a bedchamber, 2 dressing rooms, and rooms overhead for a man and a maid-servant *to each*.

One of these appartments is Lord and Lady Bute's, and 4 for strangers. Up another flight of stairs leads to the attick, where there are as many appartments as compleat, but not as lofty. The furniture well suited to all. The beds damask, and rich sattin, green, blue, and crimson; mine was white sattin. The rooms hung with plain paper, suited to the colour of the beds, except mine, which was pea green, and so is the whole appartment below stairs. The curtains, chairs, and sophas are all plain sattin. Every room filled with pictures; many capital ones: and a handsome screen hangs by each fire-side, with the plan of the room, and with the *names* of the hands by whom the pictures were painted, in the order as they stand. The chimney pieces in *good taste*; no extravagance of fancy; indeed, through-out the house that is avoided. Fine frames to the pictures, but very little gilding besides and the ceilings elegant, and not loaded with ornament. A great variety of fine vases, foreign and English, and marble tables. I think I have led you a dance

eno' to tire you, and I wish I may have given a
description plain enough to understand.
(Bulstrode, 16 September 1774)

It was down to earth and business as usual back in St.
James's Place. Mrs. Boscawen added this postscript in answer
to a query from Mrs. Delany, who was busy mending broken
china: "Quick lime and white of egg is the best ciment for
China" (Blandford Park, 27 December 1774). Mary Dewes
was next in line for Mrs. Delany's assistance:

> I will look out all my blue muslin; I believe I
> have eno' for another chair and a bottom to that
> you have. I wish, my dear child, I could *as easily
> give you* a month's work as provide you with the
> materials, but, as I have said before, there are
> *greater* difficulties to surmount than climbing
> your stupendous hills ... [these "difficulties"
> referred to the estrangement from Bernard
> Granville, who lived close to Ilam]. (St. James's
> Place, 10 March 1775)

At seventy-five years of age, on uncertain roads, in bad
weather and in an uncomfortable cold coach, she was prepared
to make a journey to visit her brother-in-law John Dewes at
his home, Welsbourne. She determined on a good night's
sleep at the end of it though, as she explained to Mary:

> I must get you to make an apology for an
> impertinent thing I shall do by your father,
> which is, sending down a mattrass for the bed
> that may be allotted me, as I am not a very good
> sleeper, and must have the sort I am used to.
> (Bulstrode, 11 June 1775)

The following year she was making chair covers:

> I believe after all I must dunn you for your *sprig'd chintz* (not the pettycoat), for I have been obliged to add two more chairs in my drawing-room, and want it to complete my set of covers, and I *can't match* it with *anything* the least like it. (St. James's Place, 6 March 1776)

She was indefatigable almost to the end, wallpapering and painting again in her eightieth year, a task she undertook every four years or so. She wrote:

> After this week I shall be montrous busy, as I am under a necessity of whitewashing, new papering, and painting my drawing room; and I have delayed in hopes of a more convenient time, but can do it no longer; and removing pictures, books and China etc. etc. will find me a good deal of busyness. (St. James's Place, 24 May 1780)

Four years later she was at it again for the umpteenth time:

> I must soon set about a very disagreeable work — removing china, pictures, and books in my drawing-room, to have it new-papered and whitewashed; and tho' I thank God enjoy as much health as I can expect at my age, I am very soon sensible of fatigue. (1 May 1784)

She overdid it, and the Duchess of Portland wrote to her:

> My Dearest Friend, I am truly grieved to hear you have been ill, but depend upon your assuring me you are much better, I think you were in the right to go to town; *but is not* the *smell* of the paint *disagreeable* to you? And why would you not go to Whitehall? Which you know, my

dearest friend, was at your service. (Margate, 31
July 1784)

The smell of paint had never been disagreeable to Mrs.
Delany. She thrived on it. She had written some time earlier
about her house in Spring Gardens, a sentiment that charac-
terises her life:

> I lard all my conversation with something about
> "my house". I was not born to be a philos-
> opher: nature has not thrown in enough of
> indifference in my composition, nor has art
> attained it; in short, I like, and love, and dislike
> with all my might, and the pain it sometimes
> costs me is recompensed by the pleasure.
> (Bulstrode, 25 October 1754)

select bibliography

Accum, Freidrich Christian, *Culinary Chemistry, 1769–1838*, R. Ackermann, 1821. National Library of Ireland, J641.

Baird, Rosemary, *Mistress of the House: Great Ladies and Grand Houses*, Phoenix, 2004.

Barnard, Toby, *Making the Grand Figure: Lives and Possessions in Ireland, 1641–1770*, Yale University Press, 2004.

Bradfield, Nancy, *Costume in Detail: Women's Dress 1730–1930*, Eric Dobby Publishing, 1968.

Buchan, Dr. William, *Domestic Medicine*, printed by H. Saunders, W. Sleater, J. Potts, D. Chamberlaine and R. Moncrieffe, booksellers, 1774.

Byrne, Michael, *Memoirs of Robert Goodbody, of Mountmellick, Clara and Tullamore, 1781–1860*, Offaly Historical and Archaeological Society, www.offalyhistory.com.

Chapone, Hester, *Letters on the Improvement of the Mind*, Dix Dublin, 1773.

Clarkson, L.A. and E. Margaret Crawford, *Feast and Famine: A History of Food and Nutrition in Ireland 1500–1920*, Oxford University Press, 2001.

Corson, Richard, *Fashions in Hair: The First Five Thousand Years*, Peter Owen Ltd, 1965.

Cosnett, Thomas, *The Footman's Directory, and Butler's Remembrancer; or the advice of Onesimus to his young friends: comprising hints on the arrangement and performance of their work; rules for setting out tables and sideboards; the art of waiting at table, and conducting large and small parties; directions for cleaning plate, glass, furniture, clothes, and all other things which come within the care of a man-servant, and advice respecting behaviour to superiors, tradespeople, and fellow-servants. With an appendix, comprising various useful receipts and tables*, Simpkin and Marshall, and H. Colburn, 1825.

Craig, Maurice, *Dublin, 1660–1860*, Allen Figgis & Co. Ltd., 1980.

Day, Angelique, *Letters from Georgian Ireland: The Correspondence of Mary Delany 1731–1768*, Friar's Bush Press, 1992.

Dublin Society for the Improvement and Encouragement of Servants, *First Report from Its Institution, May 5, 1825 to December 31, 1827*, Printed by Bentham and Hardy for the Society, 1828.

Dunleavy, Mairead, *Dress in Ireland*, B.T. Batsford Ltd., 1989.

Fagan, Patrick, *The Second City: Portrait of Dublin, 1700–1760*, Branar, 1986.

Farmar, Tony, *Patients, Potions and Physicians: A Social History of Medicine in Ireland*, A. & A. Farmar with the Royal College of Physicians of Ireland, 2004.

Fenlon, Jane, *Goods & Chattels: A Survey of Early Household Inventories in Ireland*, The Heritage Council, 2003.

Fitzgerald, Brian, *Lady Louisa Connolly, 1743–1821: An Anglo-Irish Biography*, Staples Press, 1950.

Foreman, Amanda, *Georgiana, Duchess of Devonshire*, HarperCollins, 1999.

Glasse, H., *The New Art of Cookery, Made Plain and Easy; Which Far Exceeds Anything of the Kind Ever yet Published*, printed by John Exshaw, 1762.

Hayden, Ruth, *Mrs. Delany: Her Life and Her Flowers*, British Museum Publications, 1980.

Herbert, Dorothea, *Retrospections of Dorothea Herbert, 1770–1806*, Town House, 1998 and 2004.

Hewson, Michael, *Eighteenth Century Directions to Servants in Co. Tipperary*, reprinted from North Munster Studies, *Essays in Commemoration of Monsignor Michael Moloney*, 1967.

Lefanu, William (ed.), *Betsy Sheridan's Journal, Letters from Sheridan's Sister 1784–1786 & 1788–1790*, Eyre & Spottiswoode, 1960.

Lehmann, Gilly, *The British Housewife: Cookery Books, Cooking and Society in Eigtheenth Century Britain*, Prospect Books, 2003.

Llanover, The Right Honourable Lady (ed.), *The Autobiography and Correspondence of Mary Granville, Mrs. Delany: With interesting reminiscences of King George the Third and Queen Charlotte*, First Series, Three Volumes, Richard Bentley, 1861.

Llanover, The Right Honourable Lady (ed.), *The Autobiography and Correspondence of Mary Granville, Mrs. Delany: With interesting reminiscences of King George the Third and Queen Charlotte*, Second Series, Three Volumes, Richard Bentley, 1862.

Marshall, Dorothy, *The English Domestic Servant in History*, published for the Historical Association by G. Philip, 1949.

Maxwell, Constantia, *Country and Town in Ireland under the Georges*, W. Tempest, Dundalgan Press, 1949.

McCarthy, Patricia, "Vails and Travails: How Lord Kildare Kept His Household in Order", *Irish Architectural and Decorative Studies: The Journal of the Irish Georgian Society*, Volume VI, 2003.

Mead, Dr. Richard, *Medical Precepts and Cautions*, National Library of Ireland, Jp. 6164.

Minter, Sue, *The Apothecaries' Garden: The History of the Chelsea Physic Garden*, Sutton Publishing, 2000.

Picard, Liza, *Dr. Johnson's London: Everyday Life in London 1740–1770*, Phoenix, 2001.

Porter, Roy, *English Society in the Eighteenth Century*, The Pelican Social History of Britain, Penguin Books, 1982.

Porter, Roy and Dorothy, *In Sickness and in Health: The British Experience 1650–1850*, Basil Blackwell, 1989.

Raffald, Elizabeth, *The Experienced English Housekeeper, for the Use and Ease of Ladies, Housekeepers, Cooks etc.*, Southover Press, 1997.

Razzell, P.E., *The Conquest of Smallpox*, National Library of Ireland, G 6144 r I.

Ribeiro, Aileen, *Dress in Eighteenth Century Europe*, Batsford, 1984.

Sexton, Regina, *A Little History of Irish Food*, Gill and Macmillan, 1998.

Skinner, David, "Flocks, Flowers and Follies: Some Recently Discovered Irish Wallpapers of the 18th Century", *Irish Architectural and Decorative Studies: The Journal of the Irish Georgian Society*, Volume VI, 2003.

Spencer, Colin, *British Food: An Extraordinary Thousand Years of History*, Grub Street with Fortnum & Mason, 2002.

Squire, Peter, *Squire's Companion to the British Pharmacopoeia*, sixteenth edition, J. & A. Churchill, 1894.

Stead, Jennifer, *Georgian Cookery: Recipes and History*, English Heritage, 2003.

Swift, Jonathan, *Directions to Servants*, Golden Cockerel Press, 1925.

The Modern Cook, or Housewife's Directory: Containing Several Hundred New Receipts in Cookery, Pastry, Pickling, Confectionary, Distilling, Brewing, etc. etc., printed by James Hoey at the Mercury in Skinner-Row, 1766. National Library of Ireland, LO 7000.

Tillyard, Stella, *Aristocrats: Caroline, Emily, Louisa and Sarah Lennox 1740–1832*, Chatto & Windus, 1994.

Waugh, Norah, *The Cut of Women's Clothes, 1600–1930*, Faber and Faber, 1968.

Willgox, William B. and Walter L. Arnstein, *The Age of Aristocracy, 1688–1830*, Eighth Edition, Houghton Mifflin Company, 2001.

index

A

B

C